WTTW11 CHICAGO\98.7 WFMT
Member Services
5400 N. St. Louis Avenue
Chicago, IL 60625

wttw11 | 98.7wfmt

Page	Date	Invoice No.
1	01/17/19	367810A

SOLD TO
20993058
Ms Anne-Marie Raab
4504 N Riverdale Dr
McHenry, IL 60051

Customer No.	Sales I.D.	Reference #
271475	/AP	

Ordered By	Warehouse	Phone Number

SHIP TO

Media Code	Terms
/IMPORT	*PACKING SLIP ONLY*

Total Wt.	Zone	# Packages	Ship Via
0.0 Lbs	NA	1	SS

Message:

Qty.	B/O	Shipped	Item #	Description	Unit Price	Disc	Extension
1	0	1	PRS13NM	Rick Steves' Tour News- Best Destinations			
1	0	1	PRSHTD	Rick Steves' Travel Skills DVD			
1	0	1	PRSPLB	BK Rick Steves' Travel as a Political Act			

Thank you for your support!
Any questions regarding your membership call 773-509-1111 ext.6

Rick Steves®

TRAVEL AS A *POLITICAL* *ACT*

Avalon Travel
Hachette Book Group
1700 Fourth Street
Berkeley, CA 94710

Third Edition
ISBN 978-1-63121-763-0
Third printing January 2019

For the latest on Rick's talks, guidebooks, Europe tours, public radio show, free audio tours, and public television series, contact Rick Steves' Europe, 130 Fourth Avenue North, Edmonds, WA 98020, 425/771-8303, www.ricksteves.com, rick@ricksteves.com.

Rick Steves' Europe

Special Publications Manager: Risa Laib
Managing Editor: Jennifer Madison Davis
Content Manager and Project Editor: Cameron Hewitt
Map, Graphics, and Design: Rhonda Pelikan, Dave Hoerlein, Mary Rostad
Photography: Rick Steves, Cameron Hewitt, Dean Cannon, Trish Feaster, Dominic Arizona Bonuccelli, Abdi Sami, Simon Griffith, Steve Smith, Sandra Hundraker, Michael Potter, Wikimedia Commons. Page 12 © Heinrich Hoffman; page 17, Everett Collection Inc/Alamy Stock Photo; page 148 Agencja Fotograficzna Caro/Alamy Stock Photo Photos are used by permission and are the property of original copyright owners.

Avalon Travel

Senior Editor and Series Manager: Madhu Prasher
Editor: Jamie Andrade
Associate Editor: Sierra Machado
Copy Editor and Proofreader: Kelly Lydick
Production & Typesetting: Domini Dragoone
Cover Design: Faceout Studio, Lindy Martin

Contents

Introduction

On a visit to Turkey, I met a dervish. Dervishes—who are sort of like Muslim monks—follow Rumi, a mystic poet and philosopher of divine love. (I like to think Rumi and St. Francis, who both extolled the virtues of simplicity, would hit it off well.) They're called "whirling dervishes" because they spin in a circle as they pray. The dervish allowed me to observe his ritual on the condition that I understood what it meant to him.

The dervish led me to his flat rooftop—a peaceful oasis in the noisy city of Konya—where he prayed five times a day. With the sun heavy and red on the horizon, he explained, "When we pray, we keep one foot in our community, anchored in our home. The other foot steps around and around, acknowledging the beautiful variety of God's creation…touching all corners of this great world. I raise one hand up to acknowledge the love of God, and the other hand goes down like the spout of a teapot. As I spin around, my hand above receives the love from our Creator, and my hand below showers it onto all of his creation." As the dervish whirled and whirled, he settled into a meditative trance. And so did I. Watching his robe billow out and his head tilt over, I saw a conduit of love acknowledging the greatness of God. This man was so different from me, yet very much the same. This chance interaction left me with a renewed appreciation of the rich diversity of humanity…as well as its fundamental oneness.

Experiences like this one can be any trip's most treasured souvenir. When we return home, we can put

what we've learned—our newly acquired broader perspective—to work as citizens of a great nation confronted with unprecedented challenges. And when we do that, we make travel a political act.

I enjoyed perhaps my most profound travel experience ever on my first trip overseas. I was a 14-year-old with my parents, visiting relatives in Norway. We were in Oslo's vast Frogner Park—which, then as now, is filled with Gustav Vigeland's great stony statues of humans of all ages, shapes, and sizes.

Immersed in this grand, chiseled celebration of family and humanity, I gained a new insight into my little world. I noticed how much my parents were loving me. Their world revolved around me. They would do anything to make me happy and help me enjoy a fulfilling life. At great expense to their meager family budget, they were making it possible for me to travel. Then I remember looking out over that park. It was speckled—like a Monet painting—with countless other parents…all lavishing love on their children. Right there, my 14-year-old egocentric worldview took a huge hit. I thought, "Wow, those parents love their kids as much as my parents love me. This planet must be home to billions of equally lovable children of God." I've carried that understanding with me in my travels ever since.

On that same 1969 trip, I sat on the carpet with Norwegian cousins, watching the Apollo moon landing. As Neil Armstrong took that first step on the moon, my relatives heard his famous sentence translated into Norwegian: *"Ett lite skritt for et menneske, ett stort sprang for menneskeheten."* Sharing the excitement of everyone in that room, I realized that while this was an American triumph, it was also a human one—one giant leap for mankind indeed—and the entire planet was celebrating.

As an idealistic young adult, I struggled with what I'd do with my one life. I wanted to work hard at something worthwhile and contribute to society. I wondered if it was really noble to teach wealthy Americans to travel. As a child, my earliest image of "travel" was of rich Americans on fancy white cruise ships in the Caribbean, throwing coins off the deck so they could photograph what they called the "little dark kids" jumping in after their nickels. They'd take these photos home as souvenirs of their relative affluence. That was not the kind of travel I wanted to promote.

Even today, remnants of that notion of travel persist. I believe that for many Americans, traveling still means seeing if you can eat five meals a day and still snorkel when you get into port. When I say that at a cruise convention, people fidget nervously. But I'm not condemning cruise vacations. I'm simply saying I don't consider that activity "travel." It's hedonism. (And I don't say that in a judgmental way, either. I've got no problem with hedonism…I'm a Lutheran.) Rather than accentuate the difference between "us" and "them," I believe travel should bring us together. If I'm evangelical about the value of travel, it's the thoughtful and challenging kind of travel—less caloric, perhaps—but certainly much more broadening.

And so, since that first trip, I've spent a third of my life overseas, living out of a backpack, talking to people who see things differently than me. It makes me a little bit of an odd duck.

For the last 40 years, I've taught people how to travel. I focus mostly on the logistics: finding the right hotel, avoiding long lines, sampling local delicacies, and catching the train on time. But more important than the "how" we travel is the "why" we travel: Thoughtful travelers do it to have enlightening experiences, to meet inspirational people, to be stimulated, to learn, and to grow.

Travel has taught me the fun in having my cultural furniture rearranged and my ethnocentric self-assuredness walloped. It has humbled me, enriched my life, and tuned me in to a rapidly changing world. And for that, I am thankful. In this book, I'll share what has made my travels most rewarding, and how they have helped shape my worldview and inspired my activism.

As a travel teacher, I've been fortunate to draw from a variety of rich overseas experiences. And, since just after 9/11, I've been giving a lecture I call "Travel as a Political Act." I enjoy giving this talk all over the USA—to peacenik environmentalists in Boulder, to high-society ladies' clubs in Charlotte, to homemakers in Houston, to Members of Congress and their aides on Capitol Hill, and at universities across the country.

With this book, I flesh out the message of that talk and trace the roots of my ideas to the actual personal travel experiences from which they originated. While I draw from trips all over the globe, my professional focus is Europe—so that's where many of my anecdotes are set. Europe is not that exotic, but it's on par with the USA in development, confidence, and impact on the developing world. Consequently, Europe provides an instructive parallel-yet-different world from which to view the accomplishments of our society and the challenges we face.

We can learn more about our own country by observing other countries—and by challenging ourselves (and our neighbors) to be broad-minded when it comes to international issues. Holding our country to a high standard and searching for ways to better live up to its lofty ideals is not "America-bashing." It's good citizenship.

I'm unapologetically proud to be an American. The United States has made me who I am. I spend plenty of time in other countries, but the happiest day of any trip is the day I come home. I'd never live abroad, and I'd certainly not have as much fun running my business overseas as I do here at home. America is a great and innovative nation that the world understandably looks to for leadership. But other nations have some pretty good ideas, too. By bringing these ideas home, we can help our society confront its challenges more wisely. As a nation of immigrants, whose very origin is based on the power of diversity ("out of many, one"), this should come naturally to us…and be celebrated.

This book isn't a preachy political treatise. (At least, I hope it isn't.) Since I'm a travel writer at heart, this book is heavy on travel tales and people-to-people connections. My premise is that thoughtful travel comes with powerful lessons. With this book, I hope to inspire others to travel more purposefully.

By the nature of this book, you'll get a lot of my opinions. My opinions are shaped by who I am. Along with being a traveler, I'm a historian, Christian, parent, carnivore, musician, capitalist, minimalist, member of NORML, and a workaholic. I've picked up my progressive politics (and my favorite ways to relax) largely from the people I've met overseas. And, I seem to end up teaching everything I love: history, music, travel…and now, politics.

Your opinions will differ from mine because we draw from different life experiences. As a writer, I'll try not to abuse my bully pulpit. Still, rather than take the edge off of my opinions, I'll share them, with the assumption that good people can respectfully disagree with each other. I've always marveled at how passionate I am when my Dad and I disagree on some political issue. He's my flesh and blood. Often his political assessment of something will exasperate me. I love him—but how can he possibly believe these things? While I don't necessarily want him to change his mind, I want him to understand my perspective. Sharing it with him consumes me. In writing this book, I've discovered a similar passion. I want to share what I've learned with my fellow Americans, because I consider us all part of one big family. And, I assume that you're reading this book for the same reason that I wrote it: because we both care.

In the decade since I wrote the first edition of this book—in the waning days of the George W. Bush administration—our world has changed dramatically. Pivoting from his predecessor, President Obama set this country on a clear course for eight years. And then Donald Trump was elected, and drastically changed course. In the decade to come, we can be sure of plenty more changes. Our presidents can propel our country forward, or set us back. But no matter who's in power, my fundamental message remains the same: Traveling as a political act is always worthwhile. It feels more important in challenging times, but—regardless of who's making the headlines this year—the fundamentals are always the same.

In the following chapter, I lay out the framework—those fundamental skills—that have helped me open up my perspective. Then we'll travel together to very different destinations. By the time we return home, I hope that—as on any good trip—we'll have a richer understanding of our world.

Chapter 1
How to Travel as a Political Act

If this book is a trip featuring exciting destinations, this first chapter is the flight over—a great time to mentally prepare for the trip. To get the most value out of your travels, plan to get out of your comfort zone, meet the people, and view other cultures—as well as our own—with an open mind. Here's how I do it. (I'll try to make it worth missing the in-flight movie.)

Travel like a Medieval Jester

I'm a travel writer. According to conventional wisdom, injecting politics into your travel writing is not good for business. Isn't travel, after all, a form of recreational escapism? Maybe…but it can be much more.

For me, since September 12, 2001, the role of a travel writer has changed. I see the travel writer of the 21st century like the court jester of the Middle Ages. While thought of as a jokester, the jester was in a unique position to tell truth to power without being punished. Back then, kings were absolute rulers—detached from the lives of their subjects. The court jester's job was to mix it up with people that the king would never meet. The jester would play in the gutter with the riffraff. Then, having fingered the gritty pulse of society, he'd come back into the court and tell the king the truth. "Your Highness, the people are angered by the cost of mead. They are offended by the queen's parties. The pope has more influence than you. Everybody is reading the heretics' pamphlets. Your stutter is the butt of many rude jokes." The king didn't kill the jester. Quite the contrary: In order to rule more wisely, the king needed the jester's insights.

Many of today's elected leaders have no better connection with real people—especially ones outside their borders—than those "divinely ordained" kings did centuries ago. And while I'm fortunate to have a built-in platform for sharing the lessons I've learned from my travels, I believe that any traveler can play jester to their own communities. Whether visiting El Salvador (where people *don't* dream of having two cars in every garage), Denmark (where they pay high taxes with high expectations and are satisfied), or Iran (where many willingly compromise their freedom to be ruled by clerics out of fear that otherwise, as they explained to me, their little girls would be raised to be sex toys), any traveler can bring back valuable insights. And, just like those truths were needed in the Middle Ages, this understanding is needed in our age.

Choosing to Travel on Purpose

Ideally, travel broadens our perspectives personally, culturally, and politically. Suddenly, the palette with which we paint the story of our lives has more colors. We realize there are exciting alternatives to the social and community norms that our less-traveled neighbors may never consider. Imagine not knowing you could eat "ethnic." Imagine suddenly realizing there were different genres of music. Imagine you loved books… and one day the librarian mentioned there was an upstairs.

Whether you travel as a monk, a hedonist, or somewhere in between, you can come home better friends with our world.

But you can only reap these rewards of travel if you're open to them. Watching a dervish whirl can be a cruise-ship entertainment option, or it can be a spiritual awakening. You can travel to relax and have fun. You can travel to learn and broaden your perspective. Or, best of all, you can do both at once. Make a decision that on any trip you take, you'll make a point to be open to new experiences, seek options that get you out of your comfort zone, and be a cultural chameleon—trying on new ways of looking at things and striving to become a "temporary local."

Assuming they want to learn, both monks and hedonists can stretch their perspectives through travel. While your choice of destination has a huge impact on your potential for learning, you don't need to visit refugee camps to gain political insight. With the right approach, meeting people—whether over beer in an Irish pub, while hiking Himalayan ridges, or sharing fashion tips in Iran—can connect you more thoughtfully with our world.

Good people have different passions.

My best vacations have been both fun and intensely educational. Seeing how smart people overseas come up with fresh solutions to the same old problems makes me more humble, open to creative problem-solving, and ready to question traditional ways of thinking. Travelers understand how our worldview is both shaped and limited by our family, friends, media, and cultural environment. We become more able to respectfully coexist with people who have different norms and values.

Travel challenges truths that we were raised thinking were self-evident and God-given. Leaving home, we learn other people find *different* truths to be "self-evident." We realize that it just makes sense to give everyone a little wiggle room.

Traveling in Bulgaria, you learn that shaking your head "no" means yes, and giving an up-and-down nod can actually mean "no." In restaurants in France, many travelers, initially upset that "you can't even get the bill," learn that slow service is respectful service—you've got the table all night…please take your time. And, learning how Atatürk heroically and almost singlehandedly pulled Turkey out of the Middle Ages and into the modern world in the 1920s explains why today's Turks are quick to see his features in passing clouds.

Traveling thoughtfully, we are inspired by the accomplishments of other people, communities, and nations. Then, getting away from our home turf and looking back at America from a distant vantage point, we see ourselves as others see us—an enlightening, if not always flattering, view.

Connect with People

One of the greatest rewards of travel comes from the people you encounter—especially if you're open to letting them show off a bit and impress you with their culture. As a traveler, I make a point to be a cultural lint brush, trying to pick up whatever cultural insights I can glean from every person I meet.

In our daily routines, we tend to surround ourselves with people who are, more or less, like us. That's OK. It's the natural thing to do. But on the road, you meet people you'd normally never connect with. When I travel, I meet a greater variety of interesting people in two months than I do in an entire year back home. I view each of these chance encounters as loaded with potential to teach me about people and places so different from my hometown world.

For example, one of my favorite countries is Ireland—not because of its sights, but because of its people. Travel in Ireland gives me the sensation that I'm actually understanding a foreign language. And, the Irish have that marvelous "gift of gab." They love to talk. For them, conversation is an art form.

Actually, more Irish speak Irish (their native Celtic tongue) than many travelers realize. Very often you'll step into a shop, not realizing the locals are talking to each other in Irish. They turn to you and switch to English, without missing a beat. When you leave, they slip right back into their Irish.

The best place to experience Ireland is in a Gaeltacht, as Irish-speaking regions are called. These are government-subsidized national preserves for

---

Ireland gives me the sensation of understanding a foreign language...with people who love to talk.

traditional lifestyles. In a Gaeltacht, charming and talkative locals conspire to slow down anyone with too busy an itinerary.

I was deep into one conversation with an old-timer. We were on the far west coast of the Emerald Isle—where they stand on a bluff, squint out at the Atlantic, and say, "Ahhh, the next parish over is Boston." I asked my new friend, "Were you born here?" He thought about it, paused, and then said, "No, 'twas 'bout five miles down the road." Later, I asked him, "Have you lived here all your life?" He winked and said, "Not yet."

In even the farthest reaches of the globe, travelers discover a powerful local pride. Guiding a tour group through eastern Turkey, I once dropped in on a craftsman who was famous for his wood carving. Everybody in that corner of Turkey wanted a prayer niche in their mosque carved by him. We gathered around his well-worn work table. He had likely never actually met an American. And now he had a dozen of us gathered around him. He was working away and showing off…clearly very proud. Then suddenly he stopped, held his chisel high into the sky, and declared, "A man and his chisel—the greatest factory on earth."

Looking at him, it was clear he didn't need me to tell him about fulfillment. When I asked if I could buy a piece of his art, he said, "For a man my age to know that my work will go back to the United States and be appreciated, that's payment enough. Please take this home with you, and remember me."

I traveled through Afghanistan long before the word "Taliban" entered our lexicon. While there, I enjoyed lessons highlighting the pride and diversity you'll find across the globe. I was sitting in a Kabul cafeteria popular with backpackers. I was just minding my own business when a local man sat down next to me. He said, "Can I join you?" I said, "You already have." He said, "You're an American, aren't you?" I said yes, and he said, "Well, I'm a professor here in Afghanistan. I want you to know that a third of the people on this planet eat with spoons and forks like you, a third of the people eat with chopsticks, and a third of the people eat with fingers like me. And we're all just as civilized."

As he clearly had a chip on his shoulder about this, I simply thought, "OK, OK, I get it." But I didn't get it…at least, not right away. After leaving Afghanistan, I traveled through South Asia, and his message stayed with me. I went to fancy restaurants filled with well-dressed professionals. Rather than providing silverware, they had a ceremonial sink in the middle of the room. People would wash their hands and use their fingers for what God made them for. I did the same.

That professor's hunch was right: I thought less of people who ate with their fingers. Then, through travel, I learned otherwise. Eventually eating with my fingers became quite natural. (In fact, I had to be retrained when I got home.)

Stow Your Preconceptions and Be Open to New Experiences

Along with the rest of our baggage, we tend to bring along knee-jerk assumptions about what we expect to encounter abroad. Sometimes these can be helpful (remember to drive on the left in Britain). Other times, they can interfere with our ability to fully engage with the culture on its own terms.

People tell me that they enjoy my public television shows and my guidebooks because I seem like just a normal guy. I'll take that as a compliment. What can I say? I'm simple. I was raised thinking cheese was no big deal: It's orange and the shape of the bread. Slap it on, and *voilà!* —cheese sandwich.

But in Europe, I quickly learned that cheese is neither orange nor the shape of the bread. In France alone, you could eat a different cheese every day of the year. And it wouldn't surprise me if people did. The French are passionate about their cheese.

I used to be put off by sophisticates in Europe. Those snobs were so enamored with their fine wine and stinky cheese, and the *terroir* that created it all.

If they're evangelical about cheese, raise your hands and say hallelujah.

But, now I see that rather than showing off, they're simply proud and eager to share. By stowing my preconceptions and opening myself up to new experiences, I've achieved a new appreciation for all sorts of highbrow stuff I thought I'd never really "get." Thankfully, people are sophisticated about different things, and I relish the opportunity to meet and learn from an expert. I'm the wide-eyed bumpkin…and it's a cultural show-and-tell.

For example, I love it when my favorite restaurateur in

Family Pride and Fine Wine

I'm inspired by how the pride of a family business or regional specialty stays strong, generation after generation. In Italy's Umbria region, I have long taken my tour groups to the Bottai family vineyard. Cecilia, the oldest daughter, is no longer the little girl that I once knew. Now, as her parents are taking it easy, she greets us at the gate and shares her family's passion with us. Cecilia walks us through the vineyard, introducing grape plants if they were her children. As we follow her into the dark, cool tunnels of her vast cellar—dug a thousand years ago—she finds just the right bottle to share. And finally, we gather at the family dining table in a room that has changed little in 200 years.

On my last visit, I remember enjoying Cecilia's pride and happiness

When your name's on the label, you take great joy in sharing.

as she popped open a bottle of their fine Orvieto Classico wine. Watching my glass fill, I noticed her hand gripped the bottle in a way that framed the family name on the label. And I noticed how her mother and now-frail grandmother looked on silently and proudly as visitors from the other side of the world gathered in their home. On that remote farm in Italy, where the Bottai family had been producing wine for countless generations, my group was tasting the fruit of their land, labor, and culture. And our hosts were beaming with joy.

Paris, Marie-Alice, takes me shopping in the morning and shows me what's going to shape her menu that night. We enter her favorite cheese shop—a fragrant festival of mold. Picking up the gooiest wad, Marie-Alice takes a deep whiff, and whispers, "Oh, Rick, smell zees cheese. It smells like zee feet of angels."

Take History Seriously—Don't Be Dumbed Down

I got my history degree accidentally. I remember waking up in the dorm one morning and realizing I already had seven history classes under my belt. I thought, "Three more and I'm 'a historian'! Let's push on through." Because I had traveled, history was fun. But, back then, I still didn't fully understand its importance.

Where can a monkey spy two seas and two continents at the same time? On the Rock of Gibraltar.

Contrary to conventional wisdom, a history degree *is* practical. In college, I was encouraged to also earn a business degree, so I'd graduate with something "useful." I believe now that if more Americans had a history degree and put it to good use, this world would be better off. Yesterday's history informs today's news…which becomes tomorrow's history. Those with a knowledge of history can understand current events in a broader context and respond to them more thoughtfully.

As you travel, opportunities to enjoy history are everywhere. Work on cultivating a general grasp of the sweep of history, and you'll be able to infuse your sightseeing with more meaning. Traveling with no understanding of the local history is like going to a 3-D movie and deciding not to bother with the glasses.

I was sitting on the summit of the Rock of Gibraltar, looking out at Africa. It's the only place on earth where you can see two continents and two seas at the same time. The straits were churning with action. Where bodies of water meet, they create tide rips—confused, choppy teepee seas that stir up plankton, attracting little fish, birds, bigger fish…and fishermen balancing the risks and rewards of working those turbulent waters. The fertile straits are also busy with hungry whales, dolphins, and lots of ferries and maritime traffic. Boats cut through feeding grounds, angering environmentalists. And windsurfers catch a stiff breeze, oblivious to it all.

Looking out over the action, with the stony Pillars of Hercules in the misty Moroccan distance, I realized that there was also a historical element in this combustible mix. Along with seas and continents, this is where, for many centuries, two great civilizations—Islam and Christendom—have rubbed up against each other, creating cultural tide rips. Centuries after Muslim Moors from North Africa swept north across the Strait of Gibraltar and conquered Catholic Spain, Spain eventually triumphed—pushing the Moors back into Africa. But Spain was irrevocably changed in the process.

Where civilizations meet, there are risks…and rewards. It can be dangerous, it can be fertile, and it shapes history.

Later that day—still pondering Islam and Christendom pressing against each other like tectonic plates—I stepped into a small Catholic church. Throughout Spain, churches display statues of a hero called "St. James the Moor-Slayer." And every Sunday, good 21st-century Christians sit—probably listening to sermons about tolerance—under this statue of James, his sword raised, heroic on his rearing horse, with the severed heads of Muslims tumbling at his feet. It becomes even more poignant when you realize that the church is built upon the ruins of a mosque, which was built upon the ruins of a church, which was built upon the ruins of a Roman temple, which was probably built upon the ruins of an earlier pagan holy place. Standing in that church, it occurred to me that friction between Christendom and Islam is nothing new—and nothing we can't overcome. But it's more than the simple shoot-'em-up, with good guys and bad guys, as often presented by politicians and the media. Travel, when informed by a sense of history, helps us better understand our world in all its complexity.

Travelers can actually be eyewitnesses to history as it unfolds. I was in Moscow in 1991, watching flames coming out of a once-invincible government's windows. An ideology was falling, and the streets were filled with demonstrators both for and against the new "freedom." Many, appalled by the change and clinging to the status quo they grew up with, were standing up for their now-doomed Soviet system. These demonstrators were the aged—the generation that

In the 21st century, "St. James the Moor-Slayer" still gets a place of honor in many Spanish churches.

The new glass dome atop Germany's parliament building comes with a point.

would soon be the big loser, as an aggressive and corrupt capitalism replaced communism and the comforting stability it offered. Surrounded by old Russians, with fear in their hungry eyes and hammers and sickles on their ragtag posters, forever humanized for me the plight of the Russian people. And to this day, I have a sense of why Vladimir Putin could be so persistently popular with his electorate.

Later, in 1999, I was in Berlin just as Germany's renovated parliament building reopened to the public. For a generation, this historic Reichstag building—where some of the last fighting of World War II occurred on its rooftop—was a bombed-out and blackened husk, overlooking the no-man's-land between East and West Berlin. After unification, Germany's government returned from Bonn to Berlin. And, in good European style, the Germans didn't bulldoze their historic capitol building. Instead, recognizing the building's cultural roots, they renovated it—incorporating modern architectural design, and capping it with a glorious glass dome.

Germany's old-meets-new parliament building comes with powerful architectural symbolism. It's free to enter, open long hours, and designed for German citizens to climb its long spiral ramp to the very top and literally look down (through a glass ceiling) over the shoulders of their legislators to see what's on their desks. The Germans, who feel they've been ill-served by their politicians over the last century, are determined to keep a closer eye on their leaders.

Spiraling slowly up the ramp to the top of the dome during that festive opening week, I was surrounded by teary-eyed Germans. Now, anytime you're surrounded by teary-eyed Germans…something exceptional is going on. Most of those teary eyes were old enough to remember the difficult times after World War II, when their city lay in rubble. For these people, the opening of this grand building was the symbolic closing of a difficult chapter in the history of a great nation. No more division. No more communism. No more fascism. They had a united government and were entering a new century with a new capitol, filled with hope and optimism.

It was a thrill to be there. I was caught up in it. But then, as I looked around at the other travelers up there, I realized that only some of us fully grasped what was going on. Many tourists seemed so preoccupied with trivialities—forgotten camera batteries, needing a Coke, the lack of air-conditioning—that they were missing out on this once-in-a-lifetime opportunity to celebrate a great moment with the German people. And it saddened me. I thought, "I don't want to be part of a dumbed-down society."

I believe powerful forces in our society would find it convenient (and more profitable) if we were dumbed down. Corporations make more money in a world of mindless producer/consumers. And that goes for the mainstream tourism industry, as well. The "corporate" version of travel is about having fun in the sun, shopping duty-free, and cashing in frequent-flyer miles. But to me, those concerns distract us from the real thrills, rewards, and value of travel. In our travels—and in our everyday lives—we should become more educated about and engaged with challenging issues, using the past to understand the present. The more you know, and the more you strive to learn, the richer your travels and your life become.

In my own realm as a travel teacher, when I have the opportunity to lead a tour, write a guidebook, or make a TV show, I take it with the responsibility to respect and challenge the intellect of my tour members, readers, or viewers. All of us will gain more from our travels if we refuse to be dumbed down. Promise yourself and challenge your travel partners to be engaged and grapple with the challenging issues while on the road. Your experience will be better for it.

Overcome Fear

Travel to faraway places has always come with a little fear. But over the last several years, the US has grown even more fearful…and more isolated.

A Haunting Photo from 1932 Munich: The Normalization of Nazism

This photo haunts me. It's 1932 in Munich, at a political rally for Germany's resurgent National Socialist Party ("Nazis" for short). I imagine that the people filling this room are mostly good, decent citizens. But their thinking has become corrupted by anger, fear, and frustration. They're stinging from Germany's humiliating loss in World War I and the draconian Treaty of Versailles that is hampering the recovery of their nation. The Great Depression has left many without jobs and desperate. And their leaders are telling them that insidious "others"—Jews and Communists—are responsible for their hardships. The world, they believe, is rigged against them.

The Nazis are expert in capitalizing on the concerns of voters like these. For example, they promise an ambitious infrastructure program that will reinvigorate the once-mighty economy—a vast network of super-freeways lacing their country together. They have the backing of German industrialists, who (terrified of the Communist alternative) throw their support and their *Reichsmarks* behind the Nazis. The party's propagandists

I remember when the standard farewell when I set off on another trip was "Bon voyage!" But today, Americans tend to say, "Have a safe trip." (When I hear this, I'm inclined to say, "Well, you have a safe stay-at-home—because where I'm going is statistically much safer than where you're staying.")

Of course, there are serious risks that deserve our careful attention. But it's all too easy to mistake fear for actual danger. Franklin D. Roosevelt's assertion that we have nothing to fear but fear itself feels just as relevant today as when he first said it in 1933.

I'm hardly a fearless traveler. I can think of many times I've been afraid before a trip. Years ago, I heard that in Egypt, the beggars were relentless, there were no maps, and it was so hot that car tires melted to the streets. For three years, I had plane tickets to India but bailed out, finding other places closer to my comfort zone. Before flying to Iran to film a public television show, I was uneasy. And walking from Jerusalem through the Israeli security expertly turn hateful half-truths into tenets of the party. And, most important of all, they are led by a charismatic, dogmatic ruler, called literally "The Leader" (Der Führer)—a master at repeating lies so convincingly that his followers eventually believe him. Much of the world dismisses him as a clown, a buffoon, an outrageous showman. But just enough Germans are swayed by his *"Deutschland über alles"* ideas.

A year later, Adolf Hitler will be narrowly elected chancellor. Within weeks, the Reichstag (Germany's parliament building) will mysteriously burn to the ground, giving the Führer the perfect opportunity to justify drastic "law and order" measures—unleashing the Nazis to purge their enemies from the government and reshape the German state. Within a few years, tens of millions will be dead, and Germany—and much of Europe—will be a smoldering ruin. All because of the dangerous ideas that caught on in rallies like this one.

Being a student of history brings meaning to your travels. And traveling to learn the stories of other countries can help us recognize potential threats in their infancy. Many observers have watched with alarm the rise of populist, nativist, rabble-rousing movements on both sides of the Atlantic. These movements may or may not be "fascist," but there's no question they're using the fascist playbook. Students of history have a better understanding of how these movements can rise. They know how dangerously things can escalate if the safeguards of a healthy democracy (a free and respected press, an independent judiciary, and engaged voters) are trumped by anger and fear.

barrier into Bethlehem in Palestine made me nervous. But in each case, when I finally went to these places, I realized my fears were unfounded.

History is rife with examples of leaders who manipulate fear to distract, mislead, and undermine the will of the very people who entrusted them with power. Our own recent history is no exception. If you want to sell weapons to Colombia, exaggerate the threat of drug lords. If you want to build a wall between the US and Mexico, characterize all illegal immigrants as drug runners, criminals, and rapists. If you want to create an expensive missile-defense system, terrify people with predictions of nuclear holocaust. My travels have

taught me to have a healthy skepticism toward those who peddle fear. Fear is a tool used to keep a people down. And in so many cases, I've learned that fear is for people who don't get out much. The flipside of fear is understanding—and we gain understanding through travel.

As travelers and as citizens, we react not to the risk of terrorism, but to the *perceived* risk of terrorism—which we usually exaggerate. For travelers, the actual risk is minuscule. Here are the facts: Year after year, about 12 million Americans go to Europe. How many are killed by terrorists? Think through several high-profile terrorist events in Europe since 9/11: the 2004 Madrid bombing, the 2005 subway bombing in London, the 2015 shooting in Paris nightclubs, the 2016 Brussels bombings and truck rampages in Nice and Berlin, and the 2017 truck and stabbing rampage in London. In all of those events combined—tragic though they were—fewer than 10 American tourists were killed...out of more than 150 million trips to Europe. I'll take those odds. Another thought: An American is twice as likely to be killed in their own home by a toddler playing with a gun than by *any* terrorist event...in Europe or at home.

Terrorism is here to stay. Innocent people will be killed—some by angry Muslims. Tomorrow an American could be beheaded by ISIS in Madrid. But, tragic as that might be, it wouldn't change the fact that it is safe to travel. There were far more deaths because of terrorism in Europe in the 1970s and 1980s than in recent years—we just weren't as fearful back then. Statistically, travel to most international destinations is far less dangerous than a drive to your neighborhood grocery store.

So, why do we react so strongly to these events? The commercial media are partly to blame. (See the "Walter Cronkite and Entertainment Masquerading as News" sidebar.) Sensationalizing tragedy gets more eyes on the screen. But it also exaggerates the impact of a disaster, causing viewers to overreact. More than once, I've found myself in a place that was going through a crisis that made international headlines— terrorist bombing, minor earthquake, riots, and so on. Loved ones back home call

Terrorism by the Numbers

I believe that when we overreact to the threat of terrorism, we empower the terrorists and actually become part of the problem. By setting emotion aside and being as rational as possible, we can weigh the relative risks and rewards or costs and benefits of various American behaviors. While I realize it may seem heartless to reduce tragic deaths to mere numbers, let's try a thought experiment and be purely left-brained for a moment.

Every week, a 747's worth of people die on our American highways. And it's not worth headlines. We're a mighty nation of well over 300 million people. People die. More than 30,000 people die on our roads every year. Any expert would tell you that if we all drove 20 miles an hour slower, we'd save thousands of precious lives. But in the privacy of the voting booth, is the average American going to vote to drive 50 mph on our freeways to save thousands of lives? Hell, no. We've got places to go.

Consider guns. Every year in our country, more than 10,000 people are killed by guns (30,000, if you include suicides). You could make the case that it's a reasonable price to pay for the precious right to bear arms. We are a free and well-educated democracy. We know the score. And year after year, as a society, we seem to agree that spending these lives is a reasonable trade-off for enjoying our Second Amendment right.

Germans decided not to have that right to bear arms, and consequently, they lose around a hundred people a year to guns. Europeans (who suffer less than a quarter the per capita gun killings we do) laugh out loud when they hear that Americans are staying home for safety reasons. If you care about your loved ones and understand the statistics, you'll take them to Europe tomorrow.

If we dispassionately surveyed the situation, we might similarly accept the human cost of our aggressive stance on this planet. We spend tens of thousands of lives a year for the rights to drive fast and bear arms. Perhaps more than 300 million Americans being seen by the rest of the world as an empire is another stance that comes with an unavoidable cost in human lives.

The US spends more than $600 billion annually on its military—about $400 billion more than the second-place spender (China), and far more than the European Union. I know this is wild, but imagine we changed our priorities and de-emphasized our military might in favor of "soft power." Fantasize for a moment about the money and energy we could save, and all the good we could do with those resources if even just a fraction was compassionately and wisely diverted to challenges like climate change or the plight of desperate people—in lands that have no oil or strategic importance—whose suffering barely registers in the media. Imagine then the resulting goodwill, and what that would do to the American image abroad. We'd be tougher for our terrorist enemies to demonize...and imagine the challenge that would present to terrorist recruiters.

Walter Cronkite and Entertainment Masquerading as News

Why are Americans so fearful of the world these days—fearful enough, in some cases, that they're bullied into staying home? I think it has to do with the way our news industry has changed.

Back when Walter Cronkite brought America the news, he closed each broadcast with his famous tagline: "And that's the way it is." Back then, I believe that—to the best of the network's ability—that really was the way it was. In those days, commercial networks saw the news hour as a public service and a civic responsibility. Reporting the news in a truthful and impartial way was their contribution to our society as corporate citizens. In fact, until 1987, it was actually the law (the FCC's Fairness Doctrine). Essentially, Congress granted the broadcast networks the rights to use American airwaves with just one string attached: They had to keep the populace informed. This quid-pro-quo was respected for decades, even though properly researched and reported news doesn't come cheap. When they wrote Walter Cronkite his paycheck, they did it without regard to profit. Traditionally, network news wasn't about making money—it was about making American society smarter, and therefore stronger.

Unfortunately, those days are long gone. With the end of the Fairness Doctrine and the rise of 24-hour news, media are focused on reaching as many eyeballs as possible—so they can charge advertisers enough to pay for their good-looking anchors (no offense, Walter) and still have plenty of profit left over. If not enough people are watching, they're desperate to boost viewership. So they sex it up, bloody it up, and crisis it up until enough people watch. The result: Commercial TV news has become entertainment masquerading as news. As the news becomes more sensationalized, the viewer becomes more fearful. And eventually, all that fear metastasizes into the political realm. In the long run,

me, their voices shaking with anxiety, to be sure I'm OK. They seem surprised when I casually dismiss their concern. Invariably, the people who live in that place are less worked up than the ones watching it on the news 5,000 miles away. I don't blame my loved ones for worrying. The media have distorted the event in their minds.

I got an email recently from a man who wrote, "Thanks for the TV shows. They will provide a historical documentation of a time when Europe was white and not Muslim. Keep filming your beloved Europe before it's gone."

Reading this, I thought how feisty fear has become in our society. A fear of African Americans swept the USA in the 1960s. Jews have been feared in many places throughout history. And today, Muslims are feared. But we have a choice whether or not to be afraid. Americans who have had the opportunity to travel in moderate Muslim nations like Turkey or Morocco—and

the transformation of news from information to entertainment—making us feel that we're less safe—threatens the fabric of our democracy...and, ironically, actually makes our country less safe.

Of course, many conscientious, hardworking journalists still produce news that's designed to inform rather than to entertain. But these days, they are shouting into a chaotic, overloaded media landscape. One sad byproduct of the sensationalization of news is that it has eroded respect for all journalism—even the good kind. When you train the public to view news as entertainment, it's an easy transition to sell them trumped-up scandal and salacious rumor as "news." The decline of real news has coincided with the rise of fake news: intentionally bogus but titillating stories such as, "President Obama was born in Kenya!". These stories then spread like wildfire in social media. People can choose their news, and news itself is becoming subjective rather than "the way it is."

By dumbing down our news, we've sacrificed the credibility of journalism and the great legacy of Walter Cronkite. And in a society where journalism has always served as an unofficial "fourth estate"—to keep watch over the executive, legislative, and judicial branches—this is a tragic and troubling development indeed.

have been welcomed by smiling locals—no longer associate Islam on the whole with terrorism.

Every time I'm stuck in a long security line at the airport, I reflect on one of the most disconcerting results of terrorism: The very people who would benefit most from international travel—those who needlessly fear people and places they don't understand—decide to stay home. There's an irony here: If people stay home out of fear of violence fueled by misunderstanding between cultures, they can actually bring on the danger they fear. When we travel, we build understanding. When we know people in faraway lands, it makes it harder for their government to demonize us with their propaganda, and harder for our government to demonize them through our propaganda.

It's clear to me that if we stay home out of fear, we do nothing to build empathy, and we make a small terrorist event a bigger one. I believe the most powerful things an individual American can do to fight terrorism are to travel a lot, learn about the world, come home with a broader perspective, and then work to help our country fit more comfortably and less fearfully into this ever-smaller planet.

The American Dream, Bulgarian Dream, Sri Lankan Dream: Celebrate Them All

I fondly remember the confusion I felt when I first met someone who wouldn't trade passports with me. I thought, "I've got more wealth, more freedom, more opportunity than you'll ever have—why wouldn't you want what I've got?" I assumed anyone with half a brain would aspire to the American Dream. But the vast majority of non-Americans don't have the American Dream. They have the Bulgarian Dream, or the Sri Lankan Dream, or the Moroccan Dream. Thanks to travel, this no longer surprises me. In fact, I celebrate it.

I was raised thinking the world is a pyramid, with the United States on top and everybody else trying to get there. In fact, well into my adulthood, I actually believed that if another country didn't understand that they should want to be like us, we had every right to go in and elect a government for them that did.

While I once unknowingly cheered on cultural imperialism, travel has taught me that one of the ugliest things one nation can do is write another nation's textbooks. Back in the Cold War, I had a Bulgarian friend who attended an English-language high school in Sofia. I read his Soviet-produced textbooks, which were more concerned about ideology than teaching. He learned about "economics" with no mention of Adam Smith. And I've seen what happens when the US funds the publishing of textbooks in places such as El Salvador and Nicaragua, with ideological strings attached. Not surprisingly, they teach the economics of a banana republic in a way that glorifies multinational corporation tactics and vilifies heroes of popular indigenous movements. I think most Americans would be appalled if we knew how many textbooks we've written in the developing world.

On the road, you learn that ethnic underdogs everywhere are waging valiant but seemingly hopeless struggles. When assessing their tactics, I remind myself that every year on this planet, a dozen or so languages go extinct. That means that many heroic, irreplaceable little groups of people (who consider themselves "nations without states"—see page 70) finally lose their struggle.

There are no headlines—they just get weaker and weaker until that last person who speaks that language dies…and so does one little bit of ethnic diversity on our planet.

This family has the Sri Lankan Dream.

I was raised so proud of Nathan Hale and Patrick Henry and Ethan Allen—patriotic heroes of America's Revolutionary War who wished they had more than one life to give for their country. Having traveled, I've learned that Hales, Henrys, and Allens are commonplace on this planet—each country has their own version.

I believe the US tends to underestimate the spine of other nations. It's comforting to think we can simply bomb our enemies into compliance. This is not only untrue, it's dangerous. Sure, we have the mightiest military in the world. But we don't have a monopoly on bravery or grit. In fact, in some ways, we might be less feisty than hardscrabble, emerging nations that feel they have to scratch and claw for their very survival.

We're comfortable, secure, beyond our revolutionary stage…and well into our Redcoat stage. Regardless of our strength and our righteousness, as long as America has a foreign policy stance that requires a military presence in 150 countries, we will be confronting determined adversaries. We'd be wise to choose our battles carefully. Travel can help us understand that our potential enemies are not cut-and-run mercenaries, but people with spine—motivated by passions and beliefs we didn't even know existed, much less understand.

Growing up in the US, I was told over and over how smart, generous, and free we were. Travel has taught me that the vast majority of humanity is raised with a different view of America. Travelers have a priceless opportunity to see our country through the eyes of other people. I still have the American Dream. But I also respect and celebrate other dreams.

Pry Open Your (Christian) Blinders

The United States may be a Christian nation, but we're certainly not *the* Christian nation. Nor do our Christian values set the worldwide

Travel where few Americans venture...and locals find you exotic, too.

standard for Christian values. As a Lutheran, I was surprised to learn that there are more Lutherans in Namibia than in the US. Even though they wouldn't know what to do with the standard American "green hymnal" and don't bring Jell-O molds to their church picnics, they are as Lutheran as I am. They practice the same faith through a different cultural lens.

While European Christians likely see things as we do, travel in the developing world opens your eyes to new ways of interpreting the Bible. An American or European Christian might define Christ's "preferential option for the poor" or the notion of "sanctity of life" differently from someone who has to put their children to bed hungry every night. While a US Christian may be more concerned about abortion than economic injustice, a Namibian Christian would likely flip-flop those priorities. As for the Biblical Jubilee Year concept (where God—in the Book of Leviticus—calls for the forgiveness of debts and the redistribution of land every fifty years), rich Christians assume God must have been kidding.

Travel beyond the Christian world offers us invaluable opportunities to be exposed to other, sometimes uncomfortable, perspectives. As an American who understands that we have a solemn commitment to protect Israel's security, I am unlikely to be able to sympathize with the Palestinian perspective...unless I see the issue from outside my home culture. And the best way to do that, clearly, is to actually visit Palestine and talk to locals there. That's why I traveled as much in Palestine as in Israel during my recent visit to the Holy Land. Now I understand things better—such as how Israeli settlements in the West Bank stir sentiment in Palestine as much as terrorism stirs sentiment in Israel. And by traveling there, I can understand an unintended consequence of the wall Israel built in the name of security: keeping the younger generations on both sides unable to connect and, therefore, saddled with their parents' outlook and baggage.

I come away from experiences like this one not suddenly convinced of an opposing viewpoint, but with a creeping discomfort about my confidence in the way I've always viewed the world. Whether reading the Bible through "Third World eyes," or having your hometown blinders wedged open by looking at another religion in a new way, travel can be a powerfully spiritual experience.

Get Beyond Your Comfort Zone—Choose to Be Challenged

I've long been enthusiastic about how travel can broaden your perspective. But I didn't always preach this gospel very smartly. Back in the 1970s, in my early days as a tour organizer and guide, I drove fifty or so people each year around Europe in little minibus tours. I had a passion for getting my travelers beyond their comfort zones. Looking back, I cringe at the crudeness, or even cruelty, of my techniques.

As a 25-year-old hippie-backpacker-turned-tour-organizer, I had a notion that soft and spoiled American travelers would benefit from a little hardship. I'd run tours with no hotel reservations and observe the irony of my tour members (who I cynically suspected were unconcerned about homelessness issues in their own communities) being nervous at the prospect of a night without a bed. If, by mid-afternoon, I hadn't arranged for a hotel, they couldn't focus on my guided town walks. In a wrong-headed attempt to force empathy on my flock, I made a point to let them feel the anxiety of the real possibility of no roof over their heads.

Back when I was almost always younger than anyone on my tour, I made my groups sleep in Munich's huge hippie circus tent. With simple mattresses on a wooden floor and 400 roommates, it was like a cross between Woodstock and a slumber party. One night I was stirred out of my sleep by a woman from my group sitting up and sobbing. With the sound of backpackers rutting in the distance, she whispered, apologetically, "Rick, I'm not taking this so very well."

Of course, I eventually learned that you can't just force people into a rough situation and expect it to be constructive. Today, I'm still driven to get people out of their comfort zones and into "the real world." But I've learned to do it more gently and in a way that keeps our travelers coming back for more.

For me, seeing towering stacks of wood in Belfast destined to be anti-Catholic bonfires and talking with locals about sectarian hatred helps make

This memorial in El Salvador remembers loved ones lost fighting the United States.

a trip to Ireland more than just Guinness and traditional folk music in pubs. Taking groups to Turkey during the Iraq wars helped me share a Muslim perspective on that conflict. And I consider visiting a concentration camp memorial a required element of any trip we lead through Germany.

As a tour guide, I make a point to follow up these harsh and perplexing experiences with a "reflections time" where tour members can share and sort out their feelings and observations. I've learned that, even with the comfortable refuge of a good hotel, you can choose to travel to complicated places and have a valuable learning experience.

Not long ago, I had an opportunity to hang out on the beach for a family vacation in the ritzy Mexican resort of Mazatlán. I needed a break and was fantasizing about a pristine stretch of tropical beach, swept free of local riff-raff…just me and my rich, white friends soaking it up: plastic straps on our wrists so we didn't even need to dirty our fingers with the local currency, and all the margaritas we wanted, whenever we liked. It was going to be great. Then, some friends invited me to join them for a trip to San Salvador (the capital of El Salvador) to remember Archbishop Oscar Romero on the 25th anniversary of his assassination. But there was one problem: It was the same week as my beach break.

I told my family I'd be no fun on the beach. For my vacation, I opted for El Salvador—to share a muggy bunk-bed dorm, eat rice and beans, be covered in bug bites, and march with the Salvadorans in honor of their martyred hero who stood up to what they consider American imperialism.

The march passed a long, shiny, black monument exactly like our Vietnam Veterans Memorial. My local friends (who admitted they'd copied our design) stressed that this monument honored their heroes who died in a civil war—fighting against American interests and American-funded troops. Scanning this long list of names (as many as on our Vietnam memorial back home in DC), I recalled how, at the time, I was taught that these Salvadorans were communists and needed to be stopped. But my new friends considered them heroes fighting against structural poverty—for the noble cause of letting peasants own their own land. We can debate the merits of that war, and who was right and who was wrong. But there's no debate that El Salvador is still saddled with the weight of a national tragedy that will forever shape their outlook. Through my travels, I've learned, firsthand, how there are good people waging heroic struggles all over the world… some of them against my country.

If you've got a week to spend in Latin America, you can lie on a beach in Mazatlán, you can commune with nature in Costa Rica, or you can grapple with our nation's complex role in a country like El Salvador. I've done all three, and enjoyed each type of trip. But El Salvador was far more memorable than the others. The tourism industry has its own priorities. But as a traveler, you always have the option to choose challenging and educational destinations—to choose transformational travel.

See the Rich/Poor Gap for Yourself

After traveling the world, you come home recognizing that Americans are good people with big hearts. We may be compassionate and kind, and we may operate with the best of intentions. But as citizens of a giant, powerful nation—isolated from the rest of the world by geography, as much as by our wealth—it can be challenging for many Americans to understand that poverty across the sea is as real as poverty across the street. We struggle to grasp the huge gap between the wealthy and the poor. It may be human nature to choose ignorance when it comes to this reality, but it's better character to reckon with it honestly.

Anyone can learn that half of the people on this planet are trying to live on $2 a day, and a billion people are trying to live on $1 a day. You can read that the average lot in life for women on this planet is to spend a good part

Imagine the power of a well which, with each pump and gush of water, makes an otherwise thirsty villager think, "Thank you, America."

of their waking hours every day walking for water and firewood. But when you travel to the developing world, you meet those "statistics" face-to-face... and the problem becomes more real.

In San Salvador, I met Beatriz, a mother who lives in a cinderblock house under a corrugated tin roof. From the scavenged two-by-four that holds up her roof, a single wire arcs up to a power line that she tapped into to steal electricity for the bare bulb that lights her world each night. She lives in a ravine the city considers "unfit for habitation." She's there not by choice, but because it's near her work and she can't afford bus fare to live beyond walking distance to the place that pays $6 a day for her labor. Apart from her time at work, she spends half the remaining hours of her day walking for water. Her husband is gone, and she's raising two daughters. Beatriz is not unusual on this planet. In fact, among women, she's closer to the global norm than most women in the United States.

I went home from that trip and spent $5,000 to pay for my daughter Jackie's braces. And I had money left over for whitener. I noticed every kid in Jackie's class has a family that can afford $5,000 for straight teeth.

This is not a guilt trip. I work hard and am part of a winning economic system in a stable land that makes this possible. I love my daughter and am proud to give her straight and white teeth. But I have an appetite to understand

Beatriz's world and the reality of structural poverty. I know that for the price of two sets of braces ($10,000), a well could be dug so that a thirsty village of women like Beatriz would not have to walk for water every day. They would have far more time to spend with their children. I advocate within my world on Beatriz's behalf, and enthusiastically support relief work in the developing world. This is not because I am a particularly good person…it's because I met Beatriz.

Consider for a moment applying this logic on a much larger scale. Let's say our government has one million extra dollars to spend to make us safer—and so, of course, they spend it on a new piece of military hardware (what you might call "hard power"). What if, instead, that million dollars was spent drilling 100 wells in 100 thirsty villages—what you'd call "soft power"? Then, rather than walking across the county every morning to get water, all the mothers in each of those villages could simply walk across the square. And each morning, when they pumped that life-giving water, they'd think, "God bless America." I'd argue that this is not only the decent thing to do with our money—but that it would actually make the US safer than another new gadget for our military. (When you consider that a billion dollars is a thousand times a million, the potential reach and impact of such "soft power" investments is hard to imagine.) The choice is stark, and the consequences are real. I like to think that if decision-makers had these vivid travel experiences to draw from, the world could be both better and safer. (For more on hard power, soft power, and how the USA is perceived abroad, see the "American Empire" sidebar on page 110.)

Okay, Let's Travel…

Now it's time for us to pack up these concepts and hit the road. Through the rest of this book, I'll share specific examples of "Travel as a Political Act":

In the former Yugoslavia—Croatia, Bosnia-Herzegovina, and Montenegro—we'll wander through the psychological and physical wreckage left in the aftermath of a tragic war, take note of the recovery…and ponder the sobering lessons.

Considering the European Union, we'll see how a great society (living in a parallel world to ours) is evolving. The EU is melding together a vast free-trade zone while trying to keep alive the cultural equivalent of the family farm: its ethnic diversity. And yet, the EU is facing unprecedented challenges that threaten its continued survival. We'll consider the impact of Britain

You can travel with your window rolled up...or your window rolled down.

leaving the EU (Brexit), the rise of the populist far-right on the Continent, and the influx of war refugees.

Traveling to El Salvador, we'll learn about the impact of globalization and the reality of a poor country being at the mercy of a rich country—from its own perspective rather than ours.

In Denmark, by delving into contemporary socialism and a hippie attempt at creating a utopia in a society routinely rated the most content in the world, we'll have a stimulating chance to consider a different formula for societal success.

Visiting Turkey and Morocco, we'll witness the challenges and advances of the moderate side of Islam, along with the realities of a rising tide of authoritarianism and of Islamic fundamentalism. This helps balance our perspective at a time when the news of Islam is dominated by coverage of extremists and terrorists.

In the Netherlands, Spain, Switzerland, Portugal, and the United States, we'll compare European and American drug policies, contrasting how equally affluent and advanced societies deal with the same persistent problem in fundamentally different ways.

Exploring Iran, we'll see how fear and fundamentalism can lead a mighty nation to trade democracy for theocracy, and what happens when the "Axis of Evil" meets the "Great Satan"—and we'll do it from an Iranian perspective.

In Israel and Palestine, we'll illustrate how visiting a conflicted land helps you connect with people on both sides. You'll hear both narratives, not just the one that receives more media coverage within our society.

Finally, I'll explain why flying home from each trip reminds me how thankful I am to live in America, why I believe the rich blessings we enjoy as Americans come with certain stewardship responsibilities, and how we can enrich our lives by employing our new perspective more constructively back home.

Chapter 2
Lessons from the Former Yugoslavia: War and Peace in Modern Times

Since World War II, Europe has enjoyed unprecedented peace...except in its southeastern Balkan Peninsula. As Yugoslavia broke apart violently in the early 1990s, the rest of the world watched in disbelief, then in horror, as former compatriots tore apart their homeland and each other.

Today—just a generation later—some parts of the former Yugoslavia have already re-emerged as major tourist attractions. In recent years, I've enjoyed trips to countries that once belonged to Yugoslavia, including Croatia, Bosnia-Herzegovina, and Montenegro. As destinations, they offer profound natural beauty, a relaxing ambience, and a warm welcome. Life goes on here. Local people, while not in denial about the war, would rather not be constantly reminded of it. Many think about this ugliness in their past only when tourists ask them about it.

And yet—although I realize that, in some ways, it does a disservice to these places to view them through the lens of war—I can't help but think about those not-too-distant horrors as I travel here. Seeing the bruised remnants of Yugoslavia is painful yet wonderfully thought-provoking. And, because this book is about how travel can change the way you think about the world, I hope you (and my Balkan friends) will excuse my narrow focus on that war in this chapter.

We begin at the region's top tourist hotspot: the town of Dubrovnik, in Croatia. Nowhere else in Europe can you go so quickly from easy tourism to lands where today's struggles are so vivid and eye-opening—one of many heartbreaking sectarian conflicts all around the globe. Within a few hours' drive of Dubrovnik are several new incarnations of old nations, providing rich opportunities to study the roots and the consequences of one such struggle.

Red Roofs and Mortar Shells in Dubrovnik

I was ready for a little culture shock. Flying from France to Dubrovnik, I got it. I passed through the mammoth, floodlit walls of Dubrovnik's Old Town

and hiked up a steep, tourist-free back lane to my boutique pension perched
at the top of Europe's finest fortified port city. Upon reaching my favorite
Dubrovnik B&B, I was greeted by Pero Carević.

We bellied up to the counter in his kitchen, and Pero uncorked a bottle
of the local firewater, *orahovica*. Hoping to write that evening with a clear
head, I tried to refuse Pero's drink. But this is a Slavic land. Remembering
times when I was force-fed vodka in Russia by new friends, I knew it was
hopeless. Pero had made this hooch himself, with green walnuts. As he
slugged down a shot, he handed me a glass, wheezing, "Walnut grappa—it
recovers your energy."

Showing me the mortar that destroyed his home, Pero smiled.

As we drank, Pero told me
his story: This gorgeous stone and
knotty-wood house, where he grew
up, suffered a direct hit during the
eight-month siege of Dubrovnik in
1991-1992. After the war, Pero got a
monthly retirement check for being
wounded, but was bored and didn't
want to live on the tiny government
stipend. So, he went to work and
turned the remains of his Old Town home into a fine guesthouse.

With a twinkle in his eye, Pero reached under the counter and held up
the mangled tail of a mortar shell—the very shell that destroyed his childhood home. He put the mortar in my hands. Just as I don't enjoy holding a
gun, I didn't enjoy touching the twisted remains of that mortar.

I took Pero's photograph. He held the mortar…and smiled. I didn't want
him to hold the mortar and smile…but that's what he did. He seemed determined to smile—as if it signified a personal victory over the destruction the
mortar had wrought. It's impressive how people can weather tragedy, rebuild,
and move on. Despite the terrors of war just a couple of decades ago, life here
was once again very good and, according to Pero's smile, filled with promise.

From Pero's perch, high above Dubrovnik's rooftops, I studied the view:
countless buildings lassoed within the stout medieval walls. The city is a
patchwork of old-fashioned red-tiled roofs. Pero explained that the random
arrangement of bright- and dark-toned roof tiles indicates the damage caused
by the mortars that were lobbed over the hill by the Serb-dominated Yugoslav
National Army in 1991. The new, brighter-colored tiles marked houses that

In Dubrovnik, brighter tiles mark homes rebuilt after the shelling.

were hit and had been rebuilt. At a glance, it's clear that more than two-thirds of the Old Town's buildings were bombed.

But today, relations between the Croats and their Serb neighbors are on the mend. Pero—whose B&B now houses Serbs who may have bombed his home years ago—says that, with age, someday all the tiles will fade to exactly the same hue.

Poignant as a visit to Dubrovnik may be, rich rewards await those who push on into the interior of the former Yugoslavia. Dubrovnik—the most touristy and comfortable resort on Croatia's Dalmatian Coast—is an ideal springboard for more scintillating sightseeing…including some sobering lessons in sectarian strife. But first, it's important to understand the recent history of the region.

Balkans 101

We hear the term "the Balkans" now and then, and even if we don't know exactly where that is…we know it's a challenging place. The Balkan Peninsula—a wide swath of land in southeastern Europe, stretching from Hungary to Greece—has long been a crossroads of cultures. Over the centuries, an endless string of emperors, crusaders, bishops, and sultans have shaped a region that's extremely diverse…and unusually troubled. These troubles are most profound in the former Yugoslavia—roughly the western half of this peninsula.

Yugoslavia's delicate ethnic balance is notoriously difficult to grasp. The major "ethnicities" of Yugoslavia were all South Slavs— they're descended from the same ancestors and speak closely related languages. (In fact, the word "Yugoslavia" means, roughly, "the union of the South Slavic peoples.") The distinguishing difference is that they practice different religions. Catholic South Slavs are called Croats; Orthodox South Slavs are called Serbs; and Muslim

South Slavs (whose ancestors converted to Islam under Ottoman rule) are called Bosniaks. For the most part, there's no way that a casual visitor can determine the ethnicity of the people just by looking at them.

While relatively few people are actively religious here (because of the stifling atheism of the communist years), they fiercely identify with their ethnicity. And, because ethnicity and faith are synonymous, it's easy to mistake the recent conflicts for "religious wars." But, in reality, they were about the politics of ethnicity (just as the "Troubles" in Ireland were more about British versus Irish rule than simply a holy war between Catholics and Protestants).

"Yugoslavia" was an artificial union of the various South Slav ethnicities that lasted from the end of World War I until 1991. Following the death of its strong-arm leader Tito, Yugoslavia was plunged into war by a spate of land-hungry politicians, a storm of ethnic divisions, and a heritage of fear and mistrust. Many consider the conflict a "civil war," and others see it as a series of "wars of independence." However you define the wars, they—and the ethnic cleansing, systematic rape, and other atrocities that accompanied them—were simply horrific. It's almost miraculous that after a few bloody years (from 1991 to 1995), the many factions laid down their arms and agreed to peace accords. An uneasy peace—firmer and more inspiring with each passing year—has settled over the region.

And yet, hard feelings linger. As a travel writer, I've learned again and again that discussing this region is fraught with controversy. Every time I publish an article on the former Yugoslavia, I receive angry complaints that

I'm "taking sides." (Strangely, I typically hear this complaint from each "side" in equal numbers...which suggests I'm actually succeeding at being impartial.) I believe that if you lined up a panel of experts from this region—historians from prestigious universities, respected journalists, beloved diplomats—and asked them for their take on a particular issue or historical event, each one would have a different version of events, presented as fact. One person's war hero is another person's war criminal. One person's freedom fighter is another person's terrorist. One person's George Washington is another person's Adolf Hitler. It's aggravating, and yet so human. As an outside observer, the best I can do is to sort through the opinions, force myself to see all sides of the story, collect a few random observations to share as food for thought...and encourage readers to learn from the region's tumult.

But there's no substitute for traveling here in person. Walking with the victims of a war through the ruins of their cities gives you "war coverage" you'd never get in front of a TV. Seeing how former enemies find ways to overcome their animosity and heal; enjoying the new energy that teenagers—whose parents did the fighting—bring to the streets; and observing combatants who followed no rules now raising children in the ruins resulting from their mistakes...all of it leaves a strong impression on any visitor.

Buffalo-Nickel Charm on a Road that Does Not Exist

Looking for a change of pace from Croatia's Dalmatian Coast, I drove from Dubrovnik to the city of Mostar, in Bosnia-Herzegovina. Almost everyone doing this trip takes the scenic coastal route. But I took the back road instead: inland first, then looping north through the Serb part of Bosnia-Herzegovina.

While Bosnia-Herzegovina is one country, the 1995 peace accords gerrymandered the land to grant a degree of autonomy to the area where Orthodox Serbs predominate. This Republika Srpska, or "Serbian Republic"—while technically part of Bosnia-Herzegovina—rings the Muslim- and Croat-dominated core of the country on three sides.

When asked for driving tips, Croatians—who avoid Republika Srpska—insisted that the road I hoped to take didn't even exist. As I drove inland from Dubrovnik, directional signs sent me to the tiny Croatian border town...but ignored the major Serb city of Trebinje just beyond. But despite warnings from Croats in Dubrovnik, I found plenty past that lonely border.

As I entered bustling Trebinje, police with ping-pong paddle stop signs pulled me over to inform me that drivers need to have their headlights on at all hours. The "dumb tourist" routine got me off the hook. At an ATM, I withdrew Bosnia-Herzegovina's currency, called the "convertible mark." The name goes back to the 1980s, when, like other countries with fractured economies, they tied their currency to a strong one. It was named after the German mark and given the same value. Today, while Germany has long since switched over to the euro, the original German mark lives on (with its original exchange rate) in a quirky way in Bosnia. But like the country itself, convertible marks are divided. To satisfy the country's various factions, the currency uses both the Roman and the Cyrillic alphabets, and bills have different figureheads and symbols (some bills feature Bosniaks, others Serbs). I stowed a few Bosnian coins as souvenirs. They have the charm of Indian pennies and buffalo nickels.

Coming upon a vibrant market, I had to explore. The produce seemed entirely local. Honey maids eagerly offered me tastes—as if each believed her honey was the sweetest. Small-time farmers—salt-of-the-earth couples as rustic as the dirty potatoes they pulled out of the ground that morning—lovingly displayed their produce on rickety card tables. A tourist here was so rare that there was nothing designed for me to buy. Coming from Croatia, I was primed to think of Serbs as the villains. Wandering through the market, I saw only a hardworking community of farmers offering a foreigner a warm if curious welcome.

In spite of what some said, Bosnia-Herzegovina's Trebinje not only exists, it thrives.

High on a hill overlooking Trebinje is a stately Serbian Orthodox church, with an opulence that belies the modesty of the town filling the valley below. And, as with everything here, its symbolism is loaded: It's modeled after a historically important monastery in Kosovo, a now-independent country that Serbs still claim as their own. Exploring the grounds, I bumped into a youthful monk who had been an exchange student in Cleveland. He had a great sense of humor about our cultural differences. I explained that part of my mission was to help Americans understand, rather than fear, people who looked different. Stroking his long, black beard—which matched his long, black robe—he joked, with a knowing wink, "Around here, a priest *without* a beard looks suspicious."

As I continued along the road, it became apparent that the complex nature of things here comes across in the powerful language of flags. Just as bars throughout Europe don't want football team colors, and pubs throughout Ireland don't want the green or orange of the sectarian groups, flags in this region come with lots of pent-up political anger. Throughout the day I saw different flags, each one flying with an agenda. Croats salute their red-and-white checkerboard flag, while Serbs proudly hoist their flag with four C's (the first letter of "Serb" in the Cyrillic alphabet). But in the not-too-distant past, each of these flags was also employed by an oppressive regime—so Croats and Serbs each view the other's flag as equivalent to a swastika. Meanwhile, the country's official flag—which nobody really embraces (or is offended by)—is a yellow-and-blue, triangle-and-stars configuration dreamed up by the European Union.

While most tourists can't tell the difference, locals notice subtle clues that indicate they're entering a different ethnicity's home turf. These include those highly symbolic flags, discreet but hateful graffiti symbols, pictures of old Serbian kings stenciled onto abandoned buildings, ruined castles guarding ghosts of centuries-old threats on strategic mountain passes, new road signs with politically charged names, and even ATMs with instructions in just one language—Croatian, Bosnian, or Serbian—but not all three. During the days of Yugoslavia, these languages were all lumped together into a single, mutually intelligible mother tongue called "Serbo-Croatian." But, stoked by the patriotism of proud new nationhood, each of these groups artificially distanced its language from the others—inventing new words to replace ones they found "too Serbian" or "too Croatian."

While I met generally gentle and thoughtful people in all communities here, I can also see the potential for more of the sectarian tumult that made

Nevesinje teens gather to see graduation photos.

the 1990s so terrible. There's a certain strata of society in each ethnic community, and when you see them, you can't help but think, "For war…just add bullets and agitate." A café filled with skinhead bodybuilders made me think brains and brawn are a zero-sum game. Some were built like big tubes, with muscles that seemed to squeeze their heads really small. They lived in poverty, amidst broken concrete and angry graffiti, with little but unemployment in their futures.

Later, after a two-hour drive on deserted roads through a rugged landscape, I arrived at the humble Serb crossroads village of Nevesinje. Towns in this region all have a "café row," and Nevesinje is no exception. It was lunchtime, but as I walked through the town, I didn't see a soul with any food on the table—just drinks. In this village, where unemployment is epidemic, it seems locals eat cheaply at home…and then enjoy an affordable coffee or drink at a café.

A cluttered little grocery—with a woman behind the counter happy to make a sandwich—was my answer for lunch. The salami looked like Spam. Going through the sanitary motions, she laid down a piece of waxed paper to catch the meat—but the slices landed wetly on the grotty base of the slicer as they were cut. A strong cup of "Bosnian coffee" (we'd call it "Turkish coffee")—with loose grounds settled in the bottom—cost just pennies in the adjacent café. Munching my sandwich and sipping the coffee carefully to avoid the mud, I watched the street scene.

Big men drove by in little beaters. High-school students crowded around the window of the local photography shop, which had just posted their class graduation photos. The schoolgirls on this cruising drag proved you don't need money to have style. Through a shop window, I could see a newly engaged couple picking out a ring. One moment I saw Nevesinje as very different from my hometown…and the next it seemed essentially the same.

And then, as my eyes wandered to the curiously overgrown ruined building across the street, I noticed bricked-up, pointed Islamic arches…and realized it was once a mosque. As if surveying a horrible crime scene, I had to walk through its backyard. It was a no-man's land of broken concrete and glass. A single half-knocked-over, turban-shaped tombstone still managed to stand. The prayer niche inside, where no one prays anymore, now faced a vacant lot.

The idea that there was a bloody war in this country in your own lifetime is abstract until you actually come here. Walking these streets, I talked with locals about the cruel quirkiness of this war. The towns that got off relatively easy were the ones with huge majorities of one or the other faction. (The tiny minority group would simply be run out of town.) Towns with the most bloodshed and destruction were the most diverse—where no single ethnic group dominated. Because Nevesinje was a predominantly Orthodox town, the Serbs killed or forced out the Muslims and destroyed their mosque. Surviving Muslim refugees reportedly had to walk for a week over a mountain pass to safety in the Muslim-dominated city of Mostar—where, Serbs like to say, "They found better living conditions anyway."

Remaining impartial is an ongoing challenge. It's so tempting to think of the Muslims—who were brutalized in many parts of Bosnia-Herzegovina—as the "victims." But when traveling here, I have to keep reminding myself that elsewhere in this conflict, Serbs or Croats were victimized in much the same way. Early in the war, outcast Serbs migrated to safety in the opposite direction—from Mostar to Nevesinje. On the hillside overlooking Mostar are the ruins of a once-magnificent Serbian Orthodox church—now demolished, just like that mosque in Nevesinje. Travel allows you to fill out a balanced

A ruined mosque is a silent reminder of sectarian fighting in a now thoroughly Serbian, and therefore Orthodox Christian, town.

view of a troubled region...especially if you visit an area that your home media portrays as "the enemy."

Considering the haphazardness of war, I remembered how in France's charming Alsace (the region bordering Germany), all towns go back centuries. Some are perfectly preserved, while those with the misfortune to be caught in the steamroller of war don't have a building standing from before 1945. I recalled that in England, the town of Chester survived while the Nazis leveled nearby Coventry so thoroughly that it brought a new word into their language for bombing to smithereens—to "coventrate" a place. And I remembered the confused patchwork of Dubrovnik's old and new tile roofs. These images—and now this sad, ruined mosque—all humanized the bleak reality and random heartbreak of sectarian strife and war.

Ready to move on, I climbed into my little car, left Nevesinje, and drove out of the mountains. My destination was a city that once symbolized East and West coming together peacefully, then symbolized just the opposite, and today seems to be enjoying a tentative new spirit of peaceful coexistence: Mostar.

Bosnian Hormones and a Shiny New Cemetery

Exploring the city of Mostar—with its vibrant humanity and the persistent reminders of its recent and terrible war—was both exhilarating and emotionally exhausting.

Mostar represents the best and the worst of Yugoslavia. During the Tito years, it was an idyllic mingling of cultures: Catholic Croats, Orthodox Serbs, and Muslim Bosniaks living together in relative harmony, their differences spanned by an Old Bridge that symbolized an optimistic vision of a Yugoslavia where ethnicity didn't matter. And yet, as the country unraveled in the early 1990s, Mostar was gripped by a gory three-way war among those same groups. Not that long ago, the people I now encountered here—those who brought me a coffee at a café, stopped for me when I jaywalked, showed off their paintings, and directed the church choir—had been killing each other.

Mostar's 400-year-old, Turkish-style stone bridge—with its elegant, single, pointed arch—was symbolic of the town's status as the place where East met West in Europe. Then, during the 1990s, Mostar became the tragic poster child of the Bosnian war. Across the world, people felt the town's pain when its beloved bridge—bombarded from the hilltop above—finally collapsed into the river.

Now the bridge has been rebuilt, and Mostar is putting itself back together. But some scars of war are still evident. Most of the Serbs who once lived here have fled deeper into the countryside, into the Republika Srpska. The two groups who still live here are effectively segregated along the front line that divided them during wartime: the Muslims on the east side and the Croats on the west. While the two groups are making some efforts at reintegration, progress has been slow. In 2005, some young Mostarians unveiled a statue. Rather than celebrating a political or military hero, it was of Bruce Lee, who they saw as symbolizing the fight for positive values that all sides could identify with. Lee, who struggled with ethnic divisions between Chinese and white Americans, represented to the people of Mostar an inspirational bridging of cultures. Sadly, two days after the unveiling, even that statue was vandalized.

But there has been lots of progress. As I explored the workaday streets of the town, it seemed that—despite the war damage—Mostar was downright thriving. Trg Musala (literally "Place for Prayer Square") is designed for big gatherings. Muslim groups meet at the square before departing for Mecca on their pilgrimage, or Hajj. But on the night of my visit, there was not a hint of prayer. It was prom night. The kids were out...Bosnian hormones were raging. Being young and sexy is a great equalizer. With a beer, loud music, desirability, twinkling stars—and no war—your family's income and your country's GDP hardly matter. Today's 18-year-old Mostarians have no memory of the war that shaped their parents' lives. Looking at these kids and their dried-apple grandparents clad in dusty black, warming benches on the "Place for Prayer" square, I imagined that there must be quite a generation gap.

Mostar's beloved, Turkish-style Old Bridge is rebuilt and once again brings hope that East and West can meet and mix gracefully.

I was swirling in a snow globe of teenagers, and through the commotion, a thirtysomething local came at me with a huge smile: Alen from Orlando. Actually, he's from Mostar, but fled to Florida during the war and now spends summers with his family here. A fan of my public television series, he immediately offered to show me around his hometown.

Alen's local perspective gave Mostar meaning. He pointed to a fig tree growing out the window of a small minaret. Seeming to speak as much about Mostar's people as its vegetation, Alen said, "It's a strange thing in nature… figs can grow with almost no soil." Even along the main drag, there were still blackened ruins from the war. When I asked why—after more than two decades—that prime property still had not been touched, Alen explained, "There's confusion about who owns what. Surviving companies have no money. The Bank of Yugoslavia, which held the mortgages, is now gone. No one will invest until it's clear who owns the buildings." I had never considered the financial confusion that follows the breakup of a country, and how it could stunt a society's redevelopment.

We walked to a small cemetery congested with more than a hundred white-marble Muslim tombstones. Alen pointed out the dates: Everyone died in 1993, 1994, or 1995. Before 1993, this was a park. When the war heated up, snipers were a constant concern—they'd pick off anyone they saw walking down the street. Because of the ongoing danger, bodies were left for weeks, rotting on the main boulevard, which had become the front line. Mostar's cemeteries were too exposed to be used, but this tree-filled

On Mostar's main square, children of former combatants embrace life…and are ready to party.

This cemetery, once a park, is filled with tombstones all dated 1993, 1994, or 1995.

park was relatively safe from snipers. People buried their neighbors here…under the cover of darkness.

Weaving slowly through the tombstones, Alen explained, "In those years, night was the time when we lived. We didn't walk…we ran. And we dressed in black. There was no electricity. If the Croats didn't kill us with their bullets, they killed us with their music." That politically charged, rabble-rousing Croatian pop music, used—apparently effectively—as a kind of psychological torture, was blasting constantly from the Croat side of town.

As we wandered through town, the sectarian symbolism of the conflict was powerful. Ten minarets pierced Mostar's skyline like proud Muslim exclamation points. Across the river, twice as high as the tallest minaret, stood the Croats' new Catholic church spire. Standing on the reconstructed Old Bridge, I looked at the hilltop high above the town, with its single, bold, and strongly floodlit cross. Alen said, "We believe that cross marks the spot from where they shelled this bridge. They built it there intentionally, and floodlight it each night…like a celebration."

You can travel all the way to a place as instructive and fascinating as Mostar…and not quite cross the goal line. It's important to reach beyond the tourist-friendly zones and connect with real neighborhoods. That evening, leaving my hotel with dinner in mind, I reflexively headed for the romantic strip of touristy restaurants with English menus and glorious views of the iconic and floodlit

Firsthand Accounts Make History Spring to Life

Learning from a local who actually lived through the war made my Mostar visit a particularly rich experience. Thankful for the lessons I learned in Mostar, I considered the value of firsthand accounts in my travels over the years.

When I was a gawky 14-year-old, my parents took me to Europe. In a dusty village on the border of Austria and Hungary, a family friend introduced me to a sage old man with breadcrumbs in his cartoonish white handlebar moustache. As the man spread lard on rustic bread, he shared his eyewitness account of the assassination of Archduke Franz Ferdinand in 1914. I was thrilled by history as never before.

In Prague, my Czech friend Honza took me on the walk he had taken every night for a week in 1989 with 100,000 of his countrymen as they demanded freedom from their Soviet overlords. The walk culminated in front of a grand building, where Honza said, "Night after night we assembled here, pulled out our key chains, and all jingled them at the president's win-

dow, saying, 'It's time for you to go now.' Then one night we gathered... and he was gone. We had won our freedom." Hearing Honza tell that story as we walked that same route drilled into me the jubilation of a small country winning its freedom.

My Norwegian uncle Thor gave me a similarly powerful experience in Oslo. Gazing at mosaic murals in the Oslo City Hall that celebrate the heroics of locals who stood strong against German occupation, Thor told me stories of growing up in a Nazi-ruled Norway. He woke up one morning to find his beloved royal family in exile and German soldiers on every corner.

A lard-eater with a big moustache made history fun for a 14-year-old future travel writer.

With a local guide, like Aziz in Morocco, you'll learn more than just where to get the best tea.

Norway's resistance fighters took to the snowy mountains, coordinating with brave townspeople to smuggle children to safety. Despite the vastly stronger occupying force, Thor told how his country's national spirit remained strong, and how everyone rejoiced on the glorious day the king returned and Norwegian flags flew happily again. As Thor brought the mural to life, I wondered what I would do to win back a freedom lost.

In Northern Ireland, my guide Stephen was determined to make his country's struggles vivid. In Belfast, he introduced me to the Felons' Club—where membership is limited to those who've spent at least a year and a day in a British prison for political crimes. Hearing heroic stories of Irish resistance while sharing a Guinness with a celebrity felon gives you an affinity for their struggles. Walking the next day through the green-trimmed gravesites of his prison-mates who starved themselves to death for the cause of Irish

independence capped the experience powerfully.

El Salvador's history is so tragic and fascinating that anyone you talk to becomes a tour guide. My Salvadoran guides with the greatest impact were the "Mothers of the Disappeared," who told me their story while leafing through humble scrapbooks showing photographs of their sons' bodies—mutilated and decapitated. Learning of a cruel government's actions from those sad mothers left me with lifetime souvenirs: a cynicism about many governments (you can tell by their actions whom they really represent) and an empathy for underdogs courageously standing up to their leaders when necessary.

Tourists can go to Prague, Norway, Ireland, and Central America and learn nothing of a people's struggles. Or, they can seek out opportunities to connect with people (whether professional guides or accidental guides) who can share perspective-changing stories.

With a shrapnel souvenir embedded in her back, this shopkeeper will forever feel the pain of a senseless war.

bridge. But then, my appetite for education commanded, "Halt." Rather than the easy, no-stress dinner on the riverfront, I stopped, turned 180 degrees, walked in the opposite direction, and risked earning a lifelong memory.

I took my business to the main boulevard—the former front line, where a few tentative businesses had re-opened. I stumbled upon a new-looking café and ordered a plate of stuffed peppers and a Sarajevska beer. The young man who served me had just opened his bar here, on the Muslim side. Immediately across the street stands the new Catholic church, with its oversized steeple. He said that while bullets are no longer flying, he was worried about vandalism from young, hate-filled men across the road. He had been open two months, and so far, no problem. Eating my meal, I was surrounded by poignant sights and sounds. First a warbly call to prayer echoed across town. Then the church bells tolled determinedly across the street. All the while, a little boy with training wheels on his pint-sized bike pedaled vigorously around and around a new sidewalk by a bomb-damaged line of buildings and grass too young to walk on. He went faster and faster, gaining confidence with each circle.

The next day, I popped into a small theater where 30 Slovenes (from the northernmost part of the former Yugoslavia, which avoided the terrible destruction of the war) were watching a short film about the Old Bridge, its destruction, and its rebuilding. The persistent shelling of the venerable bridge, so rich in symbolism, seemed to go on and on. The Slovenes knew the story well. But when the video reached the moment when the bridge finally fell, I heard a sad collective gasp. It reminded me of how Americans feel, even well after 9/11, when watching video of the World Trade Center disappearing into a column of ash. This experience helped me, if not feel, at least appreciate another country's pain.

At lunchtime, I stopped at a tiny grocery store, where I was happy to see a woman I had befriended the day before. She was a gorgeous person, sad

Smells like Bosnian teen spirit.

to be living in a frustrating economy, and stiff with a piece of shrapnel in her back that doctors decided was safer left in. She made me a hearty ham sandwich and helped me gather the ingredients of what would be a fine picnic. Stooping to pick up items on shelves lower than she could bend to reach, I considered how this woman's life will be forever marred by that war.

The sentiment I hear from locals when I visit this region is, "I don't know how we could have been so stupid to wage that unnecessary war." I've never met anyone here who called the war anything but a tragic mistake. The lesson I learned from their mistake is the importance of taking pluralism within your society seriously. While Bosnian sectarianism may be particularly extreme, every society has groups that could come to blows. And failing to find a way to live peacefully together—as the people of Mostar learned—means everybody loses.

That night in Mostar, as the teenagers ripped it up at their dance halls, I lay in bed sorting out my impressions. Until the wee hours, a birthday party raged in the restaurant outside my window. For hours they sang songs. At first I was annoyed. Then I realized that a Bosniak "Beach Boys" party beats a night of shelling. In two hours of sing-alongs, everyone seemed to know all the words…and I didn't recognize a single tune. In spite of all its challenges and setbacks, I have no doubt that this Bosnian culture will rage on.

Nouveau Riche and Humble Devotion on the Bay of Kotor

Circling back to Dubrovnik, I drove south to yet another new nation that emerged from the ashes of Yugoslavia: Montenegro. During my travels through this region, my punch-drunk passport would be stamped and stamped and stamped again. While the unification of Europe has made

most border crossings feel archaic, the breakup of Yugoslavia has kept them
in vogue here. Every time the country splintered, another border was set up.
The poorer the country, it seems, the more ornate the border formalities.
And, by European standards, Montenegro is about as poor as it gets. They
don't even have their own currency. With just 600,000 people, they decided,
heck, let's just use euros.

For me, Montenegro, which means "Black Mountain," has always evoked
the fratricidal chaos of a bygone age. I think of a time when fathers in the
Balkans taught their sons that "your neighbor's neighbor is your friend" in
anticipation of future sectarian struggles. Back when, for generation after
generation, so-and-so-ovich was pounding on so-and-so-ovich, a mountain
stronghold was worth the misery.

My recent visit showed me that this image is now dated, the country is
on an upward trajectory, and many expect to see Montenegro emerging as a
sunny new hotspot on the Adriatic coastline. International investors (mostly
from Russia and Saudi Arabia) are pouring money into what they hope will
become their very own Riviera.

Unfortunately, when rich people paste a glitzy facade onto the crumbling
infrastructure of a poor country that isn't ready for it, you get a lot of pizzazz
with no substance. I stayed at a supposedly "designer" hotel that, at first glance,
felt so elite and exclusive that I expected to see Idi Amin poolside. But the hotel,
open just a month, was a comedy of horrible design. I felt like I was their first

A zigzag road leads high above the Bay of Kotor to the historic capital of Montenegro.

Montenegro's Bay of Kotor rewards the curious traveler.

guest ever. My bathroom was far bigger than many European hotel rooms, but the toilet was jammed in the corner. I had to tuck up my knees to sit on it. The room was dominated by a large hot tub for two, but I am certain there wasn't enough hot water available to fill it. I doubt it will ever be used (except for something to look at as you're crunched up on the toilet).

A huge thunderstorm hit with enough fury to keep the automatic glass doors opening and closing on their own. Nothing drained—a torrent ran down the stairs outside the front door. With the rain, a backed-up sewage smell drove me out of my room. And just as I sat down for a cup of coffee in the lounge, the lights went out. Peering past the candelabra on my table, the overwhelmed receptionist explained with a shrug, "When it rains, there is no electricity." The man who runs the place just looked at me and said, "Cows." (I think he meant "chaos.")

Eventually the rain stopped, the clouds parted, and I continued exploring. The first major stop in Montenegro when arriving from Dubrovnik is the Bay of Kotor, where the Adriatic cuts into the steep mountains like a Norwegian fjord. And there, at the humble waterfront town of Perast, young guys in swim trunks edged their boats near the dock, jockeying to motor tourists out to the island in the middle of the bay. According to legend, fishermen saw the Virgin Mary in the reef and began a ritual of dropping a stone on the spot every time they sailed by. Eventually the island we see today was created, and upon that island the people built a fine little church.

I hired a guy with a dinghy to ferry me out and was met by a young woman who gave me a tour. In the sacristy hung a piece of embroidery—a 25-year-long labor of love made by a local parishioner 200 years ago. It was as exquisite as possible, lovingly made with the finest materials available: silk and the woman's own hair. I could trace her laborious progress through the line of cherubs that ornamented the border. As the years went by, the hair

of the angels (like the hair of the devout artist) turned from dark brown to white. Humble and anonymous as she was, she had faith that her work was worthwhile and would be appreciated—as it is, two centuries later, by a steady parade of travelers from distant lands.

I've been at my work for more than three decades now. I also have a faith that it (my work, if not my hair) will be appreciated after I'm gone. That's perhaps less humble than the woman was, but her work reassured me that we can live on through our deeds. Her devotion to her creation (as well as to her creator) is an inspiration to do both good and lasting work. While traveling, I'm often struck by how people give meaning to their life by producing and contributing.

I didn't take a photograph of the embroidery that day. For some reason, I didn't even take notes. At the moment, I didn't realize I was experiencing the highlight of my day. The impression of the woman's tenderly created embroidery needed—like a good red wine—time to breathe. That was a lesson for me. I was already mentally on to the next thing. When the power of the impression opened up, it was rich and full-bodied...but I was long gone. If travel is going to have the impact on you that it should, you have to climb into those little dinghies and reach for those experiences—the best ones won't come to you. And you have to let them breathe.

Monks, Track Suits, and Europe's Worst Piano in the Heartland of Montenegro

Most tourists stick to Montenegro's scenic Bay of Kotor. But—inspired by my back-roads Bosnian experience—I was eager to get off the beaten path and headed deep into the rugged interior of the "Black Mountain."

I climbed 25 switchbacks—someone painted numbers on each one—ascending from the Montenegrin coast with its breezy palm trees, bustling ice cream stands, and romantic harbor promenades into a world of lonely goats, scrub brush, and remote, seemingly deserted farmhouses. At switchback #4, I passed a ramshackle Roma encampment. I thought about how, all over our world, nomadic cultures are struggling; they're at odds with societies that demand fences, conventional land ownership, and other non-nomadic ways. I wonder how many nomadic cultures (American Indians, Eskimos, Kurds, Bedouins, Roma) will still be here in generations to come.

At switchback #18, I pulled out for a grand view of the Bay of Kotor and, pulling on my sweater, marveled at how the vegetation, climate, and ambience were completely different just a few twists in the road above sea level.

At switchback #24, I noticed the "old road" faintly cutting up the adjacent slope. While little more than an overgrown donkey path, that was once the mountain kingdom's umbilical cord to the Adriatic…its connection to the world. The most vivid thing I remember about my last visit, decades ago, was that a grand piano had literally been carried up the mountain on that tiny lane so some big-shot nobleman could let it go slowly out of tune in his palace.

As I crested the ridge, the sea disappeared and before me stretched a basin defined by a ring of black mountains—Montenegro's heartland. Exploring the poorest corner of any European country can be eye-opening—but Montenegro's is more evocative than most. Desolate farmhouses posted handwritten signs advertising smoked ham, mountain cheese, and *medovina* (honey brandy), but I didn't see a soul.

I came into a village that looked like it had no commerce at all. Stopping at a lonely tavern, I asked the bartender, "What do people do here?" He led me to a big, blocky, white building resembling a giant Monopoly house. He opened the door and I stepped inside, under tons of golden ham aging peacefully. It was a smokehouse—jammed with five layers of hanging ham hocks. My new Montenegrin friend stoked up his fire, filling the place with smoke. Ever since, as I explore back lanes in sleepy villages, I'm mindful that more industry than I realize may be hiding out.

The drive felt somehow menacing. Because up here, the Cyrillic alphabet survives better than on the coast, most signage was illegible to me. But every hundred yards or so, the local towing company had spray-painted on a rock, in lettering seemingly designed for the stray tourist: "*Auto Šlep* 067-838-555." I had a feeling they were in the bushes praying for a mishap. Pulling off for a photo of the valley, I noticed a plaque marking where Tito's trade minister was assassinated in a 1948 ambush.

At the end of the road was Cetinje, which the road sign proclaimed as the "Old Royal Capital." I'm nostalgic about this town, a classic mountain kingdom (with that grotesquely out-of-tune grand piano) established as the capital in the 15th century. Cetinje was taken by the Ottomans several times. The rampaging Ottomans would generally move in and enjoy a little raping, pillaging, and plundering. But, quickly realizing there was little hedonism to enjoy in Cetinje, they basically just destroyed the place and moved out. With the way clear, the rugged and determined residents filtered back into the ruins of their town, rebuilt, and awaited the next invasion.

Today Cetinje is a workaday, two-story town with barely a hint of its old royal status. The museums are generally closed. The economy is flat. A shoe factory and a refrigerator factory were abandoned with Yugoslavia's breakup. (They were part of Tito's economic vision for Yugoslavia—where, in the name of efficiency, individual products were made in huge quantities by government-run plants to supply the entire country.) Kids on bikes rolled like tumbleweeds down the main street past old-timers with hard memories.

At the edge of town is the St. Peter of Cetinje Orthodox monastery—the still-beating spiritual heart of Montenegro. I stepped in. An Orthodox monk—black robe and beard flowing halfway to his waist—nodded a welcome. A service was in progress. Flames flickered on gilded icons, incense created an otherworldly ambience, and the chanting was almost hypnotic.

I stood (as everyone does in Orthodox worship) in the back. People—mostly teenagers in sporty track suits—were trickling in…kissing everything in sight. Seeing these rough and casual teens bending respectfully at the waist as they kissed icons, bibles, and the hands of monks was mesmerizing. If you saw them on the streets, you'd never dream that they'd be here standing through a long Orthodox service.

For the first time, I understood what the iconostasis (called a "rood screen" in Western Europe) is all about. Used long ago in Catholic churches, and still today in Orthodox churches, the screen separates the common worshippers from the zone where the priests do all the religious "heavy lifting." Behind the screen—which, like a holy lattice, provides privacy but still lets you peek through—I could see busy priests in fancy robes, and above it all the outstretched arms of Jesus. I knew he was on the cross, but because of the height of the screen, I only saw his arms. As the candlelight flickered, I felt they were happy arms…wanting and eager to give everyone present a big, Slavic bear hug.

Deep in Montenegro, the Monastery of St. Peter of Cetinje is an integral part of the community.

Standing through an Eastern Orthodox service in a humble church in the forgotten historic capital of a mountain kingdom, I was thankful I had zigzagged to that remote corner of Europe. All those switchbacks earned me the chance to witness a vibrant and time-honored tradition surviving the storms of globalization and modernization. It occurred to me that places like this—with virtually zero mainstream tourism—often reward the curious traveler with some of the very best "sightseeing."

Back on the main street, in the middle of this Montenegrin nowhere, I met an American family traveling with their 91-year-old grandmother. We shared stories of beautiful times we'd each enjoyed and lessons we'd learned getting to know the people in this region. The grandma said, "Traveling in places like this inspires me to keep going when I should be staying home."

Alone again, I sat on Cetinje's main square. Nursing a gritty cup of coffee, I watched kids coming home from school. Two older girls walked by happily spinning the same kind of batons my sisters spun when I was a tyke. And then a sweet younger girl walked by all alone—lost in thought, carrying a tattered violin case.

Even in a country without its own currency, in a land where humble is everything's middle name, parents can find an old violin and manage to give their little girls grace and culture. Letting that impression breathe, it made me happier than I imagined it would.

Traveling in war-torn former Yugoslavia, I see how little triumphs can be big ones. I see hardscrabble nations with big aspirations. And, I see the value of history in understanding our travels, and the value of travel in understanding our history.

Chapter 3
Europe Unites: Successes and Struggles

While I dabble in the rest of the world, my true love is Europe. Since my first trip there in 1969, I've enjoyed gaining an appreciation for Europe's history, art, culture, cuisine, music…and politics.

In my lifetime, the big news in Europe has been its gradual unification. In 1947, in the rubble of a bombed-out Europe, the Continent's leaders gathered and thought, "We've dug out after horrific wars twice in our lifetime. We need to do something creative and drastic, or our children will be digging out yet again." Their solution was to unite—to weave the economies of France and Germany together, so another big war between the two big Continental powers would be unthinkable. Of course, a union is nothing without people giving up some measure of sovereignty. Since 1947, proponents of a European Union have been convincing the people of proud and independent nations to trade away bits and pieces of their independence. It's a tough sell. But in a fitful evolution—two steps forward and one step back—over the last seven or so decades, they have created a European Union.

The European Union (EU) has succeeded in attaining its founders' two key goals: avoiding intra-European war and integrating European economies. But for some, all of the changes have been too much, too fast. And as I write this (late 2017), Europe is facing some of its most significant challenges yet—raising the question of how much longer things can hold together. I'll admit, I'm a big believer in the EU and its ideals. But in this chapter, I'll also discuss some hard realities. Today, for the first time that I can remember, the future of the European Union is in doubt.

EU worries aside, Europe is the part of the world most similar to the USA. That's why I consider it the wading pool for world exploration. Americans and Europeans are both affluent, well-educated peoples who love their freedom. But, while we have much in common, we also have fundamental differences. I learn a lot about America by studying Europe. Europeans do some things better than we do. Some things, they do worse. And, most things are open to debate. Europe doesn't have all the answers—but neither do we.

Considering innovative European approaches to persistent challenges that vex our own nation can be constructive. This chapter assembles a few of my favorite examples.

Europe's "Big Government": High Taxes with High Expectations

While Europe has its share of economic woes, there's no denying that Europeans have created a vast free-trade zone that keeps the Continent competitive with the United States and with the emerging economic giants of China and India. With the unification of Europe, hundreds of millions of people now have the same euro coins jingling in their pockets.

Although Europe has a mighty economy, they strive to balance business concerns with socialistic policies. And for most Europeans, that works well. While many American politicians present voters with two options—big, bad government or little, good government—Europeans believe there's a third option: big, good government.

In American politics, "socialism" is often perceived as an all-or-none boogeyman, evoking the stifling Soviet system of the Cold War. But this thinking ignores the full spectrum of socialism. Every country on earth—including our own—includes some socialistic elements (such as our progressive taxation and the entitlements that we've come to see as the mark of a caring and civilized society).

Like us, Europe is enthusiastically capitalistic. Europeans are just more comfortable with a higher degree of socialism. Most Europeans continue to favor their existing high (and highly progressive) tax rates. That's because they believe that collectively creating the society of their dreams is more important than allowing individuals to create the personal empires of their dreams.

While American culture tends to be individualistic—inspired by "up by the bootstraps" and "rags to riches" stories—Europe is more focused on community. While as a society we are more religious, Europe is more humanistic. In Scandinavia—the most highly taxed,

The Old World comes with a youthful energy.

socialistic, and humanistic corner of Europe—you don't find a church with a steeple on the main square. Instead, you find a City Hall with a bell tower. Inside, a secular nave leads not to a pulpit, but to a lectern. Behind that lectern, a grand mosaic tells epic stories—not from the Bible, but celebrating heroic individuals who contributed mightily to their community.

Europeans pay high taxes to buy big, good government…and they expect results. Those results include an extensive social-welfare network that puts the financial burden of childcare, healthcare, education, and retirement on the collective shoulders of society, rather than on individuals. I once asked Olle, my Swiss friend, "How can you Swiss people be so docile about paying such high taxes?" Without missing a beat, he replied, "Well, what's it worth to live

in a society where there is no homelessness, no hunger, and where every child—regardless of the wealth of their parents—enjoys equal access to quality healthcare and education?" (And Olle is no liberal firebrand. He's considered a solid conservative leader in his community.)

Olle and Maria pay high taxes with high expectations... high in the Alps.

The benefits are everywhere. A Slovenian friend of mine who had a baby was guaranteed a year's maternity leave at near-full pay…and was given a state-subsidized "starter kit" with all the essential gear she needed to care for her newborn. If anyone (even a foreign traveler) goes to a public hospital for urgent care in Europe, they often won't even see the bill. Higher education in Europe is subsidized; in many countries, it's entirely free, and students even get "pocket money" while they are learning. (Europeans consider a well-educated society fundamental to their notion of national security.) Hundreds of thousands of students and professors have traveled to other EU countries to study, teach, and build a sprawling network of intra-European relations through the EU-funded Erasmus Program.

Don't get me wrong: Europeans grumble about paying sky-high taxes as much as anyone, and tax evasion is a national pastime for many. But philosophically, they understand that when it comes to taxes, the necessity outweighs the evil. European politicians don't have to promise tax cuts to win elections. Many European voters support high taxes and big government because they like what they get in return.

A flipside of this system is that Europe doesn't have the ethic of individual charitable giving that we have in the US. We go to auctions

In Stockholm, like elsewhere in humanistic Scandinavia, the city hall's bell tower rather than a church spire marks the center of town.

and bake sales to support a good cause. We help our children raise money to subsidize school activities. Our local orchestras wouldn't exist without financial gifts from donors committed to that slice of culture. And public television is made possible through the generous support from viewers like you. You don't see that so much in Europe. Europeans expect the government to care for the needy, educate young people, and support the arts. Europe's tax-funded alternative to charity auctions, pledge drives, and school car washes works for them.

In our system, the thinking is that, after we all get wealthy, we'll be sure to make charitable contributions to the places where the fabric of our society is frayed. But Europe is more socialistic. Rather than "a thousand points of light" emanating from generous community members who care, Europeans prefer one compassionate, well-organized, and collectively funded searchlight from their entire society, orchestrated by elected officials. While we care individually, they care collectively. Features that are perceived as good for the fabric of their community (such as bike lanes, heroin maintenance clinics, quality noncommercial broadcasting, after-school childcare for working parents, paid maternity and paternity leave, and freeway art) take priority over personal interests. Through progressive taxation, everyone contributes according to their ability...and regardless of the size of their heart.

European Solutions

Throughout the world, people solve similar problems with different approaches. Here are some European answers.

1 All my life, I've paid the city for a sanitation worker to pick up my garbage. In Switzerland, the garbage bag costs more...and includes pick-up. When it's full, put it out on any curb. The next morning, it's gone. **2** An Italian law requires drivers to wear a seatbelt. Your car makes annoying noises if you don't buckle up. So the Italians, in their own creative way, have designed a handy little plug to quiet their car. *Problema finito.* **3** Junk mail exasperates us. Others don't like junk mail, either. Many Europeans have a simple solution. They put a decal on the mailbox that says simply "no" or "yes" to different types of junk mail. **4** While we have stop signs in the middle of nowhere, the British have roundabouts. You don't stop. You wing into that roundabout and take off at the exit of your choice. **5** In the Netherlands, they have four-story parking garages for bicycles. The Dutch take the train in, hop on their bike, and pedal to work. It's not necessarily out of dedication to the environment. Biking simply works well.

Both the United States and Europe are enthusiastic about "government by, for, and of the people." But I've noticed a fundamental difference: In America, this is by, for, and of the people via the corporations we own. In other words, we think a primary role of government is to create an economic atmosphere where the corporations we own can prosper. I was raised with the business mantra, "What's good for GM is good for America."

In Europe, on the other hand, they choose government by, for, and of the people in spite of the corporations they own. Their government would more likely go to bat for the environment, the poor, the future, and the long-term interests of society. Their attitude: "What's good for the worker is good for corporate Europe."

Consequently, Europe is willing to consider laws that are (at least in the narrow view) bad for business. While in Europe, the notion of paying for a car's disposal when you first buy the car makes sense, it would be dismissed in the US as bad for the economy. Because carbon taxes are considered good for the environment but bad for business, I doubt you'll see them anytime soon in the US—but several European countries already have them.

Even as Europeans accept this system, they love to complain about the heavy-handedness of big government. Cumbersome bureaucracy creeps into virtually all aspects of European life. Strict health codes for restaurants dictate that cooked food must be frozen if it's not served within three hours. My Czech friend complained, "This makes many of our best dishes illegal." (Czech specialties, often simmered overnight, taste better the next day.) A Polish farmer I know gripes that, when Poland joined the EU, he had to get "passports" for each of his cows. Italians chafed at having to wear helmets while riding their otherwise stylish *motorini*. Throughout the EU, people are struggling to compromise as one-size-fits-all governance takes a toll on some of their particular passions. (Frustration with these kinds of regulations—coming from Brussels rather than from London—helped nudge many Britons to vote for Brexit.)

While Europeans seem to find clever ways to get government on their backs, the American chorus has long been, "Get the government off our backs." We don't want regulations—especially the extreme examples cited above. America has long had a less-regulated business environment than Europe. And even smartly motivated attempts to create commonsense regulations—such as the reforms put in place after the 2008 financial crisis—are rolled back as soon as the electorate's short memory will allow.

Is Brexit Contagious?: The Rise of Populism and Nativism

I'm militantly optimistic when it comes to the European Union. But my confidence has been shaken by recent political events. In June of 2016, Britain voted yes on Brexit. If and when that vote is realized, Britain will become the first EU member to leave the union (and a big, wealthy, powerful one at that). This event has sent the rest of Europe scrambling to figure out the state of a post-Brexit EU, and—in some countries—to ask whether they should also head for the exit.

The Brexit vote also threw into high relief several looming crises that have long vexed the EU. Some Southern European states (Greece, Spain, Portugal, and Italy) have still not fully emerged from a nearly decade-long economic crisis. The expansion of the euro currency has stalled, as Europeans face pressing questions about which countries have earned—or lost— the right to use the euro, and how the currency should be managed to benefit all members fairly.

Meanwhile, Europe's increased numbers of immigrants over the last generation—arguably necessary to keep Europe vital as its native population ages—has angered many Europeans. Europe is struggling to find a clear policy on handling refugees from nearby failed states and war zones. And many "Euroskeptics" are fed up with what they see as ineffective EU bureaucracy, gumming up their lives without improving them. (As a frequent visitor, I see plenty of big improvements—but when you're an angry taxpayer, it's easy to ignore the positives.)

Writing this in late 2017, it's easy to draw parallels between Europe and the USA, with our election of President Trump. In both places, I see a rise in anger against globalization, economic malaise, and a sense that immigrants are "cutting in line" ahead of natives. And to be fair, the lives of working-class people, in both Europe and the US, have in many cases grown more difficult as the world has changed. I truly believe that these are good people, motivated by fear (of a changing world) and love (wanting a prosperous future for their families).

Trump, the pro-Brexit camp, and other nativist, populist movements in Europe ingeniously tailor their messaging to this electorate, which has often been ignored by the political mainstream. And by playing fast and loose with "facts" and "news," they've convinced these voters that they have all the answers. (On the day after the Brexit vote, some pro-Brexiters sheepishly admitted that some of their advertising had intentionally misled voters.) The result, as I see it, is that these movements have convinced voters to willingly (or unwittingly) vote against their economic self-interest.

Whether it's "Put the 'Great' Back in Britain," "A Hunger for a More Hungarian Hungary," "Keep France White and French," or "Make America Great Again," the strategy is impressively consistent. Of course, Europe will survive. But will the European Union?

More recently, a whole spectrum of regulations—designed to rein in banks, protect consumers, defend civil liberties, and protect the environment— have been branded "job-killers."

On the other hand, in Europe, workers' protection, environmental protection, and what seems like an obsession for regulations in general make it tough for a small employer to survive. Europe is a challenging, even demoralizing environment for running a small business. While I appreciate the way Europe organizes much of its society, I'm thankful I run my business in America rather than there. In Europe, I could never have the creative fun I enjoy as an entrepreneur in the USA.

Is the American approach "wrong" and Europe's approach "right"? As a taxpayer and a "job creator," I see pros and cons to both systems. We can all benefit by comparing notes.

Europeans Work Less

One priority of the European approach is striking a comfortable work-life balance. The EU has about 500 million people, with an annual economy of around $16 trillion. To put that into relative terms, the US, with around 300 million people, has an economy of approximately the same size. Proponents of the American system point out that Europeans don't make as much money as we do. It's true—with more people generating only the same gross economy, they earn less per person. But Western European workers make essentially the same per hour as ours do. They just choose to work fewer hours.

I was raised believing there was one good work ethic: You work hard. While we call this *the* work ethic, it's actually only *a* work ethic. Europeans have a different one. They choose to work fewer hours than Americans do, and willingly make correspondingly less income. In recent years, both Germany and France have made it illegal for workers to email or call each other outside of work hours, except in cases of emergency. Yes, it's a blow to productivity...at least, in the short term. But they believe it prevents long-term burnout, ultimately benefitting everyone. While this approach may not be good for business, Europeans consider it good for living. Choosing to work less is part of "family values" in Europe; meanwhile, here in business-friendly America, working less is frowned upon...almost subversive.

A Greek friend of mine spent twenty years working in New York. Only after he retired and returned to Greece did he realize that not once in all those

years in America did he take
a nap. Back in Greece, if he's
sleepy in the afternoon, he
takes a snooze. Europeans
marvel at how Americans
seem willing, almost eager,
to work themselves into an
early grave. My European
friends have told me proudly,
"We don't live to work…we
work to live."

European adults get lots of time to play.

Europeans understand
the trade-off. Because they choose to work less, most Europeans don't strive
for the material affluence that their American counterparts do. European
housing, cars, gadgets, and other "stuff" are modest compared to what an
American with a similar job might own. It's a matter of priorities. Just as
Europeans willingly pay higher taxes for a higher standard of service, they
choose less pay (and less stuff) in exchange for more time off.

Imagine this in your own life: Would you make do with a smaller car
if you knew you didn't have to pay health insurance premiums? Would you
be willing to give up the luxury of a cutting-edge TV and live in a smaller
house if you could cut back to 35 hours per workweek and get a few extra
weeks of paid vacation? Would you settle for a 10 percent pay cut if you
knew you'd never get an email or phone call from the office outside of work
hours? For most Americans, I imagine that the European idea of spending
more time on vacation and with their family, instead of putting in hours of
overtime, is appealing.

I have an American friend who runs a very small movement called Take
Back Your Time (www.takebackyourtime.org). Its mission: to teach Americans that we have the shortest vacations in the rich world, and it's getting
worse. His movement's national holiday is October 24th. That's because, by
its estimates, if we accepted only the typical European workload, yet worked
as long and hard as people do in the US, October 24th would be the last day
of the year we'd have to go to work.

However, with the pressures of globalization, Europe is rethinking some
of its "live more, work less" ideals. For example, the Spanish government is
funding incentives to keep workers from going home for a midday siesta,

which most agree hurts productivity. And, I have a theory that in Ireland (where sales of Guinness are down), the number of pubs has shrunk at the same rate that the number of cafés increased, as that society has ramped up its productivity. Drinkers of heavy stout have shifted to lighter lagers, and drinkers of lager have shifted to coffee. Replacing alcohol with caffeine is a symptom of our faster-paced, more competitive world. And now—particularly in Europe's big, business-oriented cities—American-style chains allow workers to get their coffee "to go."

An Integrated Economy: Pros and Cons

One of the most remarkable feats of a united Europe has been the integration of its economy. Trade barriers between European nations are a thing of the past, and the euro currency has replaced 19 separate national currencies. Imagine: Since 2002, the same coins are used in Lisbon, Tallinn, Dublin, and Thessaloniki, and most of Europe functions as a vast free-trade zone. However, with the global financial crisis starting in 2008, Europeans realized that what goes up together, must come down together. They've learned the hard way that neighboring countries can have vastly different philosophies about fiscal prudence.

The EU designed the euro to be a "hard" currency—with minimal inflation and maximum stability. It favors export nations that shun deficit spending, and punishes countries that like to borrow a lot to inflate their debts away. Considering these standards, some countries (like Germany) are more "worthy" of the euro than others (like Greece)...and there's no convenient way to un-invite a Eurozone member.

When a nation joins the European Union, it's either a "net contributor" or a "net receiver." While there's lots of wrangling in Brussels about just who gives and gets what, Europeans know their economic union is only as strong as its weakest link. Therefore, wealthy countries give more than they get—willingly, if not always enthusiastically. That money bolsters the poorer countries. And eventually, in theory, those countries develop to the point where, rather than weak links, they become net contributors as well.

But it hasn't quite worked out that way. Think about the vast diversity the Eurozone attempts to corral. Germans are as famous for their work ethic as Italians are for *la dolce far niente* ("the sweetness of doing nothing") and Spaniards are for their aimless *paseo* wanderings. A nation of workaholics or a nation of layabouts can function just fine, provided everyone's on the same

This bridge is in Greece, but it was paid for with mostly German money—so German trucks full of Gummi Bears could efficiently reach their market across the Gulf of Corinth, on the Peloponnesian Peninsula.

page. But when hardworking folk begin to feel that they're propping up their less productive compatriots in other countries, things get testy.

Things reached a head during the economic crisis of the early 2010s, when Europe paid the price—in the form of expensive bailouts and painful cutbacks—for what had been taken-for-granted services. It's no coincidence that the European countries that have received the most development aid (the so-called "PIIGS" countries—Portugal, Italy, Ireland, Greece, and Spain) are the ones that have been the most debt-ridden, and the ones that suffered the most with economic crises. Even with significant EU aid, their productivity has lagged far behind the stronger economies. And yet, although their workforce doesn't produce as much per capita as German workers, they still have a mighty currency that's tied to Germany. By earning wages in euros and getting aid in euros, these nations enjoyed a false prosperity that they might not have actually earned—and their bursting real-estate bubble made it worse. Before European unity, if a nation didn't produce much and slid into crippling debt, it could make itself competitive by simply devaluing its currency (and by doing so, decrease, society-wide, what laborers were paid in real terms). But the euro makes that impossible: Effectively, everyone gets the *Deutschmark*...whether they deserve it or not.

In 2012, a feisty political debate erupted between two nations with diametrically opposed fiscal worldviews. Greece grabbed headlines for the severity of its economic woes and its apparent inability to resolve them. For a while, it seemed the Greek crisis might undo the euro currency, and possibly the entire EU. Germany—which generates more than a quarter of the EU's total GDP, and is the biggest net contributor to the EU's budget—decided it would no longer bankroll other countries' debt problems without having a say in its future economic standards. Chancellor Angela Merkel was willing to help bail out Greece, but her offer had strings attached: The Greeks must embrace reforms and learn to live within their means—a new standard that would be enforced by strict fiscal benchmarks.

Many Greeks on the street chafed at the suggestion that they should give up promised vacations and retirements, and be forced to adopt a Germanic nose-to-the-grindstone work ethic. But eventually the Greeks accepted the bailout, with those strings. Things stabilized, but—many fear—the problem will likely resurface. Will there come a day when Greek voters decide that a "Grexit" (a Greek version of the Brexit) is the "least worst option" for their economic future?

Europe's Internal Marshall Plan

Periodic controversies aside, Europe strives to put its tax revenue to good use. The EU is dedicated to continually upgrading its infrastructure. After World War II, the United States invested in rebuilding Europe with the Marshall Plan. It was a smart policy designed to assure us strong and stable trading partners and allies. Over the last couple of decades, for essentially the same reasons, Europe has employed a kind of internal Marshall Plan—investing hundreds of billions of euros in roads, rail lines, communication, education, and other improvements to strengthen their union. Travelers not only see this, they benefit from it.

Among the original members of the European Union, Portugal, Spain, Greece, and Ireland were the net receivers. Back then, I remember no freeways in any of those countries. Now they're rolling out freeways in all of them. And every time you drive on a slick new thoroughfare, you see a European flag reminding locals where the funding came from.

The Cost of Policing the World

While it's easy for pacifists (at home and abroad) to grumble about the US military, the reality is that we are the world's traffic cop. Americans pay with blood and money to protect victims of tyranny and to defend democracy and free enterprise around the world. Defeating the USSR, saving people from genocide in Kosovo, and fighting the Taliban in Afghanistan and ISIS in the Middle East are expensive. Typically, the US foots most of the bill, while Europe moves in with peace-keeping forces afterward. Or, as some people put it, "The US does the cooking, and Europe does the dishes."

Given America's unique world-leadership position, our limited economic means, and the world's reliance on our military might, we need to choose our battles thoughtfully. There are cases where the world supports our involvement (Darfur, Kosovo, Afghanistan), and places where they don't (Central America and Iraq). We can do whatever we want...but it sure makes things easier on everybody when we wield our might with the support of our friends and allies.

It's not unreasonable to say that Europe is "not paying its fair share" for its defense. Perhaps the EU wouldn't have so much money for its infrastructure if it had to do its own fighting. But consider the flipside: By their judgment, sinking money into their infrastructure rather than into their military is better for their long-term security. In the European view, America is trapped in an inescapable cycle to feed its military-industrial complex: As we bulk up our military, we look for opportunities to make use of it. (As the saying goes, when your only tool is a hammer, you treat every problem like a nail.) And then, when we employ our military unwisely, we create more enemies... which makes us feel the need to grow our military even more. If an American diplomat complained to his European counterpart, "America is doing all the heavy lifting when it comes to military," the European might respond, "Well, you seem to be enjoying it. We're building roads and bridges instead."

Traveling affords a good opportunity to consider how American military might has helped make our world a better place—and how it hasn't—and what kind of fiscal and military policies end up actually making a society stronger and safer.

Europe's new high-speed train network is good for commerce...but bad for birds.

Trains are faster than ever. Recently, on a bullet train in France, I enjoyed a smooth and silent 200-mile-per-hour ride through pastoral countryside. As if the rail company was ashamed of the "slower" stretches, the speedometer was only illuminated when the train exceeded 300 kilometers per hour (186 miles per hour). On a visit to Munich, I was photographing trains pulling in to the station—with birds squished onto the windshields. Looking at those poor birds, I thought, "You'd wait all your life to see a bird squished onto a windshield of a train back in my hometown."

Consider the infrastructure: A bullet train zips under the English Channel, taking people from Paris to London in two and a half hours. Denmark and Sweden built a mammoth bridge connecting Copenhagen and Malmö, creating Scandinavia's largest metropolitan area. And cities throughout Europe seem to be forever dug up because they're constantly improving and expanding their underground transit systems.

Non-EU nations are investing, too. Norway, with fewer than five million people, has drilled some of the longest tunnels in the world to lace together isolated communities in the fjords. Istanbul scraped together the money to build a massive train tunnel under the Bosphorus to connect Asia and Europe and grease its economic engine. And there's even an effort being considered to dig a tunnel connecting Spain and Morocco under the Strait of Gibraltar.

Savvy nations understand that infrastructure is the foundation for

prosperity (and power). Hitler knew he couldn't take on Europe without a good highway system, so he built the autobahn. The United States undertook a massive investment in our interstate highway system in the 1950s, which helped our country—with rich and

Berlin's train station is the biggest in Europe, with 1,800 trains a day arriving on 14 major train lines, coming in at right angles on two different levels.

poor states enjoying equal-quality, federally funded roads—truck itself into greater economic power. And, in our generation, Europe is investing money it could be spending on its military on its infrastructure instead.

Exploring a continent with a level of affluence similar to the US's gives us a chance to see firsthand the result of allocating limited resources with different priorities. People everywhere hear the excuse "there's not enough money." But there's plenty of money. Travelers see vividly that each society makes different choices according to its own priorities: Some societies may prioritize for tax cuts, new stadiums, and next-generation bombers while others opt for universal health care, faster trains, and subsidized education.

Europe Wants Peace

So far I've focused on the economy of the European Union. But for the EU's founders, money took a backseat to their primary motivation: peace. And even today, peace is the single greatest (and most underrated) success of the European Union. Even the biggest Euroskeptic recognizes that European countries have become so interconnected that Europe will never again suffer devastation from a major war as they did twice in the last century. The French and the Germans still don't agree on many things, but they've become too financially interdependent to take up arms over their differences. Minimizing the possibility of an intra-European war is *the* triumph of the EU.

If boots do hit the ground in a war, Europeans believe it will be because they have failed to prevent it. They prefer endless diplomacy to once-in-a-while war. Europe's reluctance to go to war frustrates some Americans. I believe their relative pacifism is because Europeans know the reality of war, while most Americans do not. Of course, if you have a loved one who has fought or died in Iraq, Afghanistan, or Vietnam, you know what a war is. But as a society, the US can't remember actually hosting a war. Europeans have told me that they believe the US is more willing to use its military muscle because in the age of modern warfare, no American city has ever been bombed like Coventry, Dresden, Rotterdam, or Warsaw. It's easier to feel detached when a war is something you watch on the nightly news, rather than something that killed your grandfather or destroyed your hometown.

Europe knows what a war is. It ripped itself to shreds twice within my grandparents' lifetime. Consider France's losses in World War I. France (with one-quarter as many people as we have) lost as many people as the US lost in the entire Iraq War—over 4,400 people—in one day...many times.

If there is a national piece of art for the European Union, it is Picasso's *Guernica*, because it reminds Europe of the reality of war. After World War I, Europe was awakening to the destructive power of aerial bombardments. During the Spanish Civil War in 1937, Hitler jumped at a chance to help his fellow fascist, General Francisco Franco, by bombing the Basque town of Guernica. Surveying the rubble of that town made it clear that technology had taken the destructive power of war to new heights. This inspired Picasso to create his greatest work. His mural *Guernica* memorialized the first city destroyed by an aerial bombardment, and gave Europe a preview of the horrors of its fast-approaching war with frightening accuracy. It's also a haunting reminder that "collateral damage" is real people.

They lost as many people as we lost in Vietnam (60,000) in one month. And then it happened again and again until, by the end of World War I, an estimated half of all the men in France between the ages of 15 and 30 were casualties. When some Americans, aggravated by France's unwillingness to take up arms, call the French "surrender monkeys," I believe it shows their ignorance of history.

Fewer Borders, but More Ethnic Diversity

A key strategy for preserving peace in a sprawling, multiethnic state is to respect and celebrate diversity. As if inspired by America's *e pluribus unum* ("out of many, one"), the European Union's official motto is *in varietate concordia* ("united in diversity").

I'm charmed by Europe's diversity. Hop on a train for two hours and you step out into a different culture, different language, and different heritage. As I watched Europe unite, I (like many of my European friends) feared that this diversity would be threatened. But just the opposite is happening. Europe is actually becoming *more* diverse.

In today's Europe, there are three loyalties: region, nation, and Europe. A person from Munich could consider himself Bavarian, German and European. Ask somebody from Florence where she's from, and she could say, "I'm Tuscan," or "I'm Italian," or "I'm European."

Borders and loyalties can be messy. Modern political borders are rarely clean when it comes to dividing ethnic groups. And most of the terrorism and troubles in Europe—whether Basque, Irish, Catalan, or Corsican—have been about ethnic-minority separatist movements threatening national capitals. Appreciating the needs of these people, peace-loving European leaders strive to make the Continent's minority groups feel like they belong. While they may feel ignored at the national level, they get a seat at the table in Brussels.

Brittany, in western France, is not ethnically French. People there are Celtic, cousins of the Welsh and the Irish. Just a couple of generations ago, Paris was so threatened by the secessionist dreams of these Celts that if parents gave their newborn a Celtic name, that child would not be granted a French national identity card. Such a policy would be laughable today.

As Europe unites, established countries are less threatened by "nations without states." In 1999, Scotland convened a parliament in Scotland for the first time since 1707...and London didn't stop them.

When I first visited Barcelona in the 1970s, locals weren't allowed to speak Catalan or dance their beloved *Sardana*. The Catalan flag was outlawed, so locals showed their patriotic spirit by waving the flag of the Barcelona soccer team instead. Now, in public schools, children speak Catalan first, local flags fly proudly, and every Sunday in front of the cathedral, people gather to dance the *Sardana*. This circle dance symbolizes national unity as all differences are cast aside and Catalans raise their hands together to proudly celebrate their ethnicity. A Catalan person in Barcelona told me, "Catalunya is Spain's Quebec. We don't like people calling our corner of Iberia a 'region' of Spain...because that's what Franco called it. We do not accept subjugation as a region of Spain. We are a nation without a state."

This Tirolean archaeologist funds his vision with money from Brussels.

What's going on? Barcelona is standing up to Madrid. London is respecting Cardiff. Brittany gets along with Paris (and I don't mean Spears and Hilton). As power shifts to the EU capital of Brussels, national capitals recognize and accept that their authority is waning. And the European Union supports these "nations without states." (For more on where these groups came from, see the next section.)

A friend of mine, Armin Walch, is the "Indiana Jones" of Tirolean archaeologists. Bursting with ideas and projects, he loves to renovate castles in western Austria. When Armin wants money to excavate a castle, he doesn't go to Vienna—he goes to Brussels. If he says, "I'm doing something for Austria," he'll go home empty-handed. So instead, he says he's doing something for the Tirol (an ethnic region that spans parts of Italy and Austria, ignoring the modern national boundary)...and gets funding.

The European Union is burdened with the image of a too-politically-correct bureaucracy, notorious for dictating the proper curve of a cucumber in 24 official languages. But they don't mind the teasing. While attempting to honor the linguistic and idealistic wishes of its unruly gang of members isn't always efficient, Europe understands that watching out for its ethnic underdogs is essential for maintaining its hard-won peace.

Nations without States

Modern national boundaries don't always match up with the local ethnic breakdown. And even seemingly "homogenous" Europe has several "nations without states." That's "nations"—groups of like-minded people, united by

The EU Spreads East

On May 1, 2004, eight formerly communist nations joined the European Union...and suddenly the EU grew by 75 million people. In 2007 and 2013, three more additions boosted the population by another 35 million. In just a few short years, the geographical center of Europe shifted from Brussels to Prague.

I remember visits to the Eastern Bloc during the Cold War. Back then life was bleak, gray, and demoralizing because of ongoing political repression and their unresponsive Soviet-style command economy. Someone would dictate how many of these and how much of that would be produced, ignoring the basic laws of supply and demand. It was a fiasco. On my early visits to Poland, I remember that people lucky enough to own a car were taking their windshield wipers in with them at night. That's because the government under-produced wipers, demand exceeded supply, and the thieves knew it. They'd rip off somebody's wipers at night and sell them for a fortune on the black market—the next morning! Today the laws of supply and demand are kicking in, there are plenty of wipers produced and distributed to meet the demand, and people are leaving their wipers on their cars all night long in Warsaw.

With the fall of the Berlin Wall in 1989, Eastern Europe began a dizzying transformation. In the 1990s, societies once forced to espouse Soviet economics embraced the capitalist work ethic with gusto—as if making up for lost time. While adjusting from the security of a totalitarian system to the insecurity of freedom, younger and better-educated Eastern Europeans

Eastern Europe is enjoying freedom and a new affluence.

jumped at this opportunity to get ahead—working longer hours, having fewer children, and buying more cars. On the other hand, many older people missed the job security and sense of safety while walking down the streets that they remember from the "good old days." And many less-educated young people who saw the new system working against them joined angry and racist groups such as eastern Germany's skinheads.

But those growing pains are largely in the past. Today, more than a quarter-century after the Iron Curtain fell, freedom is old news, communism is a distant memory, and they have long since settled into the grind of capitalism. Even the notion of "Eastern Europe" feels dated; people in most countries we'd identify as "Eastern Europe" insist on being called "*Central* Europeans"—a name that's both politically and geographically correct.

But I still remember those old days. And for me, each visit to Eastern Europe is a case study in the fundamental wisdom of free enterprise, the laws of supply and demand, and how, when there's an incentive to produce more, there's also an incentive to work more and play less.

language, culture, and bloodlines—that don't have an internationally recognized country to call home: the Basques, the Catalans, the Tiroleans, the
Welsh, the Bretons, and so on.

How did these people wind up without a homeland? Either they were left
out when modern maps were drawn, or their ancestors were "planted" there
generations ago. History has demonstrated, again and again, that national borders that ignore ethnic realities will sooner or later bring big problems. That's
why the EU astutely looks out for the rights of these nations without states.

The Basques were a victim of not having a seat at the map-drawing table.
Eons ago, when they drew the line between the French and the Spanish
people, the Basques said, "What about us?" They were told, "Learn to speak
French"...or "Learn to speak Spanish." Centuries later, in the 1980s and 1990s,
"Basque" became synonymous with guerrilla terrorism, through the military
separatist group ETA. But Basque anger faded as a result of the EU fostering
more autonomy—and, therefore, dignity—for Europe's small ethnic regions.
And in 2017, the ETA finally gave up its guns and renounced violence.

The border-drawing problem extends well beyond Europe. A century
ago, after the fall of the Ottoman Empire, European colonial powers drew
lines in the sands of Africa and the Middle East. Creating countries like
Libya, Iraq, and Syria, they ignored ethnic and sectarian divisions. These
thoughtlessly created countries made little sense ethnically, and therefore—to
this day—their stability requires rule by a strongman. Decades later, when
Western powers were busy promoting democracy, they supported the overthrow of such leaders (like Libya's Muhammar Khaddaffi and Iraq's Saddam
Hussein). The result: failed states, chaos, and millions of desperate, displaced
people. (Most of the people flooding into Europe during the 2015 refugee
crisis originated from lands created by Europe that were doomed to fail.

Perhaps that's why—at least subconsciously—much
of Europe sees the moral imperative in welcoming
and housing many of these refugees. For more on
this topic, see page 80.)

Drawing borders with a respect to ethnic divisions sounds sensible. But in some places—where
sizeable minority groups are intermixed with a large

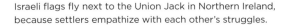

Israeli flags fly next to the Union Jack in Northern Ireland,
because settlers empathize with each other's struggles.

and dominant majority population—
it's far from simple. In many of these
cases, the minority groups didn't wind
up where they are by choice, but were
"planted" by governments.

This is a story repeated time and
again through history. For example,
in the 20th century, military families
from Soviet Russia were encouraged

Language options on an ATM show solidarity among smaller ethnic groups.

to retire in little Estonia. Moscow's agenda: to dilute the Estonian population and weaken that rebellious society by creating a large Russian minority.
Today Estonia—now independent—struggles with a big Russian minority
that refuses to integrate.

In the 16th century, the Habsburg monarchy planted Serbs—who were
escaping from the Ottomans farther south—along the Croatian-Bosnian
border, to provide a "human shield" against those same Ottomans. Many
centuries later, descendants of those Serb settlers and the indigenous Croats
were embroiled in some of the bloodiest fighting of the war following the
breakup of Yugoslavia.

Europe's "nations without states" live in solidarity with each other. In
Barcelona, the Catalan people find Basque or Galician bars a little more
appealing than the run-of-the-mill Spanish ones. They even make a point
to include the other languages on their ATMs: You'll see Catalan first, then
Spanish, Galego (the language of Galicia, in northwest Spain), Euskara (the
Basque tongue)…and then a button for all the rest (Portuguese, Swedish, and
so on). While all of these groups—Catalan, Galician, and Basque—speak
the common language of Spanish, they respect each other's native tongues
as a way to honor their shared ethnic-underdog status. These groups' affinity for each other even factors in to where they travel. On a recent trip to
Northern Ireland, I was impressed by how many travelers I met from Basque
Country and Catalunya. Because the Basques and Catalans feel a kinship
with the Catholic minority in Ireland's Protestant North, many choose to
vacation there.

The opposite is also true: Majority groups who strive to establish their
control over disputed land empathize with each other. On that same trip
to Northern Ireland, I was puzzled to see Israeli flags flying from flagpoles
in Protestant communities. It's because Protestants "planted" there in the

17th century by a bigger power (England) have struggled with their indigenous neighbors—much like Israeli settlers in the West Bank clash with the native Palestinians.

Back when Britain ruled Ceylon (present-day Sri Lanka) and used it as a big tea plantation, they couldn't get the local Sinhalese to pick the tea cheaply enough, so they imported Tamils from India (who were more desperate and willing to work for less). When colonial rule became more trouble than the tea was worth, the Brits gave the island its freedom. But, thanks in part to England's love of tea and unwillingness to pay a fair local wage, the Sinhalese and Tamils found themselves locked in a tragic, 26-year-long civil war.

When I consider the problems that come with planting Tamils in Sinhalese Sri Lanka, Israelis in Palestine, Protestants in Ireland, Serbs in Croatia, and Russians in Estonia, I'm impressed both by the spine of the people who were there first, and by the hardship borne by the original settlers. Ideally, every nation would have its own state. But in most cases, it's impossible to humanely disentangle quarreling people whose ancestors were let down by a shortsighted ruler. And so, the only viable option is to coexist peacefully—with a respect both for the mainstream cultural norms and the rights of the minority.

Travelers who observe this sort of sectarian strife firsthand better understand that respecting diversity, rather than using it as a wedge, results in a more peaceful world for everyone. And it makes me particularly thankful that the EU prioritizes the rights of nations without states.

European Challenges:
An Aging Continent Grapples with Immigration

I am a Europhile. I freely admit I have a romantic fascination with Europe and an appreciation for its way of life. But I'm not blind to the fact that Europe has its flaws and is grappling—not always very well—with some serious challenges of its own.

For years, both the US and Europe have been consuming more goods than we produce, and importing more than we export. Through the first decade of the 2000s, everybody overspent: The United States overspent on military endeavors and tax cuts, Europe overspent on infrastructure and entitlements, and individuals in both places committed to mortgages they couldn't really afford. By riding wild real-estate bubbles and creating an economy designed to generate profit by rearranging the furniture without actually producing

When European workers lose entitlements, they hit the streets.

anything, we conned ourselves into thinking we were wealthier than we actually were. When the economic crisis hit in 2008, it suddenly became clear that the world's booming economy was existing on borrowed time.

The resulting Great Recession hit people hard on both sides of the Atlantic. The collapse of the housing bubble, the huge financial hit of bailing out troubled banks, and the incalculable expense of other corporate malfeasance devastated European economies—making it even more challenging for them to finance their generous entitlements.

Further complicating matters are Europe's shifting population demographics. Europe's luxurious cradle-to-grave welfare system was conceived in a postwar society with lots of people working, fewer living to retirement, and retirees having a short life span. Originally, this plan was smart, compassionate, and sustainable: The success of Europe's social system has helped make the continent better educated and wealthier. But when a society becomes smarter and richer, two things happen: People live longer and they have fewer children. And so, the demographic makeup of Europe has flipped upside-down: relatively few people working, lots of people retiring, and retirees living a long time. In short, Europe is becoming a geriatric continent. With fewer young workers and more seniors, the arithmetic just isn't there to sustain the lavish entitlements Europeans have come to expect.

As in the USA, it's difficult to take away expected entitlements without a fight. Politicians in Europe have the unenviable task of explaining to their citizens that they won't get the cushy golden years their parents got. People who worked diligently with the promise of retiring at 62 are now told they'll need to work up to five extra years—and even then, they may not have a generous pension waiting for them.

I expect you'll see lots of marches and lots of strikes in Europe in the coming years. They're marching in opposition to policies forced by globalization.

Once, while riding the bus from Munich out to Dachau, I learned a lesson about the tyranny of the majority. En route to the infamous concentration camp memorial, I sat next to an old German woman. I smiled at her weakly as if to say, "I don't hold your people's genocidal atrocities against you." She glanced at me and sneered down at my camera. Suddenly, surprising me with her crusty but fluent English, she ripped into me. "You tourists come here not to learn, but to hate," she seethed.

Pulling the loose skin down from a long-ago-strong upper arm, she showed me a two-sided scar. "When I was a girl, a bullet cut straight through my arm," she said. "Another bullet killed my father. The war took many good people. My father ran a *Grüss Gott* shop."

I was stunned by her rage. But I sensed desperation on her part to simply unload her story on one of the hordes of tourists who tramp daily through her hometown to ogle at an icon of the Holocaust.

I asked, "What do you mean, a *Grüss Gott* shop?" She explained that in Bavaria, shopkeepers greet customers with a *"Grüss Gott"* ("May God greet you"). During the Third Reich, it was safer to change to the Nazi greeting, *"Sieg Heil."* It was a hard choice. Each shopkeeper had to make it. Everyone in Dachau knew which shops were *Grüss Gott* shops and which were *Sieg Heil* shops. Over time there were fewer and fewer *Grüss Gott* shops. Pausing, as if mustering the energy for one last sentence, she stood up and said, "My father's shop was a *Grüss Gott* shop to the end," then stepped off the bus.

Conflicts between the majority and the minority persist in today's Europe. Consider Northern Ireland, where the population is divided between Protestants (supporters of British rule) and Catholics (who identify with the Irish). While the familiar Union Jack of the UK is the "official" flag of Northern Ireland, minority Catholics who'd like to see Ireland united see it as a symbol of oppression. Unfortunately, they no longer consider it their flag. Many call it "the Butcher's Apron" instead.

For a lesson in the power of symbolism, visit a town where about two-thirds of the community is Protestant and one-third is Catholic. These towns can be decked out like a Union Jack fantasy...or nightmare, if you happen to be Catholic. The curbs are painted red, white, and blue. Houses fly huge British flags. Streets lead under trellises blotting out the sky with flapping Union Jacks. (Not too long ago, many towns like these even came with the remains of a burned-out Catholic church.) A Catholic walking down a street strewn with this British symbolism can only be quiet and accept it. To independence-minded Catholics, the Union Jack symbolizes not a united nation, but the tyranny of the majority. The result: There is no real, unified flag of Northern Ireland.

Until experiences like these in Germany and in Northern Ireland humanized the notion of "tyranny of the majority," I never really grasped the sadness of a society where a majority-rules mentality can, when

Many angry Catholics in Northern Ireland feel they have no flag. To them, the Union Jack is "the Butcher's Apron."

taken to extremes, abuse a minority and bully it into silent submission.

As the rhetoric for the Iraq War was ramping up in early 2003, a situation in Edmonds, my hometown north of Seattle, reminded me in some small way of what I'd seen abroad. This was a difficult and emotional time, with all the patriotic fervor that comes with an invasion. Perhaps a third of our town opposed the war, and two-thirds supported it. The Lions Club lined the streets of our town with American flags and declared they would stay there in support of our troops until they finished the job and came home in victory.

While I supported our troops, I opposed the war. I believed that our president knowingly lied to get us there. When the Lions Club put up all those flags—which were normally reserved for patriotic holidays—I became very uncomfortable. I wanted to embrace my flag, but was put in a regrettable position that doing so would be tantamount to supporting the war. I felt as though my flag had been demoted from something that all Americans shared (regardless of their politics) to a promotional logo for a war I didn't believe in. I knew several fellow Edmonds merchants agreed that our Stars and Stripes had been kidnapped. But in my relatively conservative town, they feared not flying it would threaten their business. They felt frightened. Their predicament reminded me of those German shopkeepers who had to stop saying "*Grüss Gott.*" And my own town reminded me of those red, white, and blue-drenched towns in Ulster. Although to a far lesser degree, I felt that here in my hometown, a minority (of which I was a part) was also being oppressed by a tyranny of the majority. In defense of our flag, I had to act.

I explained my concerns to the president of the Lions Club. He understood and agreed to have his club take down the flags after a week. It didn't happen. So, humming "Yankee Doodle Dandy" to myself, I marched through town, collecting and carefully stowing the flags. It was a small, symbolic, and perhaps overly righteous move on my part, motivated by what I considered patriotic concerns.

While some supported me, many were angry. I was shark bait on Seattle's right-wing radio talk shows for several days. But now, when my little town is a festival of Stars and Stripes on holidays like the Fourth of July, Presidents' Day, and Election Day, everybody can celebrate together because the flag flies for all of us— even the peaceniks.

They're marching because they're angry—thinking that foreigners are gaming the system and getting entitlements at the expense of good, patriotic local workers (even though, in actuality, most experts see a net contribution to societies from their immigrant population). And they are marching in protest as Europe recalibrates their long-established entitlements to fit the new (older) demographic makeup of their economy.

Europeans demonstrate with gusto. It's in their blood and a healthy part of their democracy. Workers stick up for their rights, demanding and often getting better conditions. When frustrated and needing to vent grievances, they hit the streets. I've been caught up in huge and boisterous marches all over Europe. It's not scary; in fact, it's kind of exhilarating. "*La Manifestation!*" as they say in France. All that marching is just too much trouble for many Americans. When dealing with similar frustrations, we find a website or a news outlet that affirms our beliefs...and then shake our collective fists vigorously.

Interestingly, as Europe's native population declines, its population growth may come largely from immigrants. And Europe's immigration challenges are much like America's. Around the world, rich nations import poor immigrants to do their dirty work. If a society doesn't want to pay for expensive apples picked by rich kids at high wages, it gets cheaper apples by hiring people willing to work for less. If you're wealthy enough to hire an immigrant to clean your house, you do it—you get a clean house, and the immigrant earns a wage. If you don't want to trade away your personal freedom to care for an aging parent, you hire someone else to care for them...and it's generally an immigrant. That's just the honest reality of capitalism.

In Europe, *Gastarbeiter*—German for "guest worker"—is the generic term for this arrangement. Germans famously imported Turkish people to do their scut work a generation or two ago, when Germany's post-WWII economic boom finally kicked into gear. These days, virtually every country in Western Europe has its own *Gastarbeiter* contingent. Berlin—with more than 200,000 Turks—could be considered a sizable "Turkish city." France's population includes millions of poor North Africans. And even Ireland— after its "Celtic Tiger" boom in the early 2000s—imported 120,000 Polish people to take out its trash. (At the time, it was striking to hear my Irish friends speak about their new Polish workers as if they were a new appliance.)

But invariably, wealthy people begin to realize that their "cheap labor" is not quite as cheap as they hoped. In Europe, the importation of labor creates fast-growing immigrant communities that need help and incentives to assimilate, or society at large will pay a steep price (as we saw in 2005, when the deaths of two black teenagers while being pursued by French cops ignited violent riots that rocked the underserved African and Arab suburbs of Paris).

In Europe, many immigrants melt into their adopted homelands, while others flat-out don't want to assimilate. With the increasing affordability of modern communication technologies, it's very easy for immigrants to establish insulated satellite communities that remain in constant contact with the culture and language of their homeland.

These days, it seems that immigrant groups can choose whether or not they want to integrate with their adopted countries. I've met third-generation Algerians in the Netherlands who don't speak a word of Dutch, and don't expect their children to, either. And I've met first-generation Pakistanis in Denmark who speak only Danish and know and love their adopted country just as their blond neighbors do. Like the US, Europe is suffering growing pains when it comes to its immigrants. Coming from an immigrant family in a nation of immigrants myself, I like America's "melting pot" approach. I think it works best for all if newcomers embrace their adopted culture, learn the local language, and melt in.

But the European scene is a bit more complex. The critical difference, of course, is that 99 percent of Americans descend from immigrants, whereas much of Europe has been largely homogenous for millennia. In some European countries, large-scale immigration is a fairly recent phenomenon. This makes many Europeans particularly vigilant about ensuring that Europe's homegrown culture continues to thrive. I share their concern, and yet, it's easy to fall into contradictions: If diversity is a tenet of EU beliefs, what's wrong with immigrants wanting to preserve their home cultures? Is it hypocritical to celebrate the preservation of the Catalan language, but expect Algerians to learn Dutch? Should Europe's famous tolerance extend only to indigenous European cultures?

While I'm glad I'm not a policymaker who needs to implement immigration laws in Europe, I'll be honest about my take on this dicey issue: I favor policies that promote indigenous diversity for European "nations without states," and policies that encourage assimilation for immigrants and refugees who come from outside Europe. For more on this topic, see "Immigrants: Treasure Your Heritage…and Melt" on page 130.

The Refugee Crisis and Its Impact on the EU

There's a big difference between immigration (allowing foreigners to join your country to be part of your workforce) and refugees: people literally taking "refuge"—entering a country, either legally or illegally, because it's dangerous for them to stay in their homeland. Europe has long received a steady stream of mostly "economic refugees" from miserably poor countries. But in 2015, that stream became a flood of "war refugees," as well over a million desperate people deluged the EU—mostly from war-torn Syria.

When most people use the term "refugee crisis," they mean the practical challenge of housing, feeding, transporting, and generally taking care of this huge influx of humanity. But I think the real refugee crisis is the human cost of a failed state. The refugees coming to Europe today are a direct result of poorly drawn borders by European colonial powers a century ago (as explained in the "Nations without States" section on page 70). If Europeans (or Americans) complain about the hardship of housing those refugees, they should ponder the hardship brought about by their ancestors' greedy colonial policies a century ago.

Meanwhile, caring people around the world wonder: What's the pragmatic and humane response? It calls for a two-pronged approach: First, deal humanely with the refugees who made it out. Much of Europe has risen to this occasion (especially Germany, which took in more than one million refugees in 2015). But that only addresses the result of the underlying problem, which brings me to my second point. We also have to work diligently to address the root causes of the tragedy. It's fair to assume that war refugees would rather stay in their homeland if there were a political and economic environment there where hope for a good life was realistic.

Whenever the movement of desperate people flares up, travelers ask me how their European vacation might be affected. From a practical perspective, the potential impact on travelers is essentially zero. But rather than just worrying about whether you need to show up a little early for your train at a refugee-jammed station, I'd challenge you to be open to being impacted—in the emotional sense—by Europe's new arrivals. If you meet a refugee, consider it an opportunity to put a face on the headlines. Each one of these people was forced to leave their home, and the life they'd built, to avoid being killed by the horrors of war. Try to imagine the hardships they've gone through—surviving the war at home, making the painful decision to leave, sorting out their possessions, saying goodbye to loved ones, and then having to clear hurdle after hurdle of red tape—just to get this far. And for many, their journey is far from over. If you think you're being "inconvenienced" by crossing paths with them, just imagine how they must feel.

Politically, the refugee crisis represents another big challenge for the European Union. Again, as Europe ages, it needs young labor. Europe can easily absorb the millions of refugees currently on its soil into its economy, if those refugees can just get to the more prosperous countries that might welcome them with job opportunities. And yet, the sensationalistic news media (and people's increasing inclination to get "their news" through social media) have made the refugee situation seem more dangerous and frightening than it actually is. Fear-mongering, nativist political groups are stoking that fear and anxiety—which, in turn, creates a hunger for more "law and order" and stronger borders. As one of the pet issues of ultra-nationalistic, anti-free trade, and anti-EU movements, this new dynamic will continue to be a hot-button political issue in Europe over the next few years—presenting the European Union (and its mission of celebrating multinationalism, free trade, and no borders) with a serious challenge.

Tolerance and the Futility of Legislating Morality

I'm hopeful that Europe can overcome the challenge of its new ethnic mix because of its proven track record for pluralism. While Europe has no shortage of closed-minded, knee-jerk opinions and racist, xenophobic political parties, most Europeans consider tolerance a virtue to be cultivated. At the leading edge of this thinking is the Netherlands. Historically, this corner of Europe saw some of the most devastating Catholics-versus-Protestants fighting in the religious wars following the Reformation. They learned to be inclusive—welcoming Jews when others wouldn't and providing refuge to religious refugees (such as our nation's Pilgrim founders). And, as a major maritime power during the Age of Discovery, the Netherlands became a gateway to Europe for emigrants and immigrants (and their ideas) to and from all over Asia, Africa, and the Americas. Based on lessons learned from their history, it seems the Dutch have made a conscious decision to tolerate alternative lifestyles.

When I'm in the Dutch town of Haarlem, I'm struck by the harmony and compromise people have worked out between tradition and modernity, virtuous lives and hedonistic vices, affluence, and simplicity. People live well—but in small apartments, getting around by bike and public transit. While the frugal Dutch may keep the same old one-speed bike forever, they bring home fresh flowers every day. The typical resident commutes by train to glassy skyscrapers to work for giant corporations in nearby office parks, but no skyscraper violates Haarlem's downtown cityscape, which is still dominated by elegant old gables and church spires. In Haarlem, the latest shopping malls hide behind Dutch Renaissance facades. Streets are clogged with café tables and beer-drinkers. The cathedral towers over the market square with its carillon ringing out its cheery melody as policemen stroll in pairs—looking more like they're on a date than on duty.

Two blocks behind the cathedral, a coffee shop (a business that openly sells marijuana) is filled with just the right music and a stoned clientele. People enjoying a particularly heavy strain of marijuana stare at their rolling papers as if those crinkly critters are alive. Others are mesmerized by the bubbles in their bongs.

And, down by the canal, a fairytale of cobbled lanes and charming houses gather around a quiet little church, creating a scene right out of a Vermeer painting. But this neighborhood is different. Lonely men, hands in pockets, stroll as they survey prostitutes who giggle and flirt from their red-lit windows.

While the USA is inclined to legislate morality on issues such as prostitution, gay rights, and drugs, much of Europe takes a different approach. While countries differ, the general European sentiment is not to make a

In Amsterdam's Red Light District, sex workers are unionized.

law forcing someone to be what the majority considers "moral." A European would assume that every person is a moral person, but each individual has a slightly different morality. If one group gets to make their morality the law of the land, it infringes on another person's civil liberties. So, rather than attempt to legislate morality, European law tolerates "immoral" acts as long as they don't hurt someone else.

For example, few on either side of the Atlantic would argue that prostitution is a good thing. But in most of Europe, where many people recognize that you can't just wish it away with platitudes or force it away with laws, prostitution is generally legal and regulated.

Of course, each country has its own laws...and quirks. German sex workers in Frankfurt rent rooms in multistory "Eros Towers" and essentially run their own businesses. If a Greek prostitute gets married, she must give up her license to sell sex. Portuguese call girls can lose custody of their children. Dutch hookers have a union, get a license to practice their trade, and are required to have medical check-ups to be sure they aren't passing sexually transmitted diseases. In Iceland and Switzerland, while prostitution is legal, it is illegal for a third party to profit from the sale of sex. In general, the hope is that when a prostitute needs help and pushes her emergency button, a policeman rather than a pimp comes to her rescue.

While that's the ideal, it's not foolproof. There is still sex trafficking and abuse of women in the sex trade. But Europeans figure with their more progressive, creative, and pragmatic approach to what they consider a "victimless

Part of the fun of travel is learning to respect and celebrate how different people have different passions for different things. A traveler learns that the love of life, liberty, and the pursuit of happiness comes in different colors and knows no borders. And as this photo essay shows, if there's one thing we can learn from Europe, perhaps it's new ways to enjoy life to its fullest.

▲ Like community events in my hometown are uplifting, little festivals contribute to the fabric of every community. In Verona, Italy, teenage cooks teach the little ones how to make ravioli in hopes of keeping that element of Italian culture vibrant. In spite of its modernity, Europe values its traditions. Festivals seem designed to hand these traditions from one generation to the next.

◀ In Beaune, France, the local Chamber of Commerce invests in an exhibit to help people appreciate the wine. Clearly, having a good nose in France is a life skill worth cultivating.

◀ In America, we have freezers in our garages so we can buy in bulk to save money and avoid needless trips to the supermarket. In contrast, Europeans have small refrigerators. It's not necessarily because they don't have room or money for a big refrigerator. They'd actually rather go to the market in the morning. The market visit is a chance to be out, get the freshest food, connect with people, and stay in touch. While the popularity of supermarkets is growing, Europeans who value the traditional fabric of their societies still willingly pay a little more for their bread for the privilege of knowing the person who baked it.

▶ In Italy, they love their expensive red wine—but they also love their simple, fill-'er-up-at-the-gas-station wine. Italians get their table wine cheap at filling stations like this.

▼ On the streets of Helsinki, seeing masses of people marching, I thought I might be in store for a big demonstration. Then I realized it was an annual festival where all the choirs gather on the steps of the cathedral. They sang a few hymns together, then they broke into small groups and invaded every pub in town. It's the "take choral music to the pubs" festival.

French farmers fatten their geese to enlarge their livers, considered a delicacy. They force-feed the geese four times a day. Then, when their livers grow from a quarter-pound to two pounds, they slaughter them and eat the fattened liver, or foie gras. The English travel in droves to France's Dordogne region to enjoy this gourmet treat. Animal-rights activists worldwide object to the treatment of the geese, and for a time, foie gras was actually illegal for restaurants to serve in Illinois. But French farmers don't under-

stand all the fuss. They tell me the tradition started when their ancestors caught geese who had fattened up their own livers to make the migratory trip to Egypt. They found them very tasty and decided to raise them, help them fatten those livers, and spare them that long flight. They claim that geese are designed to grow fat livers, and they pride themselves in creating fine living conditions—as the quality of the foie gras depends on the quality of life the geese lead, right up until the day they are slaughtered.

▲ The biggest single room in America is filled with airplanes. The biggest one in Europe (in Holland) is filled with flowers.

▶ The English have an impressive ability to lie on beaches—like this one, in Blackpool—and pretend it's sunny.

◀ This woman just hiked all the way from Paris to the northwest corner of Spain, Santiago de Compostela. For a thousand years, pilgrims have made this trek for reasons I don't understand. I'll never forget seeing the jubilation on the faces as triumphant trekkers of all ages and languages—walking sticks frayed, pant-legs fringed, faces sunburned—paused to savor the sweet moment when they finally reached their goal. I'm not sure why this moved me so. Perhaps it's the timeless power of individual faith. Maybe it's heritage and tradition. Or it might be the notion that people would abandon everything and move mountains for treasured feelings and beliefs that never even occurred to me.

Regardless of your journey, you can put a little pilgrim in your travels and find your own personal jubilation.

crime," they are minimizing violence, reducing the spread of AIDS
and other diseases, and allowing
sex workers a better life…all while
generating some additional tax
revenue. Social scientists have a
term for this approach: pragmatic
harm reduction.

In another example of European pragmatism, Europe's drinking age is typically lower than the
US's. While no country in the

To celebrate their graduation, Scandinavian students drink while their parents do the driving.

world has a higher drinking age than America's, most European countries
allow 16- or 18-year-olds to consume alcohol. European parents recognize
that—no matter how fiercely they moralize against alcohol—their teens will
drink. (Europeans puzzle over why 18-year-old Americans can marry, own a
gun, go to war, and vote…but can't buy a can of beer.)

Around the world, when kids graduate from high school, they party,
get drunk, and some die on the roads. When traveling through Scandinavia in May and June, you'll see a
creative solution to this problem:
truckloads of drunk high-school
graduates noisily enjoying a parent-
sponsored bash. The parents hire a
truck and provide a driver so none
of the students needs to drive. The
kids decorate their party truck. Then
the whooping and hollering grads
parade through their towns from
one family home to the next, where
parents each host one stage of the
progressive graduation kegger. Just
about everyone gets drunk. But no
one lies, and no one dies. While this
makes perfect sense to Scandinavian
parents, it would be a tough sell for
American parents.

Europe takes civil rights to extremes. Even
farm animals are guaranteed certain rights
by law. In 2008, Switzerland granted new
rights to animals, including banning the use
of live bait by fishermen, the right for sheep
and goats to have at least a visual contact
with their fellows, and a legal right for pigs
to shower after rolling in the mud.

This is just one example of pragmatic harm reduction motivating drug policy in Europe. In some parts of Europe, a joint of marijuana causes about as much excitement as a can of beer. And the Continent's needle junkies are dealt with by nurses, counselors, and maintenance clinics more than by cops, judges, and prisons. (The European approach to drug policy is covered in greater length in Chapter 7.)

Perhaps Europe's inclination to be tolerant is rooted in the intolerance of its past. In the 16th century, they were burning Protestants for their beliefs. In the 17th century, they were drowning women who stepped out of line— condemning them as witches. In the 20th century, Nazis were gassing Jews, Roma, and gay people. Now, in the 21st century, Europe seems determined to get human rights, civil liberties, and tolerance issues right. And now Europe legislates these issues rather than morality.

While the US is not likely to embrace tolerance with the sweeping idealism of some Europeans, just knowing that reasonable people endeavor to respect human diversity, promote inclusivity, and champion human rights to this degree can be empowering. Once back home, you have the option of tailoring your personal version of the American Dream with similar ideals.

European Flesh and the American Prude

On a lighter note, let's take a peek at Europe's relatively open relationship with their bodies and with sex. While not as high-minded as war and peace or taxation and social services, this is an aspect of the cultural divide that titillates any American traveler to Europe who's window-shopped a magazine kiosk, spun a postcard rack, gone to a beach or park on a sunny day, or channel-surfed broadcast TV in their hotel room late at night.

Thinking through my recent travels, I recall many examples of Europe's different attitudes about

The German Spa

When I'm traveling, there are delightful road bumps in my intense research schedule where I put away the notes and simply enjoy the moment. The classic Friedrichsbad spa in Baden-Baden is one of those fine little breaks.

Ever since the Roman Emperor Caracalla soaked in the mineral waters of Baden-Baden about 2,000 years ago, that German spa town has welcomed those in need of a good soak. And it's always naked. In the 19th century, this was Germany's ultimate spa resort, and even today the name Baden-Baden is synonymous with relaxation in a land where the government still pays its overworked citizens to take a little spa time.

I happened to be here when one of our tour groups was in town. I told the guide (who was a German) that I was excited for this great opportunity for her group to enjoy the spa. She disagreed, saying, "No one's going. They can't handle the nudity. That's how it is with American visitors."

They didn't know what they were missing. Wearing only the locker key strapped around my wrist, I began

the ritual. I weighed myself: 92 kilos. The attendant led me under the industrial-strength shower, a torrential kickoff pounding my head and shoulders...obliterating the rest of the world. She then gave me slippers and a towel, ushering me into a dry heat room with fine wooden reclining chairs—their slats too hot without the towel. Staring up at exotic tiles of herons and palms, I cooked. After more hot rooms punctuated with showers came the massage.

Like someone really drunk going for one more glass, I climbed gingerly onto the marble slab and lay belly-up. The masseur held up two Brillo-pad mitts and he asked, "Hard or soft?" In the spirit of wild abandon, I said, "Hard," not certain what that would mean to my skin. I got the coarse Brillo-pad scrub-down.

sex: My Dutch friends had, on their coffee table, a graphic government-produced magazine promoting safe sex. I was sitting on the toilet at an airport in Poland and the cleaning lady asked me to lift my legs so she could sweep. I learned that I can measure the romantic appeal of scenic pull-outs along Italy's Amalfi Coast drive by how many used condoms litter the asphalt. Soap ads on huge billboards overlooking major city intersections in Belgium show lathered-up breasts. The logo of a German travel publisher is a traveler on a tropical-paradise islet leaning up against its only palm tree, hands behind his head, reading a book that's supported

I was so soaped up, he had to hold my arms like a fisherman holds a salmon so I wouldn't slip away. With the tenderness of someone gutting a big fish, he scrubbed, chopped, bent, and generally tenderized me. In spite of the rough treatment, it was extremely relaxing.

Finished with a Teutonic spank on the butt, I was sent off into the pools. Nude, without my glasses, and not speaking the language, I was gawky. On a sliding scale between Mr. Magoo and Woody Allen, I was everywhere. Steam rooms, cold plunges...it all led to the mixed section, where the men and women come together.

This is where the Americans get really uptight. The parallel spa facilities intersect, as both men and women share the finest three pools. Here, all are welcome to glide under exquisite domes in perfect silence like aristocratic swans. Germans are nonchalant, tuned into their bodies and focused on solitary relaxation. Tourists are tentative, trying to be cool...but more aware of their nudity.

The climax is the cold plunge. I'm not good with cold water—yet I absolutely love this. You must not wimp out on the cold plunge.

Then an attendant escorted me into the "quiet room" and asked if I'd like to be awoken at any time. I told her at closing time. She wrapped me in hot sheets and a brown blanket. No, I wasn't wrapped...I was swaddled. Warm, flat on my back, among twenty hospital-type beds—only one other bed was occupied...he seemed dead. I stared up at the ceiling, and some time later was jolted awake by my own snore.

Leaving, I weighed myself again: 91 kilos. I had shed 2.2 pounds of sweat. It would have been more if tension had mass. Stepping into the cool evening air, I was thankful my hotel was a level two-block stroll away. Like Gumby, flush and without momentum, I fell slow-motion onto my down comforter, my head buried in a big, welcoming pillow. Wonderfully naked under my clothes, I could only think, Ahhhh. Baden-Baden."

by his erection. Preschoolers play naked in fountains in Norway. A busty porn star is elected to parliament in Italy. Copper-toned grandmothers in the south of France have no tan lines. The student tourist center in Copenhagen welcomes visitors with a bowl of free condoms. Accountants in Munich fold their suits neatly on the grass as every inch of their body soaks up the sun while taking a lunch break in the park...while American tourists are the ones riding their bikes into trees. During a construction industry convention in Barcelona, locals laughed that they actually had to bus in extra sex workers from France.

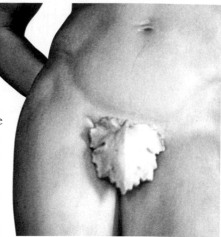

I'm not comfortable with all of this. I find the crude sexual postcards on racks all over the Continent gross, the Benny Hill–style T&A that inundates TV throughout Mediterranean Europe boorish, and the topless models strewn across page three of so many British newspapers insulting to women. And I'll never forget the time I had to physically remove the TV from my children's hotel room in Austria after seeing a couple slamming away on channel 7 (and the hotelier looked at me like I was crazy).

Compared to Europe, America is almost laughably shy about nudity. An early edition of my art-for-travelers guidebook featured a camera-toting *David*—full frontal nudity, Michelangelo-style—on the cover. My publisher's sales reps complained that in more conservative parts of the US, bookstores were uncomfortable stocking it. A fig leaf would help sales.

When it comes to great art, I don't like fig leafs. But I proposed, just for fun, that we put a peel-able fig leaf on the cover so readers could choose whether they wanted their book with or without nudity. My publisher said that would be too expensive. I offered to pay half the cost (10 cents a book times 10,000). He went for it, and I had the fun experience of writing "for fig leafs" on a $500 check. Perhaps that needless expense just bolstered my wish that Americans were more European in their comfort level with nakedness.

The last time I was at a spa in Germany's Black Forest, in one two-hour stretch, I saw more penises than I'd seen in years. All were extremely relaxed… and, I must say, I was struck by the variety. Getting Americans comfortable in the spas with naked Europeans has long been a challenge and a frustration for me as a guide. I care because, once people get used to it, they almost unanimously consider it a great experience. My first European spa visit was with some German friends—a classy, good-looking young couple. I was swept into the changing area with no explanation, and suddenly the Germans were naked. Eventually I realized everyone was just there to relax. I eased up and got more comfortably naked. It's not sexual…simply open and free.

Whether in a German spa, a Finnish sauna, a Croatian beach, or a Turkish hammam (I can't come up with a British example), a fun part of travel can be getting naked with strangers. Of course, when producing public television, we can't easily show spas, saunas, or beaches in Europe, where nudity is the norm. Even in an age where you can easily see anything, anytime on the Internet, television "standards and practices" are rigid about showing nudity or sex, or even using forbidden sexual words—and penalties for violators are severe. Any station airing anything potentially offensive (between all the ads for erectile dysfunction medications) on the public airwaves can be made to pay dearly if some of its viewers complain.

Because of strict FCC regulations on nudity, we even have to be careful of which art we film for my television show. Since I feature art that includes naked bodies, my shows are flagged by the network—and in some conservative markets, programmers play it safe by airing my shows only after 10 p.m., when things are less restrictive. As recently as the early 2000s, programmers actually got a list of how many seconds of marble penis and canvas breasts were showing in each episode. They couldn't inflict a titillating Titian painting or a buxom Bernini statue on their viewership in more conservative communities without taking heat.

As public broadcasting stations lack the financial resources to survive a major fine, they are particularly careful in this regard. Many of us who produce broadcast material on a shoestring (like me, and public broadcasting in general) have to ponder: Should we put a digital fig leaf on *David's* full-frontal nudity? Bleep Bocaccio's bawdy language? Can I film *The Three Graces* only from the waist up? Will Raphael's randy cupids be labeled "child pornography" and Bernini's *Rape of Persephone* as "S&M"? My partners in public television and I proceed gingerly—not sure if we can show Venus's breasts. Can we risk the possibility of a $275,000 fine…and is that per nipple?

You may not want to bring the more casual European approach to sex and the human body back home with you. And I'm not saying we should all run around naked. But I do suspect that children raised in America, where sex is often considered "dirty," are more likely to have an uncomfortable relationship with sex and their bodies than Europeans do. (I sense that there is more violence associated with sex here than there; in fact, Americans report at least double the incidence of rape as citizens of most European countries.) And I have a hunch that the French, who have as many words for a kiss as Eskimos have for snow, enjoy making love more than we Americans do. I like a continent where sexual misconduct won't doom a politician with anyone other than his family and friends, and where the human body is considered a divine work of art worth admiring openly.

How Europeans View Us

We've covered a lot of ground about how America perceives Europe. Now let's flip things around, to see how Europe perceives America.

Americans—mindful of the old "Ugly American" stereotype—tend to be conscientious ambassadors of their country when traveling abroad. And many are fearful that they might receive a negative welcome—especially in France, which has a reputation for being "anti-American." Through my tour business, I take several thousand Americans to France annually. Each year, I survey them in an email, asking how their experience was with the locals. Even in times when the media was telling us how "anti-American" the world was, nobody complained. The French have always given American individuals a warm welcome, even if they don't care for our foreign policy. In Europe, the mark of a real friend is not someone who constantly fawns over your obvious strengths, but someone who tells you when you are off-base and disappointing them.

When European countries refuse to support US foreign policy, many Americans say, "Don't they remember how we saved them from the Nazis?" The answer is yes, absolutely they do. I was recently filming in France's Burgundy,

at a charming little mom-and-pop château. When I'm filming, get out of my way—the sun's going down, and we've got work to do. But the aristocratic couple whose family had called that castle home for centuries insisted, "We must stop and have a ceremony because we have an American film crew here working in our castle." They cracked open a fine bottle of wine and brought out—with great ceremony, as if it were a precious relic—a beautiful

Europeans are forever thankful for America's role in freeing them from Nazi tyranny.

48-star American flag. It was the very flag they had hoisted over their château on that great day in 1944 when they were freed by American troops. They implored us, "Please go home and tell your friends that we will never forget what America did for us—winning our freedom with its heroics, its economic and military might, and its commitment to liberty." In addition to being grateful to the US for helping to free them from Hitler, Europeans also appreciate our defeat of the Soviet Union with a bold and determined battle of economic attrition during the Cold War.

I have European friends six or eight years older than me, born in the late 1940s, named Frankie and Johnny—because their parents were so inspired by the greatness of the Americans they met who came to liberate them from the Nazis.

Particularly in times of political upheaval, people ask me: Do Europeans judge us based on our current president? While I've always found a warm personal welcome—regardless of who's in the White House or which war we're currently fighting—the European view of America as a whole does rise and fall with their assessment of the current administration. Europeans are generally more liberal than Americans. During the Clinton years, the "brand of America" was soaring: With a womanizing, sax-playing, Europhile president who studied at Oxford, anything American sold, and California was always a hit. During the George W. Bush years (when speaking French was a political liability, America misled Europe into a regrettable invasion of Iraq, and the US military tortured Muslims at secret bases), the brand of America took a nosedive. European marketing firms combed anything American out of their advertising jingles. Then, with Obama, our brand was up again—in the early days of his presidency, Obama was awarded the Nobel Peace Prize...it seems, simply for liking the world. Many Europeans saw the "America first" election of Donald Trump as a sign that we'd become more ethnocentric—the dated "Ugly American" outlook is almost national policy, and Yankee Doodle no longer sells.

Many wonder how Americans are perceived during the Trump years. While Europeans understand—far better than Americans do—that oddball political figures sometimes rise to the top, they aren't used to seeing it in the US. They can't fathom how someone who loses the popular vote by nearly three million people can still become president. And they may be a little confused because the cross-section of Americans they meet are travelers, who tend to skew to the left. But, at the end of the day, most Europeans will judge you by your own actions—not by your government's.

I've found that Europeans consider it polite not to talk politics unless you break the ice. In other words, if you are a Trump supporter and don't want to get in an argument, just avoid the topic—or, if you enjoy a good debate, you've come to the right continent. And if you're a liberal and want lots of friends, tell them what you think about Trump. For an American in Europe, two new skills might be handy: an ability to explain how the Electoral College works...and a good eye-roll.

Ultimately, Europeans are inclined to like Americans. But if there is a negative aspect to their image of us, it's that we are loud, wasteful, ethnocentric, too informal (which can seem disrespectful), and a bit naive. As you travel, you may encounter what seem like strange European ways. Try to assume there is a rationale. For instance, many Italian hoteliers turn off the heat in spring and don't turn on the air-conditioning until summer. The point is to conserve energy, and it's mandated by the Italian government. You could complain about being cold or hot...or bring a sweater in winter, and in summer, be prepared to sweat a little like everyone else. While Europeans look bemusedly at some of our Yankee excesses—and with concern at others—they nearly always afford us individual travelers all the warmth we deserve.

We've taken a wide-ranging and (I hope) thought-provoking tour through the Old World. You probably found some of these ideas appealing, and others appalling. Again I'll state the obvious: Europe doesn't have all the answers. But I wonder if Europe is "out-innovating" us when it comes to finding clever new solutions. When I encourage Americans to take a look at a European approach to a problem that is befuddling us, some critics accuse me of "America-bashing"—"If you love Europe so much, why don't you just move there?" Short answer: I love America more. And because I care about our society, I challenge us to do better. In good times or bad, we should be open to considering all the solutions we can. And I find Europeans to be smart, happy, good at life, and people I enjoy learning from.

Chapter 4
Resurrection in El Salvador

There's something about visiting Central America that stirs a certain traveling soul. And my four trips to Central America—each organized and led by Augsburg College's Center for Global Education—have done much to shape my politics. It's fascinating how your impressions of a place—and the place itself—can evolve over many years of visits. My first trip, in 1988, took place during El Salvador's Civil War. By my second visit, in 1991, the leftist people's revolution had been put down, and US- and corporate-friendly forces were in control. The third trip, in 2005—the primary focus of this chapter—was built around the events memorializing the 25th anniversary of the assassination of Archbishop Oscar Romero. And, by my fourth trip, in 2010, the revolutionaries were in power, but seemed only to be proving that power corrupts—and the people were still grappling with many of the same vexing problems.

For each of these trips, I had a week or two available for a vacation. I could have enjoyed lying on a beach somewhere, but I chose to spend the time in El Salvador. Checking in on a people who lost a revolution, taking the pulse of corporate-led globalization in a poor country, collecting my impressions, and sharing them now is precisely what I consider to be travel as a political act.

I realize it's odd, as a relative novice to Latin American travel, for me to have such strong opinions—or any opinion—on these topics. Far from being an expert, I'm a classic case of someone knowing "just enough to be dangerous." It's clear: My passion is rooted in the opportunities I've had to talk with and learn from smart, impoverished people living in what I grew up considering "banana republics." Spending time with the poor in Central America, you find a wisdom, a dignity, and a humanity that radicalizes people from the rich world. I hope the following impressions and observations not only share some of what I learned, but illustrate why choosing a place like Managua over a place like Mazatlán the next time you head south of the border can create a more fulfilling travel experience.

Travel Makes You Wiser, but Less Happy

Back before my first trip to Central America in 1988, I specifically forbade my heart to get caught up in economic justice issues south of our border. I knew there were leftists fighting American-funded groups and it was a tragic mess, but that was it. There was too much pulling at me, and the competing sides, excuses, and complaints were all too complex and contradictory. I just didn't have the energy to sort it out, and I didn't need it in my life. Then I traveled there and learned what Thomas Jefferson meant when he wrote that travel "makes a person wiser, but less happy."

That first trip lit a fire in me. I realized I have the right, if not the responsibility, to form my opinions based on my own experience, even if it goes against the mainstream at home. It was liberating, empowering…and exhaust-

Top: This bus tour is filled with Americans eager to learn and hungry for inspiration. Bottom: Where and how you choose to travel determines how much you'll learn. Organizations offering "educational tours" turn the world into a fascinating classroom. (For a list of such organizations, see page 283.)

ing. After that first trip, I published my journal, flew to Washington, DC, and spent two days hand-delivering it to the office of each Member of Congress on Capitol Hill. Deep down I knew that my efforts would likely end up in congressional recycling bins, but I needed to do it. And it felt good. That little political mission marked the start of the time when my travels became more than just recreation. (That journal, and others from my Central America trips, are online at www.ricksteves.com/centam.)

In 2005, I returned to El Salvador for the first time since 1991. Landing in the capital city, San Salvador, I was met by my guide, César, who whisked me away in his car. In his coin dish, I saw shiny Lincolns and Washingtons. I'm never very confident upon arrival in a new country, and this confused me. César explained, "We've been dollarized now since 2001." American coins had become the local coins. (In a kind of voluntary colonization, local elites chose to adopt the US currency to avoid losing their personal fortunes in case of a radical change in their government.) My hunch was that, since my last visit, much more had changed in El Salvador than just the currency.

El Salvador politics line up on two sides: The left includes the FMLN guerillas-turned-politicians, students, labor groups, Protestant churches, and many Catholic priests and nuns (especially those who espouse a Liberation Theology approach). The right includes the establishment ARENA party, the military (and Civil War–era death squads), big business, wealthy elites, Evangelical churches, and the official Catholic Church hierarchy. These two forces are locked in a seemingly endless battle for the souls of El Salvador's *campesinos* (peasants). During its 20 years of rule, the ARENA party created a highly regressive tax code that strongly favored wealthy Salvadorans and international business. Traditionally, the US has supported the right wing, both to protect its own economic interests and—back in the 1980s—to fight the perceived "communist threat" of the left.

While the players remain the same, the game has changed. The peace that ended El Salvador's Civil War also ushered in an era of globalization. By my 2005 visit, North American chains—from Pizza Hut to Texaco to Subway—appeared to be thriving. The Marlboro Man looked good on his horse. And, as I cruised through town past a cancan of American-owned franchises and a cheering squad of billboards, it seemed the victory of the US-supported faction had been a huge success.

And yet, it was also immediately clear that living in San Salvador—a city of a million and a half people—was still no picnic. Through the 2000s, El Salvador was running neck-and-neck with Honduras for the highest homicide rate of any country in the Western Hemisphere, and gang violence was rising steadily. Exploring San Salvador, it was clear that any nice home came with a fenced-in and fortified front yard. Rolls of razor wire were on sale in the newspaper. In the wealthy neighborhoods, each street had an armed guard.

The relative lack of news about Latin America since the 1980s had lulled me into thinking that perhaps things were getting better for people there. But suffering that's not covered on the daily news is still suffering. This trip reminded me of the power of our media—even over those of us who are determined not to be misled. If the media chooses not to cover something, that issue becomes invisible, and its victims become mute. In a sense, silence is violence.

Under a Corrugated Tin Roof with Beatriz

El Salvador provides the *norteamericano* with a hot and muggy welcome. After one day, I had settled in quite well. I was speckled with bug bites and accustomed to my frail cold shower, noisy fan, and springy cot. I knew to brush my teeth with bottled water and to put used toilet paper in the wastebasket to avoid clogging the plumbing. I was ready for some serious education…and I got it. I was shocked to learn how amazingly blind I was to people's daily reality just a short plane ride south of the border.

Since my previous visit, Salvadorans had been dealt some miserable cards. When coffee prices crashed in the early 2000s, it sent the economy into a tailspin; many desperate young people joined gangs, while well-off people built bigger and bigger walls around their property. Eventually the *maquiladora* industry (sewing clothing for rich world corporations) moved in to provide jobs—but only after the government agreed to lower the minimum wage. By my 2005 visit, the minimum wage was about $1 an hour. While in the US, minimum wage is considered a starting point, most Salvadorans aspire only to minimum wage…and that's all they get: $144 a month.

To make ends meet, many Salvadoran families struggle to send one person abroad to earn money. These expats seek a menial labor job in the US and send back what's called "remittances." Nearly 20 percent of El Salvador's economy is money wired home from the USA. The remittances these laborers send home is common throughout the developing world. In fact, each year throughout the world, refugees working in rich countries send about half a trillion dollars to their families back home.

The Western Union office is a busy place in El Salvador. Money wired home from immigrant laborers in the US keeps many Central American families afloat.

But there's a huge cost to this phenomenon of the strongest, brightest young men leaving dangerous homelands with dead-end economies for work abroad: The home countries suffer an expensive "brain drain." Half of El Salvador's university students aspire to leave their country. They see higher education as their ticket out. And, while immigrants send home lots of money, the resulting broken families—poor single mothers trying to raise children alone—leaves a society ripe for the growth of street gangs.

In 2001, two huge earthquakes destroyed or badly damaged a quarter of the private homes in El Salvador, leaving 1.5 million homeless (in a nation of about six million people). Of course, in a big shake, it's the poor whose homes crumble—seismic safety is a luxury only the privileged can afford. (An earthquake of the same magnitude hit my hometown of Seattle that same year, and there was almost no damage.) For protection, the most that shantytown residents can do is to live in what they call "miniskirt housing"— cinderblocks for the lower half of the walls, and then light corrugated tin for the upper walls and roof. If a miniskirt house tumbles down, it won't kill you. And when it's over, you just scavenge a few two-by-fours, reassemble the frame, and nail your sheets of tin back in place.

Exploring the city's poor neighborhoods, I found myself in an urban world where it seemed that solid jobs were rare and half the workforce was in the informal economy—basically selling things on the street. In most of the old center of San Salvador, sidewalks were taken up by shanty retail stalls jammed against the walls of local businesses, forcing pedestrians to share the streets with cars.

People with no disposable income entertain themselves creatively. I joined one gang of men gathered around a rustic checkerboard in a tiny park. There

Player-supported checkers game

was no table—they were holding the board up together. It was a spirited gang, using bottle caps—turned either up or down—for pieces. With the end of the game, I was invited to play the winner. It was fun…until my opponent got what they call a "queen," and I learned that in Central American checkers, the queen has vastly more powerful moves than the "king" where I come from. With his Salvadoran queen on the rampage, I was swept from the checkered battlefield…and finished in no time.

My opponent gave me no mercy. And, beating an American tourist that day is probably as vivid a memory for them as it is for me. I find it easier to connect with people in poor countries than in rich ones. Perhaps that's because when there's almost nothing to earn, time is not money. The key: A good traveler needs to be the extrovert.

In the midst of relative affluence, Americans seem to operate with a mindset of scarcity—focusing on what we don't have or what we might lose. Meanwhile, the Salvadorans I met, who have so little, embrace life with a mindset of abundance—thankful for the simple things they do have. They're extremely generous, considering their tough economic reality.

We dropped in on Beatriz and her daughter Veronica, who live in a miniskirt shack on El Salvador's minimum wage. The place was as clean and inviting as a tin-roofed shack with a dirt floor can be. Beatriz sat us down and told of raising a family through a Civil War: "The war moved into the capital, and our little house happened to sit between the police headquarters and the guerillas. At night, I hid with my children under the bed as bullets flew. For ten years, the war put us in never-ending fear. Mothers feared the forced recruitment of our sons. Finally, we arranged a peace. But the peace accords didn't benefit us poor people." She explained how this "peace" was no more than an acknowl-

edgment of the futility of a
continued struggle.

About her life, she said,
"My house becomes a lake
in the rainy season. Still,
we are thankful to have this
place. Our land was very
cheap. We bought it from a
man receiving death threats.
He fled to America. While

we make $144 a month in the city, the minimum out in the countryside is
much less—only $70 a month. Nearly half the families in our country are
living on $1 a day per person. To survive, you need a home that is already in
your family. You have one light bulb, corn, and beans. That is about all. Living
on minimum wage is more difficult now than before the war. Before, electricity cost about $1 a month. Water was provided. Today electricity costs $19
and water $14—that's about one-quarter of my monthly wage. My mother
has a tumor in her head. There is no help possible. I have no money."

Beatriz's strikingly beautiful 22-year-old daughter, Veronica, dreamed
of going to the US. But the "coyote" (as the guy who ferries refugees across
Mexico and into the US is called) would charge $6,000, and she would
probably be raped before reaching the US border as a kind of "extra fee."

As a chicken with a bald neck pecked at my shoe, I surveyed the inge-
nious mix of mud, battered lumber, and corrugated tin that made up this
house. It occurred to me that poverty erodes ethnic distinctions. Wherever
you travel, there's something uniform about desperation.

Beatriz and Veronica prepared for us their basic meal: a corn tortilla.
As I ate a thick corn cake hot off the griddle, it felt like I was taking com-
munion. In that tortilla were tales I'd heard of peasants who bundled their
tortillas into a bandana and ran through the night as American helicopters
swept across their skies.

For me, munching on that tortilla provided a sense of solidarity—
wimpy…but still solidarity. I was what locals jokingly call a "round-trip
revolutionary" (someone from a stable and wealthy country who cares
enough to come down here…but only with a return plane ticket zipped
into his money belt). Still, having had the opportunity to sit and talk with
Beatriz and Veronica, even a round-trip revolutionary flies home with an

indelible understanding of the human reality of that much-quoted statistic, "Half of humanity is trying to live on $2 a day."

Globalization: The -Ism of Our Time

Beatriz and Veronica—and you and I—are players in a vast global chess game of commerce. As the world's economy evolves, modern technology is shrinking the planet, putting the labor, natural resources, and capital of distant lands in touch with each other and revolutionizing the way products are

made and distributed. Globalization is a complicated process that, frankly, nobody can control—or even fully understand. But the people I met in El Salvador made it more meaningful for me than any book or lecture ever could.

The rich world likes to imagine that globalization brings more efficiency, more profits, and needed resources to poor nations. And often, it does. In this equation, a company from a wealthy country decides to have their product manufactured in a poor country. The company enjoys a much lower payroll than if they employed workers back home, they pay a wage that's considered generous in the local economy, and rich world consumers get things really cheap. It's a win-win-win. At least, that's the hope.

But in reality, all too often, globalization is driven not by altruism, but by an ambition to open new markets to firms and products. The legally mandated responsibility of a corporation is to maximize profits. And if that means exploiting cheap labor in poor countries, they do it. That's why, if you talk with people in El Salvador, even proponents of globalization don't claim anything compassionate about it. It's presented simply as unstoppable: "Globalization is a big train, and it's moving out. Get on board or get run over."

In Central America, egregious examples of mishandled globalization are numerous. An American biotech giant forced the people of Honduras to sell the patent rights for plants that produce local folk cures. Now, those poor *campesinos* (who can't begin to afford international pharmaceuticals) can be legally charged for using their own traditional remedies. Another example: trade levies, which increase with processing, make it easy for a poor country

What's a Banana Republic?

The term "banana republic" originated a century ago as an insulting nickname for a Central American country run by a corrupt dictator whose economy was limited to the export of a single resource, and dominated by an American multinational corporation. (For example, in Guatemala, the United Fruit Company—which had the support of the local elites and their government—owned nearly all of the arable land, which grew only bananas for export to the USA.) In a "banana republic," trade arrangements are such that the natural resource (whether agricultural or mineral) must be exported raw—meaning that local businesses are not allowed to process it domestically, which would be more profitable. This makes it easy for the dominant corporation to manipulate the price of the raw material. (When the wholesale price of bananas goes down in a banana republic, the cost of everything else goes up.) And the vast majority of the workers are landless peasants, with no alternative to working the fields at whatever wage

the plantation offers. The system effectively keeps the entire country underdeveloped, at the expense of the local population and to the benefit of a company in another country. A consumer in the rich world may enjoy cheaper fruit that's grown in a "banana republic"... but if you really think about it honestly, you start to realize that your "cheap" banana comes at a huge cost to someone half a world away.

to export raw peanuts—but make it prohibitively expensive to produce far more profitable peanut butter.

Many participants like to think of globalization as "tough love," as the rich world tries to pull up the poor world. The scorecard tells a different story. In the last 40 years, the average annual income in the world's 20 poorest countries—places where people make on average less than $1,000 a year—has barely changed. In that same period, the average per capita income in the richest 20 nations has nearly tripled to over $30,000. The bottom 40 percent of humanity lives on roughly 5 percent of the planet's resources. The top 20 percent lives on over 75 percent. The greatest concentration of wealth among economic elites in the history of the human race is happening at the same time our world is becoming a global village. Meanwhile, even in the countries that benefit (such as the United States), the spoils go mostly to the already wealthy—padding profits for shareholders even as working-class American jobs are exported south of our borders, leaving many citizens of the rich world underemployed and disillusioned.

So what am I? Anti-globalization? No. I'm just anti–*bad* globalization. Many believe that, if implemented thoughtfully and compassionately, globalization could be the salvation of the developing world. Progress can include or exclude the poor. And, as wealthy people who reap the benefits of globalization, I believe we have a moral obligation to be responsible.

As a businessman who manufactures some of my travel bags in South Asia, I'm keenly aware that globalization can be either a force for good or a force for harm. I have struggled with and understand the inevitability and moral challenge of it—there's simply no way to produce a bag that will sell in the USA without finding the least expensive combination of quality, labor, and materials. I contribute to globalization only because I'm confident that the people who stitch and sew my bags are treated well and paid appropriately. If I believed that the factory conditions were bad for that community or for its workers, I'd take my business elsewhere. To ensure this, I fly one of my staff to the factory for a periodic re-evaluation. It's a carefully weighed decision that I make with my humanitarian principles (and with the plight of Beatriz and Veronica) in mind.

Privilege brings with it the luxurious option of obliviousness. No comfortable American enjoys being told how her cat has more "buying power" than

Painted clay figurines featuring a bloody, slain peasant (the "Christ figure") at the feet of two camouflaged, US-equipped-and-funded soldiers (considered "the new centurions," tools of empire) filled Central American Christmas markets during my earlier visits. During the heat of the Civil War, poor Salvadoran children scooted these gory trios into their manger scenes along with Mary, Joseph, and the shepherds. They were a vivid Liberation Theology reminder of Roman Empire/American Empire parallels and how Christ knows their struggles. While I didn't see them on my later visits, I keep this statue—my favorite souvenir from El Salvador—on a prominent shelf in my office.

some hungry child just south of the border, how his investments may be contributing to the destruction of the environment, how the weaponry we sell and profit from is really being used, or how—if you really knew its story— there's blood on your banana (see the sidebar). But here in the rich world, the choice is ours: awareness and concern, or ignorance and bliss.

The City Built Upon a Garbage Dump

San Salvador's poorest neighborhood—a place that makes Beatriz's neighborhood seem almost posh—is built upon a garbage dump. We wandered for an hour around this "city" of 50,000 inhabitants, dusty frills of garbage blowing like old dandelion spores in the wind.

It was a ramshackle world of corrugated tin, broken concrete, and tattered laundry. I'll never forget the piles of scrap metal, the ripped and shredded sofas, tire parts, and filthy plastic bowls I saw stacked neatly at one point. This was a nickel-and-dime retail store entirely stocked by junk scavenged from the city dump. Even the store's chairs, tables, walls, and roof were scavenged—made of battered tin.

Overlooking the shacks was a slap-in-your-face billboard from a local bank, advertising home loans for the wealthy. It read, "With every day that passes, your house is closer to being yours."

Older kids watch younger kids while dads scavenge and moms walk for water.

American Empire?

In my travels—whether to El Salvador, Europe, or Iran—I find that many people outside our borders think of the US as an "empire." But anytime I mention this back home, I get a feisty response.

You could debate long and hard about whether the US is an empire. But in reality, what you and I think is irrelevant. The fact is, much of the world *views* us as an empire, and therefore, we'll be treated as one. We might not literally claim other countries as part of our own territory, but only we can declare someone else's natural resources on the far side of our planet "vital to our national security." When others look at us, rather than see a hardworking, freedom-loving policeman of the world, they see a nation with less than 5 percent of this planet's people shelling out 40 percent of the world's military spending, and maintaining military bases in 150 countries.

Every empire in history has been plagued by angry forces on its fringes that refused to play by its rules. Romans were pestered and ultimately defeated by barbarians. The British dealt with and lost to colonial American guerilla patriots. The Habsburgs were plagued by what they derided as "anarchists"...and were eventually defeated. And today, if you're hugely outgunned—as all enemies of America are—you get creative. You shoot from the bushes like we did when we fought the Redcoats. Our enemies know that if someone decides to fight the US, they have two choices; be dead, or be "a terrorist." Our challenge in combatting terrorism is that there's always been terrorism and there always will be terrorism. It's a technique, not an enemy.

Some might brush off American military might by saying, "Well, that's just the government." *We* are our government. We cannot rest on the notion of the "innocent civilian." If I pay taxes, I am a combatant. Any American bullet that flies or any bomb that drops—whether I agree with it or not—has my name on it. That's simply honest, responsible citizenship.

I find it's helpful to view questions of US military involvement through a prism of "hard power" (employing military might) versus "soft power" (earning goodwill through humanitarian acts). For example, imagine using our military to build bridges and highways instead of blowing them up. It'd be better for the innocent people who live in those places (not to mention better for our troops). Improving the "Brand of America" in this way would make it much harder for foreign terrorists or bombastic leaders to mobilize people against us. While this might seem a little too "touchy-feely" for our militaristic society, it's less expensive—and certainly less destructive—than hard power.

We passed through a "suburb" of tin shacks housing people who lived off the dump, passing yards where they sorted out saleable garbage, stacked broken glass, and pounded rusty metal scraps into cooking pots and pans. The people had done what they could to make their slum livable. There was greenery, cute children bringing home huge jugs of water (two cents each), and lots of mud, bamboo, and corrugated tin buildings. As we approached the ridge overlooking the main dump, I started thinking that this really wasn't all that awful.

Then things changed, and we entered a kind of living hell. We'd heard of the people living off garbage dumps, and now we were in for a firsthand look: huge bulldozers, circling black birds, and a literal mountain of garbage ten stories high with people picking through it. It was a vast urban fruit rind, rotting in the sun and covered with human ants.

A policeman with a machine gun kept the people away from one half of the garbage mountain. That was where aid items that the government figured would cost them too much to disperse were being buried under the garbage. About thirty people gathered. Our guide said they were waiting for the guard to leave. I couldn't believe him. Then the guard left, and all thirty scavengers broke into a sprint and dashed into the best part of the dump. The smell was sweet and sickening.

Overwhelmed by the uncomfortable realities I was confronted with, I retreated to a strip mall in a wealthy part of town. I was just settling into a nice, peaceful, comforting latte, like I get each morning back home, when a US military helicopter surged over the horizon. It hovered above for a moment and then clumsily landed. A jolly Santa Claus hopped out to the delight of the children wealthy enough to have moms shopping here.

Looking at those kids and thinking of their dump-dwelling cousins, I realized that, even if you're motivated only by greed, if you know what's good for you, you don't want to be filthy rich in a desperately poor world.

Feeling the breeze of the chopper as Santa climbed back in and it flew away, I took another sip of the drink that cost a day's local wages. Pulling out my little notebook, I added a few more observations, and continued my education.

In 1492, Columbus Sailed the Ocean Blue...

Our Salvadoran hosts gave us a history lesson unlike any I got in school. In 1524, the Spaniards arrived in El Salvador. They killed the indigenous people, burned villages, and named the place "The Savior" after Christ. Enslaving the locals—branding them with hot irons like cattle—those first conquistadors established a persistent pattern. Fields of local staples were replaced by more profitable cash crops (indigo, then coffee), as locals were repeatedly displaced from desirable farmland. Rebellion after rebellion was put down as the land was Christianized. Making religion the opiate of the masses, the priests preached, "Don't question authority. Heaven awaits those who suffer quietly."

While political murals are dangerous these days, indigenous Salvadorans—who call themselves "people of corn"—celebrate their ethnicity instead.

El Salvador finally won its independence from Spain in 1821. The local victors were not the indigenous people, but the descendants of those first Spanish conquistadors. They wanted to continue harvesting El Salvador... but without giving Spain its cut. Indigenous Salvadorans gained nothing from "independence."

After the popular uprisings of 1932 and the massacres that followed, indigenous culture was outlawed, the left wing was decimated, and a military dictatorship was established. Those who spoke the indigenous language were killed. Traditional dress was prohibited. After 1932, when a white person looked at an Indian, the Indian's head would drop. To be indigenous was to be subversive. And today, the word *indígena* still comes with negative connotations: illiterate, ignorant, savage. If a Mestizo (mixed-race Latin American) loses his temper or does something violent, rather than say, "The devil made me do it," he'll say, *"Se me salió el indio"* (The Indian came out of me).

A monument much like America's Vietnam Veterans Memorial stands in San Salvador, remembering people killed in its most recent popular uprising.

Interested to connect with this important facet of Central American culture, I drove deep into the countryside, to a village where 90 percent of the people are indigenous and the economy is based on pottery. I spent some time with Valentín López, a potter who's passionate about keeping the pre-Colombian local art alive in his craft.

At his wheel, he demonstrated the traditional way pottery is made, painted, and burnished. It's all organic: clay pounded by bare feet, brushes made of a woman's hair, and giant seeds as burnishers. He explained how important it is for indigenous potters to be in tune with nature. In the US, a potter orders clay online. Here, they hike to the clay pit and gather it themselves. As his son kick-started the potter's wheel, Valentín pointed out that there's no electricity involved—he said, "It's people power...our gas is rice and beans." Watching the boy getting the wheel really ramped up with his muscular leg, he added, "This town produces very good soccer players."

Then came a chance for a tourist to be humiliated...and I jumped at the opportunity. Climbing into the potter's chair felt like saddling a strange animal. I pushed the heavy stone wheel with my feet. It was awkward. With images of Fred Flintstone trying to start his car, I struggled to get it going. My foot nearly got pinched and dragged by the rough wheel under the brace of the table—which would have made me, quite likely, the first person to lose a leg to a potter's wheel.

The potter's son helped me get the wheel turning full-steam, and then slammed a blob of clay onto my spinning work table. I cupped it, and it

wobbled. He showed me how to be gentle with the clay. As he trickled on some water and guided my fingers and thumbs, the clay came to life. But my creation was still a clumsy little mess... eventually made elegant, effortlessly, by my teen-aged teacher.

Glancing down the row of eight stations like the one I was sitting at, all under the shade of a corrugated tin roof, I imagined this cottage industry in full swing. And I appreciated the timelessness of the technology. While the advent of plastic must have done to pottery what the advent of cars did to blacksmithing, indigenous people want vessels that are of the earth, made by hand, and ornamented with the iconography of their ancestors. And, as long as there are indigenous people—even if there are no tourists seeking souvenirs—there will be potters in Latin America.

I grew up fascinated by Pancho Villa, but always considered him a "Mexican bandit." Indigenous Latin Americans view him as a hero who stood up against white dominance. As long as indigenous Latin Americans are kept down, my hunch is that the headlines will be filled with the Pancho Villas of the 21st century as they stand up for their rights in an aggressive and often uncompromising modern world.

As I watched Valentín and his son turn, polish, and bake their pottery with a stronger spiritual connection to their ancestors than the connection I have with my ancestors, I gained a new respect for the strength of indigenous culture in our hemisphere.

El Salvador's Civil War and Bonsai Democracy

There's a popular saying in the poor world: Feed the hungry and you're a saint. Ask why they are hungry and you're a communist. In the 1970s, some Central American priests started asking why. These Liberation Theologians threatened the powerful...and were killed.

Resurrection in El Salvador

When Oscar Romero was made archbishop in 1977, wealthy Salvadorans breathed a sigh of relief. If his reputation as a fairly conservative priest was any indication of how he would run the Church here, they believed the right wing (and the corporations who funded them) had nothing to fear. But the growing violence against the poor and the assassinations of church leaders who grappled with economic injustice drove Romero to speak out. Even-

El Salvador's Archbishop Oscar Romero

tually this mild-mannered priest became the charismatic spokesperson of his people.

As a Liberation Theologian, Romero invited his followers to see Christmas as the story of a poor, homeless mother with a hungry baby. Romero taught that the lessons and inspiration offered by the Bible were tools for the faithful as they dealt with the struggles of their day-to-day lives.

Because Archbishop Oscar Romero asked why, he was gunned down in 1980 in front of his congregation. Then, dozens of worshippers were murdered at his funeral.

After the killing of Romero, the poor—emboldened by their Liberation Theology—rebelled, plunging El Salvador into their long and bloody Civil War. The united guerilla front (FMLN) was on its way to a quick victory, but the US under President Reagan spent $1.5 million a day to keep that from happening. With the success of the Sandinistas in Nicaragua in July 1979, Reagan was determined to stop the spread of what he considered a communist threat.

Salvadoran forces assumed, because the guerillas were maintaining their strength, that innocent

If economic elites use religion as the "opiate of the masses," Liberation Theology is the opposite. Liberation Theology is a politicized view of Christianity popular among those trying to inspire the poor to fight for economic justice. Liberation Theologians preach that every person is created in God's image, and God intended them to have dignity. They believe that economic injustice and structural poverty are an affront to God, and it is right for the downtrodden to mobilize and fight for their God-given rights now rather than docilely wait for heavenly rewards. In short, Liberation Theologians believe that the Church should be about justice, not rituals.

What I call "Escape theology"—the apolitical yin to Liberation Theology's yang—is fundamentalism imported from the USA. This "suffer now, enjoy later" theology keeps the opiate in religion.

While it has given hope to millions of previously hopeless people, Liberation Theology also has had many critics. Mingling religious authority with social, political, and even military power, the movement could lead to armed revolution. And it had a potentially corrupting influence on local charismatic priests, who created a cult of personality to empower themselves and their followers. Still, many people see Liberation Theology as the only viable option for those dissatisfied with what they consider a social and economic order that keeps them poor.

As Liberation Theology took hold in Latin America in the 1970s, many Americans thought it smelled like communism. President Nixon established an American Cold War stance that considered this politicization of Christianity a direct challenge to American interests in Central America. From this point on, the story of El Salvador's struggle became a story of martyrs. First, politically active peasants were killed. From the 1970s on, Church leaders were targeted. "Be a patriot...kill a priest" was a bumper sticker-like slogan popular among El Salvador's US-funded national guard.

Liberation Theology surged through the warfare of the 1980s. But since the peace accords and (marginal) reforms of the 1990s, it seems to have gone dormant as a political force. Once-activist Christians are spent. They have accepted peace without as much justice as they once demanded. These days, in many El Salvador churches, it's taboo to talk politics.

Traveling—whether in Christian, Muslim, Hindu, or Buddhist lands—I've seen how religion injects passion into local politics...and I've developed a healthy respect for the importance of separation of religion and state. And yet, when a politicized Church (such as the one that stood by the revolutionaries of Central America in the 1980s) fights for economic justice, I find myself rooting for the politicization of religion. My heart makes my politics inconsistent.

civilians in leftist-controlled territory were no longer innocent. Civilian women and children were considered combatants—fair game—in order for the popular revolt to become less popular. Right-wing forces targeted and terrorized civilians with a brutal vengeance. Implementing a policy nicknamed "draining the fishbowl to kill the fish," notorious "death squads" wrought havoc on El Salvador's poor.

For example, the University of Central America's six leading Jesuit professors were the intellectual leaders of Liberation Theology—and, therefore, they were considered leaders of the revolution. Early one morning in 1989, government death squads came into the Jesuits' humble quarters and dragged them into the garden. One by one, they were shot in the brains with exploding bullets (because they were considered the "brains of the people's movement"). Before the death squad left, they took time to shoot a bullet through the heart of a photo of Romero hanging on the wall…still trying to kill him nine years after his death.

My visit to the university grounds where those six Jesuit priests were shot was poignant. Reading about events in faraway lands in the newspaper, you learn what happened. Then you can flip to the sports pages or comics. But hearing the story of an event from people who lived through it, you *feel* what happened. Right there behind the bedrooms of those professors, the smell of the flowers, the hard labor of the hunched-over gardener, the quiet focus of students whose parents lost a revolution, the knowledge that my country provided those exploding bullets…all combined to make this experience both vivid and enduring.

When asked "Who really runs El Salvador?," most Salvadorans would say simply, "The Embassy" (as the American Embassy is called here). You can't miss it: It's just above San Salvador, built upon the ruins of the old pre-Columbian Indian capital.

While the FMLN (the party of the leftist guerillas) could have fought on, the toll on their country was too great. Eight years of negotiations finally led to a 1992 peace accord. Suddenly, the guerillas shaved, washed, and found themselves members of parliament representing a now-peaceful FMLN party. For many years, the FMLN played a role in government, but was effectively marginalized. They were welcome… as long as they didn't get too powerful.

Salvadorans fill the streets in honor of their beloved archbishop, Romero.

Democracy in these countries reminds me of a bonsai tree: You keep it in the window for others to see, and when it grows too big, you cut it back. And who does the cutting? It has traditionally been the USA—first through active military involvement, and later through strong-arm political pressure, including (in 2004) outright threats to deport El Salvador guest workers if ARENA didn't win.

You can argue whether American meddling in Latin American politics is justified. It makes me uncomfortable to think that our nation, founded on the principles of liberty and freedom, wields such a strong influence over fledgling democracies. Father Jon Sobrino is a leading Jesuit priest and scholar at the University of Central America, who happened to be out of the country the night his six fellow professors were murdered. When I asked him about America's influence on Salvadoran politics, he said, "These days, when I hear the word 'democracy,' my bowels move."

Romero, Martyrdom, and Resurrection

The primary reason for my 2005 visit to El Salvador was to remember Oscar Romero on the 25th anniversary of his assassination. Marching with thousands of his followers through the streets of San Salvador, it was clear to me: Just as Romero prophesized, they killed him, yet he lives through his people.

I'll never forget the parade that day. Everyone in our group crayoned *Romero Vive* ("Romero lives") on our white T-shirts. We piled into a repainted but obviously recycled circa 1960s American school bus (the standard public transport in Central America today), drove as close as we could, and then spilled into the streets. Joining masses of Salvadorans, we funneled through their capital city and to the cathedral, which held the body of their national hero. Entrepreneurs sold bananas from woven bins and drinks in clear plastic bags pierced by paper straws. Parents packed along children born long after Romero's day. Prune-faced old ladies who couldn't handle the long march filled the backs of beat-up pickup

Americans march with Salvadorans 25 years after the assassination of Romero.

trucks, adding slow-rolling "granny floats" to the parade of people. Banks, Western Union offices, strip malls, and fast-food joints seemed to stand still and solemnly observe as the marchers shut down the city. Soldiers looking on appeared humbled by the crowd.

Just being there put me in solidarity with a powerful and surging people's spirit. Being a head taller than anyone else and clearly a *norteamericano*, I had lots of friends. Judging from the smiles I encountered, my presence was appreciated.

Archbishop Oscar Romero said, "If I am killed, I will be resurrected in my community." Today, he lives in his people, depicted here symbolically wearing his bullet holes.

The parade culminated at the cathedral where, in his last sermon there, Romero had directed his words to the soldiers: "You are brothers of the poor. These are your people. More important than any order from your commanders is God's order: Thou shalt not kill. I beg you. I implore you. In the name of God, I command you. Stop the killing." The next week, while leading a Mass, Romero was shot dead.

Just as he predicted, Romero rose again in his people. That symbolic resurrection is depicted in colorful murals showing the people of El Salvador rising like tall stocks of corn with big smiles and bullet wounds in their hands. In Latin America, crosses are decorated with peasants and symbols of their lives—healthy stocks of corn. While this is a land of martyrs, it's also a fertile land of resurrection.

Roman Catholic priests and nuns are routinely excommunicated in Central America for their political activism. While technically booted from their Church, they continue their work without missing a beat, believing, as one priest told me, "Part of our vow of obedience to the Church is disobedience to the Church."

Over the last several years, the local Catholic hierarchy has gradually sanitized Oscar Romero's image to be less offensive to the rich, and the slow bureaucracy of the Vatican finally made him a saint in 2018. But Salvadorans weren't waiting around. For years, priests, nuns, and people throughout the region had already been calling him "San Romero."

Lie Flat and Strum Your Guitar

Gathering at a hotel on the last night of our educational tour of El Salvador, we enjoyed a trio of guitarists. They were "100 percent *popular*" (the safe term used for anything perfectly in tune with the peoples' struggle). Enjoying their performance, I thought of the guerillas who once lay flat on the floors of their shacks under flying bullets. Strumming guitars quietly on their bellies, they sang forbidden songs. Music is the horse that carries the message of poems—the weapons of a people's irrepressible spirit.

Listening to their music—love songs to their country—I stared at the musicians and considered the ongoing struggle. Watching those slender Latino fingers crawl between the frets like guerillas quietly loping through the jungle, I thought of the courageous advocates of the people throughout the developing world, not running from the forces of globalization but engaging them.

They sang, "Our way of life is being erased…no more *huevos picados*, we now have omelets…no more *colones*, we now have dollars." They wondered musically,

"How can a combo meal at a fast-food chain cost $8, while $20 gathered at church feeds 200 hungry mouths? Why did God put me here?"

Wrapping up my El Salvador visit with this inspirational concert, I considered how the superstars of nonviolence (Gandhi, Martin Luther King Jr., John Lennon, Oscar Romero) all seem to get shot. Are the pacifists losers? As a competitive person, I don't like this idea.

My 1988 visit to Central America was filled with hope. I came again after the defeat of people's movements in both El Salvador and Nicaragua in 1991. The tide had turned, and I wondered how the spirit of the people's movements—so exuberant just three years before—would fare after the American-funded victories of their opponents. Then, in 2005, after 14 years of globalization, it was clear: That was only one game in town.

Refocusing on the troubadours, I heard them sing, "It's not easy to see God in the child who cleans the windshields at a San Salvador intersection... but we must."

Epilogue: Back to the Barrio

In 2010, after the publication of this book's first edition, I returned to El Salvador. While my first visit, in 1988, was to witness and understand an actual war, today that struggle has become a political one. The problems caused by the gap between rich and poor, which fueled the revolutions and civil wars of the recent past, now fill the docket in parliament. And today, both headlines and peoples' minds are filled with the struggles caused by that persistent gap—petty crime, the drug war, and gang violence.

Driving from the airport into the harsh urban scene of San Salvador, I saw a big banner proclaiming, "Nothing will intimidate El Salvador: Government and society united against crime and violence." Since my last visit, the already rising tide of gangs in El Salvador had gotten even worse. (Many believe this is driven by Salvadorans who go to find work in the US, and bring back their shiny new gang memberships. In a sense, El Salvador exports labor and imports gangs.) I was told it was unwise to walk around after dark, for fear of being robbed at knifepoint by a group of young thugs. It was clear that the fear and violence that wracks a society because of a huge gap between rich and poor is bad for the economy. It's terrible for tourism, and, more importantly, good people who would otherwise dedicate themselves to building their nation become hopeless, and, instead dream of escaping to the USA.

Excited to reconnect with someone who'd meant a great deal to my understanding of El Salvador—and global poverty concerns in general—I headed to the barrio to see Beatriz. Right down to the hardscrabble chicken roaming the yard, her home seemed unchanged after five years. It was fun to give her a copy of this book and watch her daughters read the passage about their illiterate mom to her.

We sat down to a lunch of brawny chicken, chicken soup, delicious fresh-ground corn tortillas, and a tall plastic bottle of Coke to share. Their Christmas tree looked a little funny; they explained that it was the bottom half of a fake tree that they shared with an uncle—they just bent up one of the big branches to give it a "top."

Like many families, Beatriz's husband had emigrated to the USA with the promise of sending home money. Eventually the money stopped flowing, and he established his own life in the States. He's now married again, with a second crop of children.

Beatriz's daughters are now well into their twenties and, I imagine, would like to live on their own. But that's not possible. They each work 48-hour weeks and make about $300 per month (about $1.50 per hour). It's typical for

young women to work in textile plants sewing garments for international corporations. As part of a globalized labor force, they are competing with the most desperate labor on the planet. These *maquiladora* plants, while pretty miserable by US standards, are considered a blessing here, as they bring relatively solid jobs to a land otherwise without much industry.

The driving daily concern for Beatriz and her daughters is no longer the old war against a military dictatorship, but the new war against crime and the rising cost of living. The daughters told of the daily fear they experience riding the bus to work. Routinely thieves stop

Top: When a society fails to mind the gap, you have armed guards welcoming you at shops, hotels, and finer residential neighborhoods. Bottom: San Salvador's informal economy bullies pedestrians off the sidewalks and into the streets.

the bus and enter from each end, extorting all of their valuables. They don't leave home with anything of value without considering, "Do I want to risk losing this?"

We discussed one of the biggest changes since my last visit: The scrappy, can't-get-no-respect FMLN party had finally taken power in 2009. Only by offering up a less political candidate for president—Mauricio Funes, who was better known as a journalist than as a politician—could the former guerillas win a slim majority. Their priorities were to improve education and health care; to address gang violence; and to reform the tax codes that aggressively favored the rich.

But the FMLN's win set up a startling reality check. It's easy to be the guerilla opposition and just complain. But once in power, it's a delicate balancing act: staying true to your populist past, accepting the reality that capitalism drives our globalized world, and being constantly tempted by the inherently corrupting trappings of power. Showing a grasp of local politics that seemed surprising to me for such a poor and illiterate woman, Beatriz

explained how every guerilla has his price. In the view of many poor Salvadorans, the FMLN's ideals have been compromised, and the new leaders are
only marginally better than the old. Beatriz explained that the social and
economic justice voice of the Church is now gone—a symptom of a society
tired of political struggle. People complain that there's no way to organize.

My hunch is that the wealthy elite in the fancy suburbs are hardly
mindful of the downtown realities because they can function fine without
ever crossing paths with this humble side of their society. The fortified
housing compounds of the wealthy—with their stout walls, razor wire,
and armed guards—had been beefed up even more since my previous
visit. Wealthy locals (and tourists) happily pay triple for a reputable taxi
to hop from one "safe zone" to another.

To get a better look at El Salvador's upper crust, I went to La Gran
Vía, one of several top-end malls serving San Salvador's wealthy. These are
more than just malls;
they function as a city
center for people who
live in gated communi-
ties. The mall had the
fantasy aura of Disney
World, with a happy
pedestrian boulevard
flanked by two floors
of restaurants, shops,
children's playgrounds,
and a multistory
garage filled with very

La Gran Vía Mall: Imagine a slice of San Salvador where everyone's rich.

nice cars. Little sightseeing trains took visitors on the rounds. The Starbucks
had a vast terrace—clearly a place to see and be seen.

I ended up sharing a drink with a Salvadoran couple. It became clear
that in my two days of sightseeing, I had experienced more of San Salvador's
pithy core than these residents had in years. They peppered me with questions
about their own city. As they considered it too dangerous to go downtown,
it mystified them that an outsider had ventured there.

I capped my Gran Vía night at the cinema, enjoying an American
comedy alongside Salvadorans for whom razor wire is a status symbol.
Sitting in that air-conditioned comfort, munching on popcorn, I thought

back to Beatriz's dirt floors and handmade tortillas. Actually experiencing contrast makes abstract lessons picked up in our travels not only concrete and human, but more lasting.

El Salvador, along with the rest of Central America, is evolving. Their fragile democracies are maturing. The revolutionary force in El Salvador (like the one in neighboring Nicaragua) has morphed into a pragmatic and moderately corrupt political party that actually won an election. Hollow as that victory may seem, the brutality of earlier strongman governments is a thing of the past. It seems to me that the country, exhausted by extremism, is determined to be peaceful.

The more I travel, the more it seems to me that different societies (whether El Salvador, Iran, Egypt, China, or the USA) are on parallel evolutionary tracks. Absent impatient external forces, if left to their own devices, societies develop in a way that is good for their people. As we capitalists believe in the invisible hand of the marketplace, I see this as the invisible hand of the political arena.

In talking with so many local experts over the years, it has occurred to me that US liberals coming to Latin America in search of understanding (like me) want the story to have black-and-white clarity. But the sobering reality is much more complex. Seeing how things have changed—and yet stayed the same—over more than two decades of visits, I realize that some of the easy answers I've espoused in the past now seem naive and unhelpful. I returned home from my latest trip without the clean epilogue I sought. But at least my visit gave me a sense of optimism: A pluralistic society is trying to work things out without war. El Salvador is moving fitfully but steadily forward. As Martin Luther King, Jr., often remarked, "The arc of the moral universe is long, but it bends towards justice." You can't help but fly home from Central America rooting for its beautiful people…and wanting to do more.

Chapter 5
Denmark: Highly Taxed and Highly Content

Traveling through Denmark, I enjoy a constant barrage of experiences that give me food for political thought. Scandinavia (including Denmark) is Western Europe's most sparsely populated, most literate, most prosperous, most socialistic, and least churchgoing corner. This most highly taxed corner of Europe likes its system. An exceptionally affluent society, it chooses to sip rather than to gulp. It's a traditionally blond corner of Europe that struggles with immigration issues. And Copenhagen's famous hippie commune, now approaching a half-century old, is standing strong against a rising tide of free market trends.

There's plenty in Denmark that Americans who travel as students of the world can ponder in order to spice up their take on well-worn social and economic issues back home. This chapter delves into a few of the joys and challenges of Danish life. It also serves as a practical example of how one European country embraces that continent's more socialistic system and faces the immigration challenges that I discussed in Chapter 3. This snapshot of Danish life is a reminder that you can glean powerful lessons even when you travel to more comfortable countries that don't seem so different from back home.

Everything's So...Danish

Wherever you travel, you encounter societies that are driven by a desire for their people to live well. Denmark seems particularly adept at this feat. In survey after survey, when asked whether they're content with their lives, the Danes are found to be among the happiest people on earth. With each visit to Denmark, it's become my mission to figure out: What makes those Danes so darned happy?

Expensive, highly taxed, and highly efficient Denmark confuses me. The affluence of Denmark's Scandinavian cousins in Norway can be explained by their North Sea oil bonanza. But the Danes' leading natural resources are wind power, pigs, and pickled herring. Considering the very high cost of living here, the Danish lifestyle seems richer than their modest after-tax incomes would suggest. In fact, the Danes live extremely well. Traveling through what seems to be a fantasyland, you keep wondering, "How do they do it?"

First off, there's the obvious: Denmark is, simply, pleasant. I'm impressed by how serene things are, even in the bustling capital of Copenhagen. Their subway is silent, automated, on the honor system (with random ticket checks rather than turnstiles), and frequent—trains go literally every two minutes. The streets are so quiet (thanks to downtown pedestrian-only zones) that I don't yell to my friends from a distance…I walk over to speak to them in a soft "indoor voice." On my last visit, I saw an angry young man at the Copenhagen train station barking into his mobile phone—and it occurred to me that in a

week in the country, that was the only shouting I'd heard.

When you get beyond Copenhagen and travel into the Danish countryside, you find yourself saying "cute" a lot. Thatched-roof farms dot a green landscape of rolling hills and fields. Tidy sailboats bob in tiny harbors. Parents push kids in prams along pedestrian-only streets. Copper spires create fairy-tale skylines. The place feels like a pitch 'n' putt course sparsely inhabited by blond Vulcans. Travelers here find the human scale and orderliness of Danish society itself the focus of their sightseeing. Everything is just so…Danish.

The local Disneyland—Legoland—is a wildly popular place featuring 35 million Lego bricks built into famous landmarks from around the world. (They claim that if you lined them all up, they'd stretch from here to Italy.) The place is crawling with adorable little ice-cream-licking, blond children. Although stoked with piles of sugar, the scene is strikingly mellow. Kids hold their mothers' hands while learning about the Lego buildings and smile contentedly as they ride 'round and 'round on the carousel.

Riding Danish trains is also thought-provoking. Wandering into a nearly empty, sleek train car, I noticed that each seat was marked *Kan reserveres*.

I figured that meant "not reserved," and sat down. Then I was bumped by a friendly Dane with a reservation. He said, "The sign means the seat 'could be' reserved…we don't promise too much." Noticing several young men with shaved heads and the finest headphones as they made clockwork connections on their commute to work, I thought that Denmark seemed so minimalistic and efficient…and so well-ordered.

On another train ride, I was filming a segment for a public television show. I'd look into the camera and say, "A fun part of exploring Denmark is enjoying the efficiency of the great train system." As usual, I needed about six or eight takes to get it right. My Danish friend was chuckling the whole time. He finally explained that our train was running eight minutes late, and each time I said my line, all the Danes on the train around me would mutter, "No, no, no." Clearly, it's all relative. While only two trains a day serve my town back home, these trains go six times an hour. And while many Danes go through life without ever getting around to buying a car, they still grouse about things like public transit. My friend said, "We Danes are spoiled. We love to complain."

Danish "Social-ism" and the Free Rider Problem

Of course, there's much more to Danish contentedness than being quaint and orderly. It's all built upon a firm cultural foundation. Danish society seems to be a finely tuned social internal-combustion engine in a glass box: highly taxed, highly connected, and highly regulated, with all the gears properly engaged. Their system is a hybrid that, it seems, has evolved as far as socialism can go without violating the necessary fundamentals of capitalism. It's socialistic…but, with its unique emphasis on society, it's also social-istic.

What happens when a tune-up is needed? My Danish friends tell me they rely on their government. Rather than doing what's best for corporations, the Danish government clearly looks out for the people's interests. The Danes say, "If our government lets us down, we let ourselves down."

Immigrants: Treasure Your Heritage...and Melt

I've painted a rosy picture of Denmark. But the country is not without its challenges. One key issue facing Denmark, along with the rest of Europe and the US, is immigration.

When my grandparents migrated from Norway to the US, they lost contact with their Norwegian relatives, and had little choice but to melt into American society. (And, while they arrived speaking barely a word of English, just two generations later, I barely speak a word of Norwegian.) Today they could go online to read Norwegian news, watch television shows from home, and video chat with relatives around the world. Modern telecommunications advances allow communities of foreigners to settle in more comfortable places while remaining in close contact with far-flung friends and family back in the "old country." Like the Algerian family I mentioned in Chapter 3 (who've been in the Netherlands for three generations, speak barely a word of Dutch, and are still enthusiastically Algerian), these people have no interest in assimilating. Consequently, rather than "melting pots," wealthy countries such as Denmark are becoming cafeteria plates with dividers keeping ethnic groups separate.

Immigration can be a major wedge issue—especially in formerly homogenous nations. Only 40 years ago, there were virtually no foreigners in Denmark. As in many European countries, part of the population, especially older and more insular Danes, fears immigrants and gravitates to right-wing, racist parties. Meanwhile, progressive Danes—who celebrate a multicultural future—wonder why their wealthy nation of high-tech, multilingual globalists is still struggling to get along with their relatively small community of Muslim immigrants. While some Danes view their growing Muslim

This strong social ethic permeates the whole of Danish society. A traveler can find it in its raw and indigenous form in the rural corners and small towns—places where anyone is allowed to pick berries and nuts, but "no more than would fit in your hat."

On a recent visit to a Danish small town, I saw this social ethic in the way a local friend of mine reacted to a controversy. The biggest hotel in his town started renting bikes to compete with Mrs. Hansen's bike rental shop. My friend was disappointed with the hotel manager, saying, "They don't need to do that—bike rental has been Mrs. Hansen's livelihood since she was a little girl." Of course, there's no law forbidding it. And with our American business ethic, we'd just say that competition is good. But in Denmark, to look out for Mrs. Hansen's little bike rental business was a matter of neighborly decency.

Other countries have struggled to become more social-istic...and failed. So how do the Danes pull it off? I think their success relates to

A Muslim Dane catches the changing of her country's guard.

minority as a problem, others are willing to see a more colorful society as an opportunity.

At Copenhagen's City Museum, I met a Pakistani Dane who worked there as a guide. He spoke Danish like a local and talked earnestly about the exhibit, as if his own ancestors pioneered the city. Thinking of assimilation, I got emotional. Surprised at being choked up, I was struck by the beauty of a Pakistani Dane as opposed to a Pakistani living in Denmark.

Am I wrong to wish that a Muslim living in Denmark would become a Dane? Am I wrong to wish the US would speak only English, rather than Norwegian or Spanish as well? Am I wrong to lament districts of London that have a disdain for all things British? Immigrants energize a land—but they do it best (as is the story of the US) when their vision is a healthy melting pot. Melt, immigrants... treasure your heritage while embracing your adopted homelands. But it's more than just an "immigrant issue." Europeans (like Americans) fearful of encroachment, change, and differing hues of skin need to show tolerance, outreach, and understanding. From what I've seen, with these attitudes, it works better for all involved.

their acceptance of their social contract. Any society needs to subscribe to a social contract—basically, what you agree to give up in order to live together peacefully. Densely populated Europe generally embraces Rousseau's social contract: In order to get along well, everyone will contribute a little more than their share and give up a little more than their share. Then, together, we'll all be fine.

The Danes—who take this mindset to the extreme—are particularly conscientious about not exploiting loopholes. They are keenly aware of the so-called "free rider problem": If you knew you could get away with it, would you do something to get more than your fair share? The Danes recognize that if everyone did this, their system would collapse. Therefore, they don't. It seems to me that the Danes make choices considering what would happen to their society (not just to themselves) if *everyone* cheated on this, sued someone for that, freeloaded here, or ignored that rule there.

In contrast, the United States subscribes to John Locke's version of the social contract: a "don't fence me in" ideal of rugged individualism, where you can do anything you like, as long as you don't hurt your neighbor. Just keep the government off our backs. In some ways, this suits us: As we have always had more elbow room, we can get away with our independent spirit. Thanks to our wide-open spaces, determination to be self-sufficient, and relative population sparsity, it's easier—and arguably less disruptive—for us to ignore the free rider problem.

If I had to identify one major character flaw of Americans, it might be our inability to appreciate the free rider problem. Many Americans practically consider it their birthright to make money they didn't really earn, enjoy the fruits of our society while cheating on their taxes, drive a gas-guzzler just because they can afford it, take up two parking spots so no one will bump their precious car, and generally jigger the system if they can get away with it. We often seem to consider actions like these acceptable…without considering the fact that if everyone did it, our society as a whole would suffer.

The consequences of ignoring this reality were thrown into sharp relief with the crippling financial crisis that began in 2008. In the lead-up to the crisis, smart people knew deep down that existing policies would not be sustainable if everyone jumped in, trying to make money from speculation rather than substance. They gambled that they could pull it off, and the free rider problem wouldn't kick in. But then it did. As Europe, too, got caught up in this "casino capitalism," we saw how interconnected our world has become, and how—with globalization—there's now only one game in town.

A good example of how the Danish social ethic differs from others is a simple one: Danes are famous for not jaywalking. Even if the roads are empty at 3 a.m., pedestrians still stop and wait at a red light. If there's no traffic in sight, my American individualism whispers, "Why obey a silly rule?" And so I jaywalk, boldly, assuming that my fellow pedestrians will appreciate my lead and follow me. In most countries, they do. But when I jaywalk in Denmark, the locals frown at me like I'm a bad influence on the children present. That social pressure impacts even a hurried, jaywalking tourist. So, rather than feel like an evil person, I wait for the light.

I don't know how well I'd fit in if I lived in Denmark. But their personal and societal formula intrigues me. On my last visit, I asked Danish people I met about their society—and why they're so happy. Here's a sampling of what they told me:

"Regular workers pay on average a 35 percent income tax—big shots pay more than 50 percent. Of course, we expect and we get a good value for our taxes. We've had national healthcare since the 1930s. We know nothing else. If I don't like the shape of my nose, I pay to fix that. But all my basic health needs are taken care of. Here in Denmark, all education is free. And our taxes even provide university students with almost $1,000 a month in educational support for living expenses for up to six years. We Danes believe a family's economic status should have nothing to do with two fundamental rights: the quality of their healthcare or the quality of the education their children receive. I believe that Americans pay triple per person what we pay as a society for healthcare. Your system may be better for business…but ours is better for people. Perhaps a major negative consequence of our socialism is that since Danes are so accustomed to everything being taken care of by the government, we may not be very helpful or considerate towards each other when in need." (For a more in-depth conversation on these topics, see "Interview with a Copenhagener," later.)

When I saw a tombstone store with *Tak for Alt* ("Thanks for Everything") pre-carved into each headstone, I figured it was a message from the dearly departed after enjoying a very blessed life in Denmark. But I asked a Dane, and learned that it's a message from the living bidding their loved one farewell (similar to our "Rest in Peace"). Still, I think when a Dane dies, it's a good message from both sides: *Tak for Alt.*

Living Large While Living Small

An interesting side effect of the Danish system is that sky-high taxes make things so costly that people consume more sparingly. The society seems designed in a way that encourages people to use less, waste less, chew slower, appreciate more, and just sip things. A glass of beer can cost more than $10. A cup of coffee can run $7—and refills are unheard of. A big box economy à la Wal-Mart is just not very Danish. I think Danes know they could make more money if they embraced the "Big Gulp" track and started super-sizing things. But the collective decision is based on what's good for the fabric of their society rather than what's good for the economy.

One example that's obvious to any visitor is cars…or the lack thereof. Figuring in registration fees and sales tax, Denmark levies a 100 percent tax on new automobiles. So to buy one car, you have to pay for two cars. As a result, throughout Denmark, a third dimension zips along silently between pedestrians and drivers: bicycles. With so many bikes, traffic congestion and pollution are reduced, parked cars don't clog the streets, and people are in shape. (What's safe for the environment can be dangerous for absentminded pedestrians. On my last visit to Copenhagen, on two occasions I was nearly flattened as I stepped from a taxi into the bike lane.)

London and Paris have taken lanes away from drivers to create bike lanes. But so far, the lanes are underused, and the entire effort just seems to make things worse. Somehow, Copenhagen has it figured out. During Copenhagen's rush hour (rain or shine), there are more bikes on their roads than cars, and everything moves smoothly.

While walking through one of Copenhagen's main squares, I noticed it was dominated by people, cobbles, and buildings. It felt calm, spacious, and inviting. I looked again and saw that there were also about fifty parked bikes—blending into the scene almost unnoticed—and absolutely no cars. If instead of bikes, those were parked cars, the charm would be replaced by chaos and congestion.

Many hotels even provide their guests with loaner or rental bikes. I find having a bike parked in my hotel's bike rack is a great way to fit in and literally "go local." Copenhagen has as many bike lanes as car lanes, and I can get anywhere in the town center as fast on my two wheels as by taxi. When you get out of the city to explore the Danish countryside, you'll see that newly

---

You'll see more bikes than cars on Copenhagen's squares.

paved roads are lined by perfectly smooth bike lanes—one for each direction. Even out in the country, it seems that bikes outnumber cars.

Interview with a Copenhagener

For insight on the Danish way of life, I talked to Richard Karpen—a friend and tour guide who leads tours around the city, educating visitors both about Denmark's history and its current social reality. Richard, a long-time resident of Copenhagen, calls himself a social historian. He agreed to chat with me about the issues in this chapter. Here are a few highlights of our conversation.

Denmark is famous for being happy. Why, exactly, are the Danes so darned happy?

Richard responds: Danish values are human values. Three important elements are trust, the freedom to be yourself, and finding purpose in life.

I think in America, trust is a big issue these days. Well, Danes are a trusting and trustworthy people. In Denmark, "social trust"—a general feeling that you trust your fellow citizens and the pillar institutions of government, law courts, police, hospitals, and so on—is generally found to be the highest in the world. A perfect example of Danish "social trust" is the image of babies sleeping in carriages outside a restaurant while the parents eat inside. You might say, "But no one is watching!" A Dane will say, "Everyone is watching."

If anyone accidentally leaves a wallet, purse, or backpack in a café, and a Dane finds it, it will be returned with the money, credit cards, and passport intact. You can throw a found wallet in any postbox, and the post office will return it. If someone tips over in the bicycle lane, Danes will stop to help the person, call an ambulance, and wait until the ambulance arrives.

Most Danes feel they are able to find purpose in life. In fact, Danes share a collective purpose: forming a cohesive and effective society. Danes pay some of the highest taxes in the world, and seven out of ten in a recent survey said they would be willing to pay more in order to keep the system functioning to protect the most vulnerable in their society. They feel individually responsible and committed to social welfare. They are connected to something bigger than any individual. This gives them a sense of purpose and helps them feel contented in life. They are not victims of the system—they are part of it.

In Denmark, people have the freedom to be themselves. Danes feel that the main purpose of education is to develop the personality of the child. Danes

teach their children that no
matter what they're good at,
they're making a contribution to society. You're not a
lesser human being because
you struggle with math or
science; you can be the best
in your class in creativity or
cooking. This gives Danish
children an extraordinary
base in choosing a life that
corresponds to who they are.

Richard Karpen explains the Danish way of life.

According to the Social Progress Index, Denmark ranks as number
one out of 128 countries because it's considered best at addressing the basic
human needs of life, equipping citizens to improve the quality of their lives,
protecting the environment, and providing opportunities for everyone to
make personal choices and reach their full potential.

Denmark also happens to be a wealthy nation, but wealth is a poor
estimator of happiness. The GDP per capita in the US is $10,000 higher
than in Denmark—but the US is ranked a distant 13th in the global study
of happiness and well-being.

*Denmark is one of the Scandanavian nations (along with Norway and
Sweden). Tell me about the "Scandanavian Model" and why it works.*
Richard responds: The Scandanavian countries score high on any list of economic and life quality indicators. The success of the so-called "Scandanavian
Model" is commonly attributed to several factors: income equality, a high
level of trust, a high willingness to pay tax (which is tightly coupled with
strong social security), a blend of governmental regulations and capitalism,
and cultural homogeneity.

An American might scoff at what they see as an overly regulated, overly
taxed, and overly restrictive society. A Dane might point out that the USA is
called the "land of the free" and the "land of opportunity"—but is "freedom"
staying at a job you hate because you don't want to lose your health insurance?
Is "independence" putting your career on hold, and relying on your spouse's
income, so you can take care of a young child when your employer doesn't offer
paid parental leave or day care is too expensive? Does "opportunity" mean

depending on the resources of your parents, or a bundle of loans, to get a university degree? Is realizing the American Dream supposed to be so stressful?

You could make a case that the notion of the US as a land of freedom and opportunity is trailing behind reality. The choices Scandanavian countries have made in arranging society over the last 30 years have ended up bringing people a lot more freedom—and a lot more equality of opportunity. For example, in America, gender roles are more traditional than in Scandanavian countries. This is partly because of the way a society supports—or doesn't support—families. American women often become much more dependent on their husbands once they have children, because they're more likely to put aside their career to care for the kids. In Scandanavia, in many cases, society provides support for women and men to work and take care of their families, and for children to be able to rise above their parents' educational levels or income levels. This is, ironically, traditionally what the American Dream has been about.

There's an interesting "happiness gap" in families: In America, people who don't have children tend to be happier than people who do. But in Nordic countries, people who have children are happier than those who don't. Why is this? It boils down to affordable day care, paid sick days, paid vacation days, and not having to constantly worry about paying for health care and college. That's the Danish version of "family values."

What do you think is the most misunderstood part of the Scandanavian Model among Americans?
Richard responds: Many Americans think the Scandanavians are socialists. They are actually quite capitalistic, but they prioritize in social areas. One of the wonderful things about Americans is they have this huge faith in everyone's ability. It's like, "Let's go to the moon." And they do! But to me, the curious thing is how Americans lose that faith immediately when they discuss something like affordable day care. It's like, "Oh, no, if we give this to people, they will never work again!"

Many Americans might say, "This all sounds great, but you guys are paying sky-high taxes. We don't want anything to do with that." What would you say to that?
Richard responds: First of all, the taxes are not necessarily as high as many Americans think. For someone who lives in the US—where you have federal taxes, state taxes, city taxes, and property taxes—the tax burden is not

very different than the tax burden in Denmark.

And secondly, to smartly compare relative taxation, you need to consider what you get for your taxes. Americans might pay lower taxes initially. But then, on top of that, they pay for day care, they pay for health insurance, they pay for college tuition—all these things that Danes get for their taxes.

Finally, on a lighter note, the Danish idea of "hygge" has become trendy stateside. What is hygge?

Beach huts are *hygge*.

Richard responds: *Hygge* is an approach to living that encompasses warmth, togetherness, safety, intimacy, peacefulness, simplicity, enjoyment, and contentment. It's about an atmosphere and an experience, rather than about things. It's about being with the people we love—the feeling that we are safe, shielded from the world, and can let our guard down. *Hygge* is sitting around a friendly dinner table by the glow of candlelight, a good book, and a cup of tea. It's preparing for a family Christmas. It's baking bread in a warm kitchen. It's a winter walk on the beach. It's cocoa by candlelight. The key is to embrace these experiences fully, live them in the moment, and appreciate that they bring spiritual rewards along with the more tangible benefits of, say, having read a good book. *Hygge* draws meaning from ordinary living. It's a way of acknowledging the sacred in the secular—of giving something ordinary a special context, spirit, and warmth, and taking time to make it extraordinary. For me, *hygge* is a big part of being Danish.

Christiania: Copenhagen's Embattled Commune

I was strolling through the commotion of downtown Copenhagen, past chain restaurants dressed up to look old and under towering hotels that seem to sport the name of a different international chain each year. Then, as if from another age, a man pedaled by me with his wife sitting in the utilitarian bucket-like wagon of his three-wheeled "Christiania Bike." You'd call the couple "granola" in the US.

Looking as out of place here in Copenhagen as an Amish couple wandering the canyons of Manhattan, they were residents of Christiania.

While Denmark sounds wildly innovative in the way it takes socialism to its logical extreme, that system only works as long as the complete society is on board: Everyone obeys the laws so that all can be safe, affluent, and comfortable. And yet, Denmark also hosts Europe's most inspirational and thriving nonconformist hippie commune. Perhaps being content and conformist is easier for a society when its nonconformist segment, rebelling against all that buttoned-down conformity, has a refuge.

In 1971, the original 700 Christianians established squatters' rights in an abandoned military barracks just a 10-minute walk from the Danish parliament building. Two generations later, this "free city" still stands—an ultra-human communal mishmash of idealists, hippies, potheads, non-materialists, and happy children. The population today: 600 adults, 200 kids, 200 cats, 200 dogs, 17 horses, and a couple of parrots. Seeing seniors with gray ponytails woodworking, tending their gardens, and serving as guardians of the community's ideals, I'm reminded that 180 of the original gang that took over the barracks four decades ago still call Christiania home. The Christianians are fighting a rising tide of materialism and conformity. They are determined to raise their children to be free spirits.

Everyone knows utopias are utopian—they can't work. But Christiania, which has evolved with the challenges of making a utopia a viable reality, acts like it never got the message. It's broken into 14 administrative neighborhoods on land still owned by Denmark's Ministry of Defense. Locals build their homes but don't own the land; there's no buying or selling of property. When someone moves out, the community decides who will be invited in to replace that person. A third of the adult population works on the outside, a third works on the inside, and a third doesn't work much at all.

For the first few years, hard drugs and junkies were tolerated. But that led to violence and polluted the mellow ambience residents envisioned. In 1979, the junkies were expelled—an epic confrontation now embedded in the community's folk history. Since then, the symbol of a fist breaking a syringe is as prevalent as the leafy marijuana icon. Hard drugs are emphatically forbidden in Christiania.

Christiania says yes to marijuana and no to hard drugs.

But not pot. Marijuana has always been the national plant of the free city. "Pusher Street" (named for the sale of soft drugs here) is Christiania's main drag. It was once lined with stalls selling marijuana, joints, and hash. But in the 2000s, Pusher Street came under fire. To pre-empt city forces from shutting down the entire community for its open sale of pot, residents bulldozed the marijuana stalls lining Pusher Street in 2004. Since then, in spite of regular police raids, marijuana remains prevalent. But the retailing, while still fragrant, is no longer flagrant. On my last visit, I found a small stretch of Pusher Street—dubbed the "Green Light District"—where pot was openly, if cautiously, being sold. Signs acknowledged that this activity was still illegal, and announced three rules: 1. Have fun; 2. No photos; and 3. No running—"because it makes people nervous."

The crackdown provided a classic case study in the regrettable consequences of a war on marijuana: For the first time in years, the Copenhagen street price for pot went up, gangs started moving into the marijuana business, and street crime became associated with pot. There was actually a murder in 2005, as pushers fought to establish their turf—almost unthinkable in mellower times. (For more on marijuana laws, see Chapter 7.)

Get beyond the touristy main drag of Christiania, and you'll find a fascinating, ramshackle world of peaceniks shuffled with some irony among the moats, earthen ramparts, and barracks of the former military base. Alternative housing, carpenter shops, hippie villas, cozy teahouses, children's playgrounds, peaceful lanes, and interfaith stupa-like temples serve people who believe that "to be normal is to be in a straightjacket."

There are a handful of basic rules, along with the prohibition against hard drugs: no cars, no guns, no explosives, and so on. A few "luxury hippies" have oil heat, but most use wood or gas. The community has one mailing address. A phone chain provides a system of communal security because Christianians have had bad experiences calling the police. As a reminder of the constant police presence lately, my favorite Christiania café, Månefiskeren ("Moon Fisher"), has a sign outside saying, "The world's safest café—police raids nearly every day."

Meanwhile, an amazing thing has happened: Christiania—famous for its counter-culture scene, geodesic domes on its back streets, and vegetarian cafés—has become one of the most-visited sights among tourists in Copenhagen. Move over, *Little Mermaid*.

I recently got an email from some traveling readers. They said, "We're not prudes, but Christiania was creepy. Don't take kids here or go after dark."

I agree. It's not a pretty place. But hanging out with parents raising their children with Christiania values, and sharing a meal featuring home-grown vegetables with a couple born and raised in this community, I find a distinct human beauty in the place. And I have come to believe more strongly than ever that it's important to allow this social experiment and give alternative-type people a place to live out their values.

As I biked through Christiania, it also occurred to me that, except for the bottled beer being sold, there was not a hint of any corporate entity in the entire "free city." There was no advertising and no big business. Everything was handmade. Nothing was packaged. People consumed as if how they spent their money shaped the environment in which they lived and raised their families. It's not such a far cry from their fellow Danes, who also see themselves as conscientious participants in and shapers of their society.

But ever since its inception, Christiania has been a political hot potato. No one in the Danish establishment wanted it. And no one has had the nerve to mash it. While once very popular with the general Copenhagen community, Christianians have lost some goodwill recently as they are seen more as a clique, no longer accepting others to join and looking out only for themselves. Mindful of their need for popular support from their Copenhagen neighbors, Christianians are working to connect better with the rest of society. Its residents now pool their money, creating a fund to pay for utilities and city taxes (about $1 million a year) and an annual budget of about $1 million to run their local affairs.

Recently, Denmark's government has tried to "normalize" Christiania—pressured by developers salivating at the potential profits of developing this once nearly worthless land. There's talk about opening the commune to market forces and developing posh apartments to replace existing residences, according to one government plan. Increasingly, this community of peaceniks is in danger of being evicted. But Christiania has a legal team, and litigation will likely drag on for many years.

With little money, advertising, or styles to keep up with, Christianians do a lot of swapping.

Many predict that Christiania will withstand the government's challenge, as it has in years past. The community, which also calls itself Freetown, fended off a similar attempt in 1976 with the help of fervent supporters from around Europe. *Bevar Christiania*—"Save Christiania"—banners fly everywhere, and locals are confident that their free way of life will survive. As history has shown, the challenge may just make this hippie haven a bit stronger.

As I left Christiania and headed back into clean, orderly, and conformist Denmark, I looked up at the back of the "Welcome to Christiania" sign. It read, "You are entering the EU."

Later that day, on the bustling streets of downtown Copenhagen, I paused to watch a parade of ragtag soldiers-against-conformity dressed in black and waving "Save Christiania" banners. They walked sadly behind a WWII-vintage truck blasting Pink Floyd's "Another Brick in the Wall." (I had never really listened to the words before. But the anthem of self-imposed isolation and revolt against conformity seemed to perfectly fit the determination of the Christianians to stand up against corporatism, against thought control and against stifled individuality.) On their banner, a slogan—painted onto an old bedsheet—read: *Lev livet kunstnerisk! Kun døde fisk flyder med strømmen* ("Live life artistically! Only dead fish follow the current"). Those marching flew the Christiania flag: three yellow dots on an orange background. They say the dots are from the o's in "Love Love Love." (For a fascinating documentary on Europe's longest surviving squat, see www.busno8.com.)

While I wouldn't choose to live in Christiania, I would feel a loss if it were shut down. There's something unfortunately brutal about a world that makes the little Christianias—independent bookstores, family farms, nomadic communities, and so on—fight aggressive giants (such as developers, big chains, agribusiness, and centralized governments) to the death. Those economic and governmental behemoths always seem to win. And when corporatism wins, we may become safer and wealthier and even more comfortable...but it all comes at a cost.

The need for a Christiania is not limited to the Danes. After that trip, from the comfort of my suburban Seattle living room, I stumbled upon live TV coverage of the finale of the Burning Man Festival (the annual massing of America's artistic free spirits each Labor Day in the Nevada desert). Watching it, I heard the cry of an American fringe community that—much like the tribe at Christiania—wants to be free in an increasingly interconnected world that demands conformity.

Traveling in Denmark, considering well-ordered Danish social-ism and reflecting on the free-spirited ideals and struggles of Christiania, gives me insight into parts of my own society that refuse to be just another brick in the wall. Hopefully when the pressures of conformity require selling a bit of our soul, travel experiences like these help us understand the potential loss before it's regrettably gone.

Denmark is a riddle that I love puzzling over. On the one hand, their dedication to their social contract is the bedrock of their insistent happiness. On the other, in their longstanding acceptance of Christiania, the Danes seem to be unusually tolerant of free spirits. I imagine that the dramatic tension between these extremes is part of what keeps Danish life interesting...both for the Danes and for us visitors. As all societies vie to win the "most content" surveys, traveling reminds us that contentment is based not on surrendering to conformity, but in finding that balance between working well together and letting creative spirits run free.

Chapter 6
Turkey and Morocco:
Sampling Secular Islam

My Dad used to be absolutely distraught by the notion that God and Allah could be the same. Years ago, I couldn't resist teaching my toddler Andy to hold out his arms, bob them up and down, and say, "Allah, Allah, Allah" after table grace just to freak out his Grandpa. Later, rather than just torture my Dad, I took a more loving (and certainly more effective) approach to opening him up to the Muslim world: I took him to Turkey. Now—while he's still afraid of ISIS—my Dad is no longer afraid of Islam.

While violent Islamic fundamentalists represent a tiny fraction of all Muslims, the threats they pose are real—and they get plenty of media coverage. To help balance my understanding of Islam, I make a point to travel and learn about its reasonable, mainstream side—where embracing secularism is not seen as being anti-Muslim, but simply the mark of a modern democracy. Two of my favorite destinations for doing that have been Turkey and Morocco.

Visiting moderate developing nations that happen to be primarily Muslim provides a safe and fascinating look at our globe's fastest-growing religion, practiced by more than 1.5 billion people worldwide. Through travel, we can observe Islamic societies struggling (like our own society) with how to navigate a rough-and-tumble globalized world. In doing so, we gain empathy.

I have long considered Turkey—one of my favorite countries—an ideal classroom for better understanding our world and its struggles. My company has offered tours of Turkey, through good times and bad, since before the first Gulf War (in 1990). We've followed Turkey's torrid modernization, its battles with separatist Kurds, and its internal tug-of-war between modern urban secularists and fundamentalists. And, for many years, I've worried with my Turkish friends about the persistent rise of Islamic fundamentalism in a country that has always taken such pride in the modern secularism of its beloved founder, Kemal Atatürk.

Today, Turkey—like Europe and the US—faces a rising tide of populism, nativism, and nationalism. But in Turkey, this trend is especially extreme—and especially troubling. Turkey's president since 2014, Recep Tayyip Erdoğan, has embraced "law and order" fear-mongering as an excuse to cut down on personal freedom and bulk up the military. He's incrementally dismantling the safeguards that have kept Turkey secular and moderate for nearly a century. Today's Turkey is at a crossroads—deciding what kind of country it wants to be, going forward.

For many years, the predictable question I'd get from loved ones was, "Why are you going to Turkey?" With each visit to Istanbul—one of my favorite cities in the world—all I could think was, "Why would anyone *not* travel here?" Now, with the darkness of Erdoğan settling over 80 million Turks, Western tourism is essentially dead in a country where it once thrived. Hotels are shut down, squares that thrived with guests from around the world are quiet, and there's barely a foreigner in sight. From a safety point of view, I'd pack my bags for a trip to Istanbul tomorrow, confident that I'd receive a warm welcome. But I'd be sad, as the free spirit I expect to find in Turkey would be in hiding behind building-sized Erdoğan banners.

This chapter is—I'll admit—largely nostalgic, reflecting on a happier and simpler time in pre-Erdoğan Turkey. But the lessons are as true as ever—and hopefully, when the spirit of Atatürk retakes its place as the guiding light of the Turkish people, we'll be traveling there again soon. I'll also take you on a brief visit to Morocco, another gateway to the Muslim world. In general, I hope this chapter inspires you to travel boldly into the Muslim world... because the experiences you enjoy there come with lessons you'll draw upon for the rest of your life.

Istanbul Déjà Vu

When I was in my twenties, I finished eight European trips in a row in Turkey. I didn't plan it that way—it was the natural finale, the subconscious cherry on top of every year's travel adventures. In recent trips to the city where East meets West, I've been struck both by the similarities and by the jarring differences between the city I knew back in the 1980s and the one I've enjoyed in recent years. My memories of those trips are filled with both nostalgia and vivid examples of how gradual and positive change was sweeping our planet.

It was 2015, and I was excited to reacquaint myself with Turkey. The moment I stepped off my plane, I remembered how much I've always enjoyed

Istanbul, a sprawling metropolis with one foot in Asia and the other in Europe, is a fascinating cauldron of activity—offering a rich travel experience to visitors.

this country. Marveling at the efficiency of Istanbul's Atatürk Airport, I popped onto the street and into a yellow *taksi*. Seeing the welcoming grin of the unshaven driver who greeted me with a *"Merhaba,"* I just blurted out, *"Çok güzel."* I forgot I remembered the phrase. It just came to me—like a baby shouts for joy. I was back in Turkey, and it was "very beautiful" indeed. My first hours in Turkey were filled with similar déjà vu moments like no travel homecoming I could remember.

As the *taksi* turned off the highway and into the tangled lanes of the tourist zone—just below the Blue Mosque—all the tourist-friendly businesses were still lined up, providing a backdrop for their chorus line of barkers shouting, "Yes, Mister!"

I looked at the kids in the streets and remembered a rougher time, when kids like these would earn small change by hanging out the passenger door of ramshackle vans. They'd yell "Topkapı, Topkapı, Topkapı" (or whichever neighborhood was the destination) in a scramble to pick up passengers in the shared minibuses called *dolmuş*. (The *dolmuş*—a wild cross between a taxi and a bus—is literally and so appropriately called "stuffed.")

While Turkey's new affluence has nearly killed the *dolmuş*, the echoes of the boys hollering from the vans bounced happily in my memory: "Aksaray, Aksaray, Aksaray...Sultanahmet, Sultanahmet, Sultanahmet."

President Erdoğan vs. a Pluralistic Turkey

Turkey is not exactly living in Mr. Rogers' neighborhood. It shares borders with Syria, Iraq, and Iran. Ten percent of its society is Kurdish, many of whom have aspirations to secede and form an independent Kurdistan. In the mid-2010s, two million Syrian refugees—fleeing their war-torn homeland—flowed through Turkey, many on their way to Europe. And, as the easternmost member of NATO, Turkey finds itself caught in the middle of growing tension between the USA and Russia.

Because of its unique position, I've long considered Turkey a model for balancing the needs of a strong leader with Western ideals of pluralism and secularism. For years, Muslims in neighboring countries who dreamed of a more democratic system looked to Turkey for inspiration. But after Recep Tayyip Erdoğan was elected president in 2014, it gradually became clear that he had a different vision: to make Turkey less free, less Western-oriented, and less secular. When Kemal Atatürk founded modern Turkey in 1923, he anticipated such a leader. In fact, Turkey's constitution calls for a strict sepa-

ration of mosque and state—and even requires the Turkish military to overthrow its own president if ever he violates that tenet (which they've actually had to do, on several occasions).

President Erdoğan needed an excuse to shore up his power...and he got it, on July 15, 2016. On that night, a faction of Turkey's military attempted a coup, ostensibly to stop Erdoğan's overreach. It failed, and Erdoğan responded with a harsh crackdown. Erdoğan declared an extended state of emergency, replacing leading generals, silencing professors, shutting down the press, and locking up thousands of

I remembered my favorite call was for the train station's neighborhood: "Sirkeci, Sirkeci, Sirkeci." After dropping off my bag at my hotel, I stopped for tea—served in the customary small, tulip-shaped glass—before heading out to explore.

Istanbul, a city of over 10 million, was thriving. The city was poignantly littered both with remnants of grand empires and with living, breathing reminders of the harsh reality of life in the developing world. Sipping my tea, I watched old men shuffle by, hunched over as if still bent under the towering loads they had carried all of their human-beast-of-burden lives.

Western-minded Turks. He essentially criminalized his political opposition.

Before the coup attempt, Erdoğan—who was then focused on getting Turkey admitted to the EU—had been praised for his support of religious freedoms and civil rights. Suddenly, things changed. The leaders of the military were replaced by Erdoğan cronies. The military and the judiciary, both counted on for their defense of secularism, were effectively muzzled. Erdoğan moved to stop the public from organizing. He blocked or limited Internet access and social media. Turks were arrested on charges of simply insulting the president. Erdoğan, named by the *European Voice* "European of the Year" in 2004, had now moved Turkey—its populace thoroughly frightened and submissive—closer to autocracy. Joining the EU is no longer a Turkish priority. Instead, Erdoğan is cozying up to Russia and, like Putin, uses any conflict with the West as a way to boost his popularity and empower him to make more fundamental changes in Turkish society.

Erdoğan further consolidated his power in April of 2017, when a narrowly passed referendum increased the president's reach and effectively neutered the checks and balances among the branches of Turkish government. This scares moderate and progressive Turks, because it legitimizes Erdoğan's hold on power as "the will of the people." And observers of history see recent events in Turkey lining up with a frightening pattern that allows autocrats to take control of a democratic state: First comes a flashy crisis (the failed coup), which sets the stage for the strongman to legally amplify his power (the referendum). A police state with a silenced opposition follows.

I find Erdoğan fascinating as an example of the impact that a single individual can have on history. It feels good to celebrate the power of grassroots activism to bring change, but, sadly, history and travel both teach us that one person—put into power by a quirky election, an assassination, or a convenient excuse to throw out a constitution—can derail an entire democratic society.

And yet, this ancient city was striding into the future. During my visit, everyone was buzzing about the new tunnel under the Bosphorus, giving a million commuters in the Asian suburbs of Istanbul an easy train link to their places of work in Europe. This tunnel was emblematic of modern Turkey's commitment to connecting East and West, just as Istanbul bridges Asia and Europe. I also see it as a concrete example of how parts of the developing world are emerging as economic dynamos.

Stepping out of my shoes, I entered the vast, turquoise (and therefore not-quite-rightly-named) Blue Mosque. Hoping for another déjà vu, I didn't get it. Something was missing. Yes…gone was the smell of countless

sweaty socks, knees, palms, and fore-
heads soaked into the ancient carpet
upon which worshippers did their
quite physical prayer work-outs. Sure
enough, the Blue Mosque had a fresh
new carpet—with a subtle design that
keeps worshippers organized in rows
the same way that lined paper tames
printed letters.

The prayer service let out, and a
sea of Turks surged for the door. Being
caught up in a crush of locals—where
the only way to get any personal space
is to look up—is a connecting-with-
humanity ritual for me. I seek out these
opportunities. It's the closest I'll ever
come to experiencing the exhilaration of
body-surfing above a mosh pit. Going

The Blue Mosque is down-to-earth and
sublime, from its stocking-feet carpets to
its soaring domes.

outside with the worshipping flow, I scanned the dark sky. That scene—one
I had forgotten was so breathtaking—played for me again: hard-pumping
seagulls powering through the humid air in a black sky, surging into the light
as they crossed in front of floodlit minarets.

Walking down to the Golden Horn inlet and Istanbul's churning waterfront, I crossed the new Galata Bridge, which made me miss the dismantled
and shipped-out old Galata Bridge—so crusty with life's struggles. Feeling
a wistful nostalgia, I thought of how all societies morph with the push and
pull of the times.

But then I realized that, while the old bridge is gone, the new one has
been engulfed with the same vibrant street life: boys casting their lines, old
men sucking on water pipes, and sesame-seed bread rings filling steamy
glass-windowed carts.

Strolling the new Galata Bridge and still finding old scenes reminded
me how stubborn cultural inertia can be. If you give a camel-riding Bedouin
a new Mercedes, he still decorates it like a camel. I remember looking at
tribal leaders in Afghanistan—shaven, cleaned up, and given a bureaucrat's
uniform. But looking more closely, I could see the bushy-gray-bearded
men in dusty old robes still living behind those modern uniforms. On a

trip to Kathmandu, I recall seeing a Californian who had dropped out of the "modern rat race"—calloused almost-animal feet, matted dreadlocks, draped in sackcloth as he stood, cane in hand, before the living virgin goddess. Somehow I could still see Los Angeles in his eyes. The resilience of a culture can't be overcome with a haircut and a shave—or lack of one—or a new bridge.

On the sloppy adjacent harborfront, the venerable "fish and bread boats" were still rocking in the constant chop of the busy harbor. In a humbler day, they were 20-foot-long open dinghies—rough boats with battered car tires for fenders—with open fires for grilling fish literally fresh off the boat. For a few coins, the fishermen would bury a big white fillet in a hunk of fluffy white bread, wrap it in newsprint, and I was on my way…dining out on fish.

In recent years, the fish and bread boats had been shut down—they had no license. After a popular uproar, they came back. They're a bit more hygienic, no longer using newspaper for wrapping, but still rocking in the waves and slamming out fresh fish.

In Turkey, I have more personal rituals than in other countries. I cap my days with a bowl of *sütlaç*. That's rice pudding with a sprinkle of cinnamon—still served in a square and shiny stainless-steel bowl with a matching spoon, not much bigger than a gelato sampler.

And I don't let a day go by in Turkey without enjoying a teahouse game of backgammon with a stranger. Boards have become less characteristic; they're now cheap and mass-produced, almost disposable. Today's dice— plastic and perfect—make me miss the tiny handmade "bones" of the 20th century, with their disobedient dots. But some things never change. To test a fun cultural quirk, I tossed my dice and paused. As I remembered, a bystander moved for me. When it comes to backgammon, there's one right way…and everybody knows it. And in Turkey, as if a result of its ruthless history, when starting a new game, the winner goes first.

With each backgammon game, I think of one of my most precious possessions back home: an old-time, hand-hewn, inlaid backgammon board, with rusty little hinges held in place by hasty tacks, and soft, white wood worn deeper than the harder, dark wood. Twenty years after taking that backgammon board home, I open it and still smell the tobacco, tea, and soul of a traditional Turkish community. There's almost nothing in my world that is worn or has been enjoyed long enough to absorb the smells of my life and community. It's a reminder to me of the cost of modernity. And when the feel and smell of my old backgam-

mon board takes me back to Turkey, I'm reminded how, in the face of all that modernity, the resilient charm of traditional cultures is endangered and worth preserving.

With that visit, I observed how the people—like those dots on the modern dice—line up better. The weave of a mosque carpet provides direction. There's a seat for everyone, as the *dolmuş* are no longer so stuffed. Fez sales to tourists are way down, but scarf wear by local women (a symbol of traditional Muslim identity) is way up. Each of my déjà vu moments shows a society confronting powerful forces of change while also wanting to stay the same.

My hotel's inviting terrace was open at night, ideal for gazing past floodlit husks of forts and walls, out at the sleepy Bosphorus, with Asia lurking just across the inky straits. The strategic waterway was speckled with the lights of freighters at anchor stretching far into the distance.

Noticing the power of the moonlight shimmering on the water, I recalled the legend of the Turkish flag—a white star and crescent moon reflected in a pool of bright-red blood after a great and victorious battle. From my perch, it seemed that now the crescent moon shone over not blood, but money: trade and shipping…modern-day battles in the arena of capitalism.

At breakfast, the same view was lively, and already bright enough to make me wish I had sunglasses. An empty oil tanker heading north for a Romanian fill-up was light and riding high. Its prow cut through the water like a plow—a reminder of how, today, trade is sustenance and oil is a treasured crop. As I scanned the city, it occurred to me that Istanbul is physically not that different from my home city. I could replace the skyline of domed mosques and minarets with churches and steeples, and it could be the rough end of Any Port City, USA.

Rather than my standard bowl of cereal, for my Turkish breakfasts I go local: olives, goat cheese, cucumbers, tomatoes, bread, and a horrible instant orange drink masquerading as juice. Gazing at my plate, I studied the olive oil. Ignoring the three olive pits, I saw tiny, mysterious flakes of spices. They were

doing a silent and slow-motion do-si-do to a distant rhythm with lyrics that told of arduous camel-caravan rides along the fabled Silk Road from China.

Later that day, I took an aimless stroll, as I love to do here...to immerse myself in Turkey, collecting random memories. Wandering under stiletto minarets, I listened as a hardworking loudspeaker—lashed to the minaret as if a religious crow's nest—belted out a call to prayer. Noticing the twinkling lights strung up in honor of the holy month of Ramadan, I thought, "Charming—they've draped Christmas lights between the minarets." But a Turk might come to my house and say, "Charming—he's draped Ramadan lights on his Christmas tree." I marveled at the multigenerational conviviality at the Hippodrome—that long, oblong plaza still shaped like the chariot racecourse it was 18 centuries ago. Precocious children high-fived me and tried out their only English phrase: "What is your name?" Just to enjoy their quizzical look, I'd say, "Seven o'clock." As I struggle to understand their society, I guess my mischievous streak wanted them to deal with a little intercultural confusion as well.

It's in this environment that, as a tour guide, I spent many trips introducing tour members (like my father) to Turkish culture and Islam. I recall well-educated professionals struggling to get things straight. People would quiz me: "So, where did they get the name 'Quran' for their Bible? Could it be considered a Bible?" Turkish guides love to tell stories of tourists who ask, "Was this church built before or after Christ?" But all guides repeat to themselves the first rule of guiding: "There are no stupid questions." After all, it's in environments like Istanbul—in countries all around the world—that thoughtful travelers get out of their comfort zones and enjoy the easy educational rewards that come with being steep on the learning curve.

Turkish Village Insights in Güzelyurt

Big cities can be relatively cosmopolitan and homogenized by modern affluence. But small towns, with their more change-averse residents, are cultural humidors—keeping fragile traditions moist and full of local flavor.

Güzelyurt, an obscure-to-the-world but proud-of-itself village in central Turkey, has long taught me the richness and nobility of rustic village life in the developing world. Students of the world find that, in any country, remote towns and villages can be wonderful classrooms.

On my last visit, Güzelyurt was all decked out. I happened to arrive on the day of everybody's favorite festival: a circumcision party. It's a wonderful celebration. Turks call it "a wedding without the in-laws." The little boy, dressed like a prince, rode tall on his decorated donkey through a commotion of friends and relatives to the house where a doctor was sharpening his knife. Even with paper money pinned to his fancy outfit and loved ones chanting calming spiritual music, the boy looked frightened. But the ritual snipping went off without a glitch, and a good time was had…at least, by everyone else.

On a different trip, I learned that Turkish weddings are also quite a spectacle. I'll never forget being a special guest at a wedding in Güzelyurt. The entire community gathered. Calling the party to order, the oldest couple looked happily at the young bride and groom and shared a local blessing: "May you grow old together on one pillow."

Whenever there's a family festival, village Turks turn on the music and dance. Everybody is swept onto their feet—including visiting tourists. It's easy: Just follow the locals as they hold out their arms, snap their fingers, and shake their shoulders. During one such Güzelyurt party, the man of the house came over to me—the foreigner—and wanted to impress me. Waving me to a quiet corner, he said, "Here on my wall, the most sacred place in

my home, is my Quran bag, where I keep my Quran. And in my Quran bag I also keep a copy of the Bible and a copy of the Torah—because I believe that we Muslims, Christians, and Jews are all 'children of the Book'…children of the same good God."

Leaving the party, I walked down the street. The town seemed cluttered with ugly unfinished concrete buildings bristling with rusty reinforcement bars. While I love the Turks, I couldn't help but think, "Why can't these people get their act together and just finish these buildings?" That was before I learned that in Turkey, there's an ethic among parents—even poor ones—that you leave your children with a house. Historically Turks are reluctant to store money in the bank because it disappears through inflation. So instead, they invest bit by bit by constructing a building. Every time they get a hundred bucks together, they put it into that ever-growing house. They leave the rebar exposed until they have another hundred bucks, so they make another wall, put on a window, frame in another door…and add more rebar. Now, when I look at that rusty rebar, I remember that Turks say, "Rebar holds the family together"…and it becomes much prettier.

At the edge of Güzelyurt, I came upon a little boy playing a flute. Just like in biblical times, it was carved out of an eagle bone. I listened. And I heard another eagle-bone flute, out of sight, coming from over the hill, where his dad was tending the sheep. As they have for centuries, the boy stays with the mom and plays the eagle-bone flute. The dad tends the flock and plays his flute, too, so the entire family knows that all is well.

I hiked up the shepherd's hill and sat overlooking the town. On a higher hill, just beyond the simple tin roof of its mosque, I saw the letters G Ü Z E L Y U R T spelled out in white rocks. Listening to the timeless sounds of the community, I thought how there are countless Güzelyurts, scattered across every country on earth. Each is humble, yet filled with rich traditions, proud people, and its own village-centric view of our world. Güzelyurt means "beautiful land." While few visitors would consider it particularly beautiful, that's how the people who call it home see it. They'd live nowhere else. And for them, it truly is a *güzel yurt*.

Defending the Separation of Mosque and State…for Now

When visiting eastern Turkey, you don't have a list of sights. It's a cultural scavenger hunt. Years ago, I was exploring with a tour group when we came across 300 kids in a stadium. They were thrusting their fists into the air,

People around the world are passionate about their struggles.

screaming in unison, "We are a secular nation! We are a secular nation!" I asked my local guide, "What's going on? Don't they like God?" She said, "Yes, we love God here in Turkey, but—with the rising tide of Islamic fundamentalism just over the border in Iran—we are very concerned about the fragile and precious separation of mosque and state in our country."

Turkey has long modeled how a nation can be both Muslim and secular. But in recent years, with the rise of President Erdoğan, the line between mosque and state gets a little more blurred. (While Erdoğan is not a religious hardliner, the sweeping changes he is making to Turkish society are, many fear, destabilizing what had been a clear-cut secularism.) Turkey, like so much of today's world, is in a tug-of-war between secular forces and fundamentalism. And, just as in other Islamic lands, Turkish fundamentalist groups use fear of perceived American meddling to win public support. With the ramped-up economic metabolism and change that comes with globalization, people whose time-honored ways are threatened cling to what makes their cultures and societies unique. They seek solace in their rituals, religion, and traditions. (Considering the widespread impact of globalism, I believe this dynamic is at work in all countries, rich and poor, east and west—including my own.)

During the holy month of Ramadan, practicing Muslims refrain from eating, drinking, or even smoking during daylight hours. As a visitor, I

find the Muslim faith all the more vivid and engaging during Ramadan. As an oblivious tourist, I kept stumbling into the subtle ways Ramadan affects everyday life. Sucking sweet apple tobacco from a water pipe, I offered my waiter a puff of my hookah. He put his hand over his heart and explained he'd love to, but he couldn't until the sun went down. During Ramadan, if you sleep lightly, you'll wake to the call to prayer and the sounds of a convivial meal just before dawn. As the sun rises, the fast begins. Later, as the sun sets, the food comes out, and the nightly festival begins. Saying, *"Allah kabul etsin"* ("May God accept our fast today"), the staff at a restaurant where I was having only a glass of tea welcomed me to photograph them, and then offered to share their meal.

Anywhere in Islam, witnessing the breaking of the day-long Ramadan fast at sundown is like watching children waiting for the recess bell. Throughout my visit, every time I witnessed this ritual, people offered to share their food. At that restaurant, I said, "No, thanks," but they set me up anyway—with figs, lentil soup, bread, and baklava.

As much as I enjoy these Ramadan experiences, my recent visits left me with an uneasy awareness of how fundamentalism is creeping into the mainstream. Mayors now play a part in organizing Ramadan festivities. During Ramadan, no-name neighborhood mosques literally overflow during prayer time. With carpets unfurled on sidewalks, it's a struggle just walking down the street. I got the unsettling feeling that the inconvenience to passing pedestrians wasn't their concern…as if they felt everyone should be praying rather than trying to get somewhere.

I don't want to overstate Turkey's move to the right, but keen and caring secular observers see an ominous trend. I have friends in Turkey almost distraught at their country's slide toward fundamentalism. To them, it's an evolution that seems difficult to stop.

Imagine watching your country gradually slip into a theocracy: one universal interpretation of scripture, prayer in school, religious dress codes, women covering up and accepting a scripturally ordained subservient role to men, judges chosen on the basis of the dominant religion, laws and textbooks being rewritten. Whether abroad or in the US, when the separation of religion and state is violated, a moralistic ruling class that believes they are right and others are wrong is set free to reshape its society.

Seeing this struggle play out in Turkey—a land that first adopted a modern, secular constitution only in 1924—is dramatic. I can feel the chill

sweep across a teahouse when a fundamentalist Muslim man walks by...
followed, a few steps behind, by his covered-up wife.

For a traveler, the move to the religious right is easiest to see in peoples'
clothes. As the father of a teenage girl who did her best to dress trendier
than her parents allowed, I am intrigued by teenage Muslim girls covering
up under scarves and, I imagine, duress. Sure, they're covered from head to
toe. But under their modest robe, many wear chic clothes and high heels.

Throughout Islam, scarves are widely used both as tools for modesty
and as fashion accessories. In a fine silk shop, I asked a young woman to
demonstrate scarf-wrapping techniques. She happily showed off various
demure styles. I asked her to demonstrate how to turn one of her scarves
into a conservative religious statement. It took some convincing before she
obliged. She tied the scarf under her chin and around her face, and then,
with an extra fold across the forehead, suddenly she became orthodox. The
power of that last fold gave me goose bumps. She took it off with a shudder.

Later that day, a local friend, Mehlika, took me to Istanbul's Eyüp Sultan
Mosque, where all of the women wore their scarves with that forehead fold.
Famous in Istanbul as the mosque attracting the most conservative worshippers, even its state-employed female security guards were wearing strict,
religious headscarves. To Mehlika (a modern and secular woman), it was
striking—even disturbing—that state employees would be seen in this garb.

The courtyard outside the mosque was filled with a kind of religious
trade fair. Stalls offering free food, literature, and computer programs (with
a do-it-yourself prayer guide) stood side by side. Using incentives to target

poor and less-educated Turks, it reminded me of the old-school strategy of Christian missionaries. The propaganda seemed mostly directed at women. Mehlika believes that women, even more than men, are pulling secular Muslim societies like Turkey to the right.

Marketers know that women make the purchasing decisions in American families. Considering this, I ponder whether women make the religious decisions in Turkish families, and to what degree women really are behind the changes in moderate Muslim societies like Turkey. I told Mehlika I found it interesting that, in both my society and in Muslim societies, women with an agenda can be at odds. She agreed, saying, "Here in Turkey, while these conservative Muslim women push their agenda in terms of 'family values,' secular women like me push our agenda in terms of 'women's rights.'"

Many things drive religious people to get political: a desire for economic justice, a moral environment in which to raise their children, equal rights, the "sanctity of life," and hopes for salvation. These are powerful forces that can easily be manipulated by clever political marketing. They can drive people to war, and they know no cultural or political boundaries.

Observing the enthusiasm of this very religious crowd in the courtyard of the mosque, I could imagine someone who had never been outside of the US dropping in on this scene—and being quite shocked by it all. I asked Mehlika, "Should a Christian be threatened by Islam?" She said, "If you have self-confidence in your system, assuming it deserves to survive, it will. Christendom should be threatened by Islam only if the Christian West seeks empire here."

I find an irony in the tensions between America and Islam. I believe we're incurring incalculable costs (both direct and indirect, tangible and intangible) because our lack of understanding makes us needlessly fearful about Islam. And sadly, I fear that because we're afraid of it, our actions may, eventually and ironically, actually create a situation where we need to be afraid. I wish every American could take a walk through Istanbul with Mehlika.

Islam in a Pistachio Shell

As our generation sorts through the tensions between Islam and Christendom, a rudimentary understanding of the Muslim faith is a good life skill for any engaged non-Muslim. Here's an admittedly basic and simplistic outline designed to help travelers from the Christian West better understand a complex and often misunderstood culture.

Muslims, like Christians and Jews, are monotheistic. They call God "Allah." The key figure in the Islamic faith is Muhammad, Allah's final and most important prophet, who lived from A.D. 570 to 632. When Muhammad's name appears in print, it's often followed by "PBUH": Peace Be Upon Him.

Just as Christians come in two basic varieties (Protestants and Catholics), Muslims come in two branches. After Muhammad died in A.D. 632, his followers argued over who should succeed him in leading his Islamic faith and state, causing Islam to splinter into two rival factions. Today Shias (a.k.a. "Shiites," less than 15 percent of all Muslims) are concentrated in Iran and Iraq, while Sunnis dominate the rest of the Islamic world (including Turkey and Morocco).

The "five pillars" of Islam are the same for all Muslims. Followers of Islam should do the following:

1. Say and believe, "There is only one God, and Muhammad is his prophet."

2. Pray five times a day, facing Mecca (denoted inside a mosque by a niche called a *mihrab*). Modern Muslims believe that, along with thinking of God, part of the value of this ritual is to help people wash, exercise, and stretch.

3. Give to the poor one-fortieth of your wealth, if you are not in debt. ("Debt" includes the responsibility to provide both your parents and your children with a good life.)

4. Fast during daylight hours through the month of Ramadan. Fasting is about self-discipline. It's also a great social equalizer that helps everyone feel the hunger of the poor.

5. Visit Mecca. Muslims who can afford it and who are physically able are expected to go on a pilgrimage (*Hajj*) to the sacred sites in Mecca and Medina at least once in their lifetime. This is interpreted by some Muslims as a command to travel. My favorite Muhammad quote: "Don't tell me how educated you are; tell me how much you've traveled."

Prayer services in a mosque are usually gender-segregated. The act of praying is quite physical (repeatedly bending over) and—as a practical matter

The Islamic equivalent of the Christian bell tower is a minaret, which the *muezzin* traditionally climbs to sing the call to prayer. While traditionally minarets were grand (as pictured here), in a kind of architectural Darwinism, they are shrinking. As calls to prayer are now electronically amplified, the *muezzin* sings into a mic at ground level, and the minaret's height is no longer necessary or worth the expense. Many small, modern mosques have one mini-minaret about as awe-inspiring as your little toe.

Call to Prayer

While the call to prayer sounds spooky to many Americans, I find that with some understanding, it becomes beautiful. Traditionally, just before the sun rises, an imam (prayer leader) stares at his arm. When he can tell a gray hair from a black one, it's time to call his community to prayer. While quality and warble varies, across Islam the Arabic words of the call to prayer are exactly the same. The first call to prayer of the day starts with an extra line:

Praying is better than sleeping
God is great (Allahhhhhh hu akbar...)
I witness there is no other God but Allah
I witness Muhammad is Allah's prophet
Come join the prayer
Come to be saved
God is great...God is great
There is no other God but Allah.

Big mosques have a trained professional singer for a *muezzin*. Many tiny mosques can't afford a real *muezzin*, so the imam himself does the call to prayer. The qualitative difference can be obvious. Invariably, my hotel seems to be within earshot of five or six mosques, which creates quite a cacophony.

My challenge is to hear the Muslim call to prayer as a beautiful form of praise that sweeps across the globe five times a day—from Malaysia across Pakistan, Arabia, and Turkey to Morocco and then to America—like a stadium wave, undulating exactly as fast as the earth turns.

of respect for women, and less distraction for both sexes—women generally worship apart from the men.

Just as pre-Vatican II Catholicism embraced Latin (for tradition, uniformity, and so all could relate and worship together anywhere, anytime), Islam embraces Arabic. Turks recently experimented by doing the call to prayer in Turkish, but they switched back to the traditional Arabic.

The Quran teaches that Abraham was a good submitter (to the will of God). The word for submitter is "Muslim"—derived from *Islam* ("submit") with a *Mu-* ("one who"). So a Muslim is, literally, "one who submits."

Wherever I travel, having just a basic grasp of the dominant local religion makes the people and traditions I encounter more meaningful and enjoyable. Exploring Muslim countries leaves me with memories of the charming conviviality of neighborhoods spilling into the streets. Like Christmas is a fun time to enjoy the people energy of a Christian culture, Ramadan is a particularly fun and vibrant time to be among Muslims. My visits to places like Turkey, Morocco, Iran (described in Chapter 8), and Palestine (described in Chapter 9) have shown me how travel takes the fear out of foreign ways.

Morocco: Everything but Pork

Islam is as culturally varied as Christendom. Turkey is unique among Muslim states because of its European orientation and because of its alliance with the US (important during the Cold War, Gulf War, and Iraq War). Morocco, another Muslim country, offers a different insight into Islam. And, while many are avoiding travel to Turkey after Erdoğan's post-coup crackdown, Morocco remains a welcoming and popular Muslim destination for Western travelers. On my last visit to Morocco, what I found pleased me: a Muslim nation succeeding, stable, and becoming more affluent with no apparent regard for the US.

Artists, writers, and musicians have always loved the coastal Moroccan city of Tangier. Delacroix and Matisse were drawn by its evocative light. The Beat Generation, led by William S. Burroughs and Jack Kerouac, sought the city's multicultural, otherworldly feel. Paul Bowles found his sheltering sky here. From the 1920s through the 1950s, Tangier was an "international zone," too strategic to give to any one nation, and jointly governed by as many as nine different powers, including France, Spain, Britain, Italy, Belgium, the Netherlands…and Morocco. The city was a tax-free zone (since there was no single authority to collect taxes), which created a booming free-for-all atmosphere, attracting playboy millionaires, bon vivants, globetrotting scoundrels, con artists, and expat romantics. Tangier enjoyed a cosmopolitan golden age that, in many ways, shaped the city visitors see today.

But because of Tangier's "international zone" status, Morocco's previous king (Hassan II, who ruled from the 1960s through the 1990s) effectively

disowned the city. He made a point to divert all national investment away from his country's fourth-largest city, denying it national funds for improvements. Over time, Tangier fell into a steep decline. It was a neglected hellhole for a generation. The place depressed me.

But the city changed radically in the first decade of the 2000s…and so has my assessment of it. When King Mohammed VI took the throne in 1999, he reinvested funds to help Tangier become a great city again. The difference is breathtaking. While Tangier is still exotic—with its dilapidated French colonial and Art Deco buildings giving it a time-warp charm—it's much more efficient, people-friendly, safe-feeling, and generally likable.

Checking into Hotel Continental, I was greeted by flamboyant Jimmy, who runs the shop there. Jimmy knows every telephone area code in the US. Many years ago, I had told him I was from Seattle. He said, "206." Now I tested him again. He said, "206, 360, 425, 564…new area codes."

Hotel Continental had me looking for the English Patient. Gramophones gathered dust on dressers under mangy chandeliers. A serene maid painted a sudsy figure-eight in the loose tiles with her mop, day after day, surrounded by dilapidation that never went away.

As I updated the information in my guidebook, I found a striking and nonchalant incompetence. My guidebook listed the hotel's phone and email data more accurately than their own printed material. It's a 70-room hotel with, it seemed, barely a sheet of paper in its office.

Morocco's new king is more modern, and with his friendly policies, Tangier is enjoying a renaissance.

Roosters and the Muslim call to prayer worked together to wake me and the rest of that world early each day. When the morning sun was high enough to send a rainbow plunging into the harbor amid ferries busily coming and going, I stood on my balcony and surveyed Tangier kicking into gear. Women in colorful, flowing robes walked to sweatshops adjacent to the port. They were happy to earn $8 a day (a decent wage for an unskilled worker here) sewing for big-name European clothing lines—a reminder that a vast and wealthy Continent is just a short cruise to the north. Cabbies jostled at the pier for the chance to rip off arriving tourists.

It's an exciting time in Morocco. Walking the streets, I enjoyed observing a modest new affluence, lots of vision and energy, and, at the same time, no compromise with being Arabic and Muslim. The king is modernizing. His queen, a commoner, is the first queen to be seen in public—Moroccans have never seen their king's mother. Imagine the dramatic societal changes in such a short time.

Women are making gains throughout Moroccan society. Until recently, a woman here couldn't open a bank account. During my visit, the general director of the stock exchange in Casablanca was a woman, and out of 21 ministers voted into office in a recent election, seven were female.

The Moroccans I encountered didn't emulate or even seem to care about the USA. Al-Jazeera blared on teahouse TVs, with a pointed critique of American culture. But people appeared numb to the propaganda, and the TV seemed to be on that channel for lack of an alternative. I felt no animosity directed toward me as an American. There was no political edge to any graffiti or posters.

When I tried to affirm my observations with my guide, Aziz, he explained to me the fundamental difference between "Islamic" and "Islamist": Islamists are expansionist and are threatened by the very existence of Israel. He explained how Al-Jazeera appeals to Islamists, but he made it clear that Morocco is Islamic, not Islamist.

Wandering in Tangier—especially after dark—is entertaining. It's a rare place where signs are in three languages (Arabic, French, and Spanish)... and English doesn't make the cut. Sometimes, when I'm frustrated with the impact of American foreign policy on the developing world, I have this feeling that an impotent America is better for the world than an America whose power isn't always used for good. Seeing those signs reminded me that there's a world that's managing just fine without us.

The market scene was a wonderland—of everything but pork: Mountains of glistening olives, a full palate of spices, children with butcher knives happy to perform for my camera.

Aziz explained that each animal is slaughtered in accordance with Islamic law, or Halal. I asked him to explain. He took me to a table with a pile of chickens and hollered, "Hey, Muhammad!" to catch the attention of a knife-wielding boy. (Aziz explained that when he wants someone's attention, he says, "Hey, Muhammad!" It's like our "Hey, you"...but very respectful. For a woman, you'd holler, "Hey, Fatima.") He asked the boy to demonstrate the proper way to slaughter an animal, and I was given a graphic demonstration: in the name of Allah, with a sharp knife, animal's head pointing to Mecca, body drained of its blood.

Before this visit, I had recommended to my guidebook readers that day-trippers from Spain just hold their nose and take the organized tour (with all the big bus groups from Spain's Costa del Sol). A Tangier guide meets you at the ferry. He takes you on a bus tour of the city and a walk through the old town, where he leads you to a few staged photo ops (camel ride, snake charmer, Atlas Mountains tribal musicians). After visiting a clichéd restaurant where you eat clichéd food while a belly dancer performs, you

In Morocco, package tourists dine with clichés and each other.

visit a carpet shop. Guides and their tour companies must make a healthy commission. Why else would they offer the round-trip ferry ride with the tour for the same price as the round-trip ferry ride without the tour?

Being here without a big tour group, I met gracious Moroccans eager to talk and share. About the only time I saw other Westerners was when I crossed paths with one of the many day-tripping groups. As they completed their visit, these tourists walked in a tight, single-file formation, holding their purses and day bags nervously to their bellies like paranoid kangaroos as they bundled past one last spanking line of street merchants and made it safely back onto the ferry.

I pondered this scene, wondering if these tourists—scared, oblivious, clutching the goodies they traveled so far to pick up on the cheap, and then sailing home without learning a thing—were dealing with Morocco this way because it's the same way their home countries deal with the developing world in general.

It was poignant for me because, until the lessons I learned from this trip, I was part of the problem—recommending the tour rather than the independent adventure. Some of those needlessly paranoid tourists likely had my guidebook in the bag they were clutching. I wished I could grab their books and update all the information that I now realized was bad advice.

While I was comfortable and enjoyed a fascinating Moroccan experience on my own, the frightened tour groups reminded me of some kind of self-imposed hostage crisis. They sailed away still filled with fear, but I was celebrating an Islamic nation that was stable, enjoying a thriving economy, and made me feel perfectly welcome. The tourists were thankful they didn't get ripped off or diarrhea. I had overcome my fear and was thankful Morocco was doing so well.

In some cases, visiting a country on a tour ruins any opportunity to really learn about that place. While that may be a lost opportunity and a costly mistake, it can also be a valuable lesson. Any one of those tourists could return and, with a different attitude (and better guidebook advice), be welcomed not as a customer, but as a friend.

The Human, the Bear, and the Forest

I am a Christian who wants to believe we can live peacefully with Islam. One thing is clear to me: What I learn about Islam from media in the US can fill me with fear and anger. What I learn about Islam by traveling in Muslim countries fills me with hope and a desire to better understand each other.

Of course there are real dangers. And rare is the religion with a fundamentalist fringe that wouldn't kill in the name of God. But no society should fear another society simply because their leaders and media say they should. Before anyone hardens their take on Islam, a little travel to a moderate Muslim country can be a good idea. (It's a sad irony that terrorism causes Americans to travel less.) If you can't visit in person, travel to Islam vicariously by seeking out connections and friendships at home with people from cultures and religions that are different from your own.

The centuries-old tension between Christendom and Islam is like a human sharing a forest with a bear. Both just want to gather berries, do a little fishing, raise their kids, and enjoy the sun. Neither wants to do harm to the other, but—because they can't readily communicate—either would likely kill the other if they crossed paths. The world is our forest and we're sharing it with others. As it gets smaller, more and more cultures will cross paths. Our advantage over the human and the bear: we can communicate.

Chapter 7
Europe: Not "Hard on Drugs" or "Soft on Drugs," but Smart on Drugs

Because of my travels, I find myself one of the most high-profile people in America advocating for the reform of our nation's marijuana laws. In 2003, I hiked the length of Seattle's Hempfest—America's largest marijuana rally—for the first time. It became clear to me: These people aren't criminals. Maybe they're doing things some people don't like. But it's not right to make them criminals. Since then, I've joined others in working to legalize marijuana. I'm a board member of NORML (the National Organization for the Reform of Marijuana Laws), and in 2012, I co-sponsored the historic Initiative 502—which legalized adult recreational marijuana use in Washington State. Then, as part of the successful 2014 and 2016 campaigns, I barnstormed Oregon, Massachusetts, and Maine to raise awareness of the wisdom of ending our government's war on marijuana in those states.

All of this does not mean that I'm "pro-drugs." I simply appreciate how most of Europe treats its drug problems in a pragmatic way, with success measured by harm reduction rather than by incarceration. While in the US, year after year, about 700,000 people are arrested with marijuana charges, in much of Europe discreetly smoking a joint is just another form of relaxation.

I speak out on this issue, in part, because most Americans cannot—out of fear of losing their job, or reputation, or both. Of the countless good causes I could get involved in, drug policy reform is a high-risk choice. When I'm interviewed about this on TV or radio, journalists ask me all the predictable, skeptical questions…and then, as soon as the mic is off, they often say, "Thanks for having the courage to speak out." My first thought is that if it seems courageous to challenge a law that you believe is wrong, that is, in itself, reason to speak out. Since I own my own business, I can't get fired…and so, when it comes to America's prohibition on marijuana, I can consider lessons learned from my travels and say what I really believe when I'm back home.

Today, while the number of states with legal recreational marijuana is approaching double digits, much of our country is still very regressive on drug policy reform. Europe offers a strikingly different approach to drug use and abuse.

The US and Europe: Two Different Approaches to Drug Abuse

There's no doubt that the abuse of drugs—whether "soft drugs" (such as marijuana, alcohol, and tobacco) or "hard drugs" (including heroin, cocaine, and methamphetamines)—is a serious problem that destroys many lives. Since the 1970s, the US approach has been to declare a "war on drugs" (with the exception of alcohol and tobacco). In contrast, Europe has attempted a wide range of solutions to the same problem. And, while Europe certainly doesn't have all the answers, their results have been compelling. I've traveled with an appetite for learning why Europe has fewer drug-related deaths, less drug-related violence, less drug-related incarceration, and less drug consumption per capita than we do here in America. (I must admit, though, that as I reviewed the numbers to back up my claims for this chapter, I discovered one irrefutable fact: Statistics on drug use and abuse are all over the map. While most of the empirical studies reinforce my conclusions, conflicting data always seem to emerge. I assume this is because most sources have an agenda—pro or con—which skews their findings.)

In an Amsterdam "coffeeshop," you won't find coffee.

To be clear, there is no Europe-wide agreement on drug policy. Some countries—including the Netherlands, Spain, Portugal, and Switzerland—categorize marijuana as a soft drug (similar to alcohol and tobacco). Others—including Iceland and Greece—strictly enforce laws against both marijuana and hard drugs (in fact, drug-related arrests are actually on the rise in some countries). But what most European countries have in common is an emphasis on education and prevention rather than incarceration. They believe that by handling drug abuse more as a public health problem than as a criminal one, they are better able to reduce the harm it causes—both to the individual (health problems and antisocial behavior) and to society (healthcare costs, policing costs, and drug-related crime).

Generally, Europeans employ a three-pronged strategy for dealing with hard drugs: law enforcement, education, and healthcare. Police zero in on dealers—not users—to limit the supply of drugs. Users generally get off with a warning and are directed to get treatment; any legal action respects the principle of proportionality. Anti-drug education programs work hard to warn people (particularly teenagers) of the dangers of drugs. And finally, the medical community steps in to battle health problems associated with drug use (especially HIV/AIDS and hepatitis C) and to help addicts reclaim their lives.

When it comes to soft drugs, policies in much of Europe are also more creative and pragmatic than America's. We'll get into an illuminating case study (the Netherlands) later in this chapter.

Meanwhile, much of the US seems afraid to grapple with this problem openly and innovatively. Rather than acting as a deterrent, the US criminalization of marijuana drains precious resources, clogs our legal system, and distracts law enforcement attention from more pressing safety concerns. Of the many billions of tax dollars we invest annually fighting our war on drugs, more than half is spent on police, courts, and prisons. On the other hand, European nations—seeking a cure that isn't more costly than the problem itself—spend a much larger portion of their drug policy funds on nurses, counselors, and clinics. According to the EU website, European policymakers estimate that they save 15 euros in police and healthcare costs for each euro invested in drug education, addiction prevention, and counseling.

Learning from Europe, the US should be open to new solutions. It's disappointing for a nation so famous for its ingenuity to simply label the drug problem a "war" and bring in the artillery. Europeans make a strong case that approaching drug abuse from the perspective of harm reduction can be more effective. And so, to find inspiration, let's take a closer look at how four European countries deal with drug use: the famously tolerant Dutch stance on the soft drug of marijuana; the clever Spanish, with their "cannabis clubs"; the pragmatic Swiss approach to the hard drug of heroin; and—most surprising—the Portuguese approach, which has simply legalized the consumption of *all* drugs, hard and soft alike.

The Dutch Approach to Marijuana

Amsterdam, Europe's counterculture mecca, thinks the concept of a "victimless crime" is a contradiction in terms. The city—and the Netherlands in general—is well-known for its progressive attitude about marijuana. Regardless of your views, it's fascinating to try to understand the Dutch system that, in 1976, decriminalized the personal recreational use of pot. I travel to Amsterdam frequently, and on each visit, as a part of my guidebook research chores, I talk to various locals about marijuana—from the guys who run shops that sell pot, to pot smokers and non-smokers, and to police officers who deal with drug problems face-to-face. Here's what I've learned.

First off, marijuana is not actually "legal" in the Netherlands—Dutch law still technically defines marijuana use as a crime. But for nearly 40 years, the nation's prosecutors have made it a policy not to enforce that law under their guiding principle of expediency: It makes no sense to enforce a law that is more trouble than it's worth.

In a Dutch coffeeshop, the menu features service with a smile—and imaginative names for its marijuana.

The Dutch are justly famous for their practice of *gedogen*—toleration. They believe that as soon as you criminalize something, you lose any ability to regulate it. So, just as we tolerate and regulate alcohol and tobacco, they tolerate and regulate recreational pot smoking.

But Dutch tolerance has its limits. The moment you hurt or threaten someone else, the crime is no longer victimless—and no longer tolerated. Dutch laws against driving under the influence—whether alcohol or marijuana—are extremely tough. The Dutch are well aware of the problems associated with drugs, especially addictive ones. (The Dutch word for addiction, *verslaving*, means "enslavement.") Because of the wide-reaching social costs of having citizens "enslaved" by hard drugs, drugs such as heroin and cocaine are strictly illegal in the Netherlands. And, while the police generally ignore marijuana use, they stringently enforce laws prohibiting the sale and use of hard drugs.

Essentially legal since 1976, an impressive variety of marijuana joints fills the sales racks in Dutch coffeeshops.

Throughout the Netherlands, you'll see "coffeeshops": cafés selling marijuana. The minimum age for purchase is 18, and coffeeshops can sell up to five grams of marijuana per person per day. As long as you're a paying customer (for instance, you buy a drink), you can pop into any coffeeshop and light up, even if you didn't buy your pot there.

Because of laws prohibiting the advertising of marijuana, the customer must take the initiative to get the menu. Locals buy marijuana by asking, "Can I see the cannabis menu?" In some coffeeshops, customers actually have to push and hold down a button to see an illuminated menu—the contents of which look like the inventory of a drug bust.

The Dutch smoke both hashish (made from the resin of the cannabis plant) and the buds or flower of the plant (which they call "marihuana" or "grass"). Pre-rolled joints are sold individually ($4-7, depending on the strain), though some places sell only small packs of three or four joints. Joints come in three varieties: pure, with a "hamburger helper" herb mix, or with tobacco. Any place that caters to Americans sells joints without tobacco, but you have to ask specifically for a "pure" joint. Shops also sell marijuana loose, in baggies. They dispense rolling papers like toothpicks, and customers can borrow a bong or a vaporizer. I'm told the better pot, though costlier, is actually a better value, as it takes less to get high—and it's a better high.

Because pot is retailed much like beer or cigarettes, varieties evolve with demand. While each shop has different brands, it's all derived from two types of the marijuana plant: *Cannabis indica* and *Cannabis sativa*. *Indica* gets you a stoned, heavy, mellow high—it makes you just sit on the couch. *Sativa* is light, fun, uplifting, and more psychedelic—it makes you giggle.

Most of the pot sold in Dutch coffeeshops is grown locally, as coffeeshops find it's much safer to deal with Dutch-grown plants than to import marijuana (the EU, as you might imagine, prohibits any international drug trade)."Netherlands weed" is now refined, like wine. The Dutch are wizards in a greenhouse, and technological advances have made it easier to cultivate exotic strains. You may see joints described as if they'd come from overseas, such as "Thai"—and, indeed, the strain may have originated elsewhere—but it's generally Dutch-grown.

While most American pot smokers like their joints made purely of marijuana, the Dutch (like most Europeans) are accustomed to mixing tobacco with marijuana. Back in the 1970s, most locals smoked hash, which needs to be mixed with something else (like tobacco) to light up. Pot was expensive, and it was simply wasteful to pass around a pure marijuana joint. Mixing in tobacco allowed poor hippies to be generous without going broke. Today, more Dutch prefer "herbal cannabis"—the marijuana bud common in the US—but they still keep the familiar tobacco in their joints. And since the Dutch don't cure their marijuana, it's simply hard to smoke without tobacco.

The Netherlands' indoor-smoking ban—designed to protect employees from secondhand smoke—pertains to tobacco, but not pot. It might seem strange to an American, but these days, if a coffeeshop is busted, it's probably for tobacco. Coffeeshops with a few outdoor seats have a huge advantage, as their customers can light up tobacco-and-marijuana joints outside. Shops without an outdoor option are in for an extra challenge, as many local smokers would rather get their weed to go than smoke it without tobacco at their neighborhood coffeeshop.

Coffeeshop baristas are generally very patient in explaining the varieties available, and try to warn Americans (who aren't used to the strength of the local stuff) to try a lighter leaf. Tourists who haven't smoked pot since their college days are notorious for overindulging in Amsterdam. Locals joke that the most dangerous thing about smoking pot is gravity. Baristas nickname tourists about to pass out "Whitey"—the color their faces turn just before they hit the floor. To keep this from happening, the key is to eat or drink something sweet. Cola is a good fast fix, and coffeeshops keep sugar tablets handy.

Legally, while each coffeeshop can sell as much as it likes, it's permitted to keep an inventory of only 500 grams (about one pound) of pot in stock. A popular shop—whose supply must be replenished five or six times a day—

The Prohibition of Our Age

Travel teaches us a respect for history, and when it comes to drug policy, I hope we can learn from our own prohibitionist past. Back in the 1920s, America's biggest drug problem was alcohol. To combat it, we made booze illegal and instituted Prohibition. By any sober assessment, all that Prohibition produced was grief. By criminalizing a soft drug that people refused to stop enjoying, Prohibition created the mob (Al Capone and company), filled our prisons, and cost our society a lot of money. It was big government at its worst. Finally, courageous citizens stood up and said the laws against alcohol were causing more problems than the alcohol itself. When Prohibition was repealed in 1933, nobody was saying "booze is good for

For decades, Seattle's annual Hempfest celebrated the civil liberty to smoke marijuana. It also provided a platform for drug policy activists to explain why the laws against pot were causing more harm than good and this prohibition had to go. (Photo by Trish Feaster)

you." Society just realized that the laws were counterproductive and impossible to enforce. In our own age, many lawyers, police officers, judges, and other concerned citizens are coming to the same conclusion about the current US government-sponsored prohibition against marijuana.

simply has to put up with the hassle of constantly taking small deliveries. The reason? Authorities want shops to stay small and not become export bases—which would bring more international pressure on the Netherlands to crack down on its coffeeshop culture. (A few years ago, Amsterdam's mayor—understanding that this regulation just has the city busy with small-time deliveries—proposed doubling the allowable inventory level to a kilo. It's striking to think of a big-city mayor grappling with a practical issue like street congestion caused by needlessly small wholesale marijuana deliveries.)

The wholesale dimension of the marijuana business is the famous "gray area" in the law. Rather than deal with that complex issue, Dutch lawmakers just left wholesaling out of the equation, taking the "don't ask, don't tell" route. Most shops get their inventory from the pot equivalent of home brewers or micro-brewers. Shops with better "boutique suppliers" get the reputation for having better-quality weed (and regularly win the annual Cannabis Cup trophy).

Everyone I've talked with in Amsterdam agrees that pot should never be bought on the street. Well-established coffeeshops are considered much safer, as their owners have an incentive to keep their trade safe and healthy.

The Dutch are not necessarily "pro-marijuana." In fact, most have never tried it or even set foot in a coffeeshop. They just don't think the state has any business preventing the people who want it from getting it in a sensible way. To appease Dutch people who aren't comfortable with marijuana, an integral component of the coffeeshop system is discretion. It's bad form to smoke marijuana openly while on the street. Dutch people who don't like pot don't have

to encounter it and rarely even smell it. And towns that don't want coffeeshops don't have them.

Easygoing as the Dutch may seem about smoking pot, many in the Netherlands want to tighten things up. In the early 2010s, there was a new movement to recriminalize. Local right-wingers, conservative Christian groups, and the American government have all pressured the Netherlands government to restrict its marijuana policies. This has pitted federal authorities in the Netherlands against mayors. Generally mayors, who are responsible for crime on their streets, advocate for the legal retail sale of marijuana in coffeeshops. They know when coffeeshops are shut down, there's a spike in the criminal activity that goes along with criminals selling pot on the streets.

A 2011 Dutch law sought to close coffeeshops near schools, and coffeeshop licenses have not been renewed in certain neighborhoods—as towns and cities want to keep a broad smattering of shops rather than a big concentration in any one area. Consequently, the number of coffeeshops in Amsterdam has fallen from a peak of more than 700 (in the mid-1990s) to about 200 today. With all of this pressure, coffeeshop proprietors are scrambling to be good citizens and nurture good relations with their neighbors.

One of the biggest concerns with the coffeeshop system is "marijuana tourism." It's no coincidence that Amsterdam has become a mecca for harmless but occasionally obnoxious backpackers eager to legally light up. And neighboring countries (France and Germany) complain that it's too easy for their citizens to make drug runs across the border. In response, some Dutch border towns have implemented a "weed pass" system, allowing pot sales only to registered Dutch citizens. But when that happens, the independent-minded Dutch who don't want to be registered as pot users end up buying it on the street, which rekindles the black market and the problems that causes.

Despite detractors, statistics support the belief that the more pragmatic Dutch system removes crime from the equation without unduly increasing consumption: After more than 40 years of handling marijuana this way, Dutch experts in the field of drug-abuse prevention agree that, while marijuana use has increased slightly, it has not increased more than in other European countries where pot smokers are being arrested. (According to EU statistics, 23 percent of Dutch people have used pot, compared to more than 30 percent of Italians, French, and Brits.) My Dutch friends also enjoy pointing out that, while three recent US presidents—Clinton, Bush, Obama—admitted or implied that they've smoked marijuana, no Dutch prime minister ever has.

Dutch parents generally agree with their country's lenient approach to marijuana. The Dutch have seen no significant change in marijuana consumption among teens (who, according to US and EU government statistics, smoke pot at half the US rate). Meanwhile, in the US states where it's still legal, many teens report that it's easier for them to buy marijuana than tobacco or alcohol—because they don't get carded when buying something illegally.

It's interesting to compare European use to the situation in the United States. According to Pew Research Center statistics, approximately half of all American adults have used marijuana at some point in their life. Various economists estimate that illegal marijuana is an approximately $100 billion untaxed industry in our country. The FBI reports that almost 50 percent of the roughly 1.5 million annual drug arrests in the US are for marijuana—the vast majority (84 percent) for simple possession…that means users, not dealers.

Many Dutch people believe that their pot policies have also contributed to the fact that they have fewer hard drug problems than other countries. The thinking goes like this: A certain segment of the population will experiment with drugs regardless. The coffeeshop scene allows people to do this safely, with soft drugs. Police see the coffeeshops as a firewall separating soft drug use from hard drug abuse in their communities. If there is a dangerous chemical being pushed on the streets, for example, the police (with the help of coffee-shop proprietors) communicate to the drug-taking part of their society via the coffeeshops. When considering the so-called "gateway" effect of marijuana, the only change the police have seen in local heroin use is that the average age of a Dutch needle addict is getting older. In fact, many people believe marijuana only acts as a "gateway" drug when it is illegal—because then, young people have no option but to buy it from pushers on the street, who have an economic incentive to get them hooked on more expensive and addictive hard drugs.

The hope and hunch is that people go through their drug-experimentation phase innocently with pot, and then the vast majority move on in life without getting sucked into harder, more dangerous drugs. Again, the numbers bear this out: Surveys show that more than three times as many Americans (1.5%) report having tried heroin as Dutch people (0.5%).

Studying how the Dutch retail marijuana is interesting. It's also helpful because learning how another society confronts a persistent problem differently than we do can help us envision how we might deal with the same problem more effectively. I agree with my Dutch friends, who remind me that a society has to make a choice: tolerate alternative lifestyles…or build more prisons. The Netherlands has made its choice. While America is still building more prisons, the Dutch are closing theirs. My Dutch friends needle me with the fact that the US has the world's highest incarceration rate—nearly

Dutch cops, happy to ignore pot smokers since 1976 (but still tough on hard drugs), measure the effectiveness of their society's drug policy in terms of harm reduction.

10 times the Dutch rate—at an annual cost of $60 billion. I also agree with New York Mayor LaGuardia. Way back in the 1930s, when it was becoming clear that America's Prohibition on alcohol wasn't working, LaGuardia said that if a society has a law on the books that it doesn't intend to enforce consistently, the very existence of that law erodes respect for all laws in general.

Spain's Cannabis Clubs

Marijuana is illegal in Spain. But Spaniards have clever ways of smoking pot without getting arrested. Traditionally, Spaniards call potheads "kangaroos," because when the police show up, smokers stow their joints not in pockets (which can be legally searched), but under their underpants, where the police can't go without a warrant. This quick stash is done so routinely that Spaniards joke they'll eventually evolve a kangaroo-like pouch just below their bellies.

Spain has also innovated its own way to get around the government's insistence on criminalizing the sale of marijuana. They can smoke with their friends and not get arrested by joining social organizations called "cannabis clubs" (*club social de cannabis*). I spent a

Spaniards join cannabis clubs to smoke marijuana legally.

delightful evening at a discreet and tasteful lounge in Barcelona's Gothic Quarter. Any night of the week, its members drop in to enjoy the privileges of being a part of their club—to smoke the weed they collectively own without getting arrested. The people I met were happy to explain their system.

Cannabis clubs are for members only and not open to the public. You technically don't buy weed; you co-own its production. Spaniards told me, "We are used to dealing with the old laws that should be changed, but aren't. We build little fantasies to dance artfully around them."

There's a huge variety of cannabis clubs in Spain, each with its own personality and style. They're funded by annual membership fees. As they can't make any profit, some actually put on impressive cultural events to spend their extra money.

Because the big risk is neighbors complaining about the noise or smell, clubs are often located in edgy neighborhoods, and are careful to keep an extremely low profile. Reputable clubs generally don't advertise, don't allow minors, keep their clientele quiet, and close at midnight (early by Spanish standards). In Spain, I was told, you can *smoke* with impunity. But if you *sell* even one joint, you might as well sell a kilo—the police take the sale of any amount very seriously.

Generally speaking, Spaniards know there's cheap stuff on the streets, but they prefer to pay more to join a club with predictable quality. Vaporizers may be the rage in the USA and much of Europe, but in Spain, they just don't sell. Whether tobacco or marijuana, Spaniards simply love the ritual of actually smoking.

While the Dutch and (to a lesser degree) the Spanish are lenient in their marijuana laws, many other European countries are also progressive on this issue. I've chatted with people passing a joint as they played backgammon in the shadow of the cathedral in Bern. They told me that marijuana enforcement is stricter in Switzerland each spring at the start of the travel season, so the country doesn't become a magnet for marijuana tourism. And I've talked with twentysomethings in Copenhagen rolling a joint on the steps of their City Hall. They explained that—because of an international trade agreement the US wrote and pushed through the United Nations—they have to be careful, because the Danish government is required to arrest a couple of pot smokers each year in order to maintain favored trade status with the United States.

The Swiss Approach to Hard Drugs

Marijuana is one thing. But hard drugs—such as heroin—are another. And, even as some European countries are liberalizing their approach to pot, they draw a clear distinction between "soft" and "hard" drugs. Hard drug abuse is a concern in Europe—with an estimated two million problem users—just as it is in the US. There is no easy solution. But the pragmatic European approach, based on harm reduction rather than punishment for an immoral act, appears to have had some success. Switzerland has been at the forefront of these efforts.

The last time I was in Switzerland, I dropped into a café in downtown Zürich, went into the bathroom…and it was all blue. I had stumbled into another example of a creative European drug policy. The Swiss, who don't want their junkies shooting up in public bathrooms, install blue lights. If you can't see your veins…you can't shoot up.

Of course, this minor frustration wouldn't stop junkies from finding a fix. Across the street is a machine that once sold cigarettes. Now it sells hygienic, government-subsidized syringes—two for a franc, less than a buck apiece. The Swiss recognize that heroin doesn't spread HIV/AIDS or other deadly diseases. Dirty needles do. Then, when addicts need to shoot up, they know they can go down the street to a heroin-maintenance clinic, where they get the services of a nurse and a counselor. Swiss society sees addicts as people who are sick rather than criminal, and would like to help addicts stay alive, get off welfare, and rejoin the workforce. Clinic workers told me that in Switzerland, crime and AIDS cases related to heroin use have decreased, while recovery and employment rates among their clients have increased.

When addicts aren't nervous about where they'll get their next fix, consumption goes down (as do overdoses). When demand on the streets goes down, so does the price. This brings down street violence…and is bad news for a pusher's bottom line. With clean needles and a source providing reliable purity, potency, and quantity, maintaining the addiction becomes less dangerous. With these provisions, you still have an addict—but you remove crime, violence, money, and disease from the equation, so you can treat it for what it is: a health problem for people who are screwing up their lives and need help. As Swiss addicts are safely dosed to maintenance levels, they begin to reclaim their lives, get jobs, pay taxes, and—in many cases—kick their habit altogether. Switzerland's heroin-maintenance centers (now also in Germany and the Netherlands) succeed in reducing the harm caused by drug abuse.

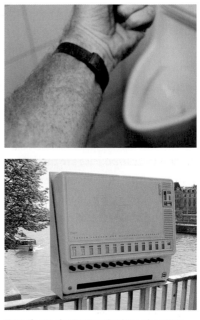

Top: If you don't want junkies shooting up in your toilet, just install blue lights. Bottom: Swiss machines that once sold cigarettes now sell government-subsidized syringes. When it comes to needles in Switzerland, no one shares.

While heroin-maintenance programs have been relatively successful, Europeans have tried and failed with other programs. For instance, experimental "needle parks" (places where the hard drug-taking community could gather) ended up attracting junkies and creating a public nuisance. These were abandoned for the more low-key maintenance centers. But at least Europeans are dealing with the challenge openly, innovatively, and compassionately.

In contrast, some observers suggest that the US's more punitive policies toward addicts cause "junkification": they marginalize addicts and drive them to dangerous, predatory behaviors—from simple stealing, to mugging, to prostitution, to selling drugs to others. In other words, if you treat heroin addicts like they're dangerous junkies…that's exactly what they'll become.

The casual American observer who sees more junkies on the streets of Europe than in the US may conclude they have a bigger drug problem because of their more lenient drug policies. In fact, according to the 2016 UN World Drug

Report, the percentage of Western Europeans who use illicit drugs is about half that of Americans. The difference is that theirs are out and about while working with these centers and trying to get their lives back on track. Ours are more often either dead or in jail. Through its busy maintenance centers, Switzerland has overseen literally millions of heroin fixes, and they've not had a single overdose death. The US is suffering a tragic opioid crisis, with well over 50,000 deaths in 2017 caused by overdoses. Meanwhile, Europe (with a larger population and roughly the same number of hard-drug addicts) loses only around 10,000. Sadly, recent White House policies are throwbacks that will make things worse, not better.

Like my European friends, I believe we can adopt a pragmatic policy toward both marijuana and hard drugs, with a focus on harm reduction and public health, rather than tough-talking but counterproductive criminalization. It's time to have an honest discussion about our drug laws and their effectiveness. I've learned from my travels that, when it comes to drug policy, you can be soft, hard…or smart.

The Portuguese Approach to All Drugs

What if *all* drugs were legal? One European country has attempted it, with results that may surprise you.

Portugal lived under a repressive right-wing dictator, Antonio Salazar, for a generation. Typical of repressed societies celebrating an end to tyranny, when the Portuguese rid themselves of their dictator (in 1974), many went overboard on their newfound freedoms. One consequence: a spike in people addicted to hard drugs.

In the 1980s and 1990s, little Portugal had about 100,000 hard drug addicts. A group of experts came together to find a solution to this problem. With the goal of establishing a legal framework for harm reduction, they enacted "Law 30," which effectively decriminalized the consumption of all drugs. As of 2001, severe criminal penalties for possessing small amounts of any drug were replaced with slap-on-the-wrist punishments.

After a decade, the new conservative government (which had, by then, replaced the more progressive government that established Law 30) assessed the law they once opposed, and deemed it to be smart and effective. The number of people who reported that they had tried various drugs increased a little (possibly because it is more comfortable to admit drug use when it's legal), but there was no significant change in routine use rates from the time when drugs were illegal. While use rates increased shortly after the new law went into effect, it dropped back down a few years later; similar use increases in Italy and Spain during this same time period suggest that the brief spike was unrelated to the new law. And drug use among adolescents actually declined with the implementation of Law 30.

Portugal now has half as many addicts, fewer people with HIV, and more people in treatment. The police, now freed up to focus on violent crime, appreciate the measure. The burden on Portugal's prisons and criminal system has lessened, and the relationship between the Portuguese government and its drug-using population went from adversarial to advocate. Even former opponents of the law have agreed that its benefits far outweigh its harms. Decriminalized drugs—both hard and soft—will continue to be Portuguese law of the land.

Every society needs to find its own solutions, and not every solution is a good fit for every society. But it is good to learn from other societies who are thinking out of the box to deal with problems that also plague our society. And Portugal's Law 30 certainly has drug policy experts paying attention.

Paths—and Barriers—to Legalization

With the thought-provoking success stories in the Netherlands, Spain, Switzerland, and Portugal, why don't more countries take a chance on experimenting with their drug laws? Simply put, they're afraid of US retribution. The United States, by way of the United Nations, has rigged the system to prevent change: If a country legalizes, it risks being "decertified" by the UN. This means it's disqualified from receiving foreign aid, and the US Congress is required to vote against them in trade policies—effectively sparking an expensive trade war. Even the United States' own drug czar is required by our government to vote to keep drugs illegal.

Europe has come up with clever ways around this. That's why you hear about "decriminalization" rather than "legalization." It's all about exploiting loopholes: Many European countries have anti-marijuana laws on the books, but choose not to enforce them. Even in the Netherlands, marijuana is still technically "illegal"; they've just legislated themselves around those laws (permitting the "gray area" of the law). Europe wants science over ideology.

Wealthy countries who want to legalize can tinker around this way because if they go too far, they can absorb the potential cost of a trade war with the USA. But poor countries, scraping to get by, simply can't afford the risk of trade sanctions and must carefully toe the line. In 2012, several Latin American countries (including Mexico, Costa Rica, Guatemala, El Salvador, and Colombia) began talking about the wisdom of taking the crime out of the drug equation to help alleviate some of the violence wracking their societies. The White House sent emissaries with a strong message to cool off, and Latin American leaders found themselves between a rock and a hard place when trying to take the violence and money out of their local drug wars. Observers note that in many ways, current drug laws are enriching organized crime throughout the world.

Perhaps this might change if some bold American states took the initiative to legalize marijuana and test the system. Oh, wait…that already happened.

Legal Pot in the United States

While decriminalization efforts in various European countries have tested the waters, legalization on US soil would be a game-changer worldwide. Like our international neighbors, American drug policy reformers have used loopholes to create provisions for medical marijuana in more than a dozen states. For example, in 2003, my hometown of Seattle voted to make enforcement of laws against recreational pot smoking the lowest priority for its police force.

After years of studying this topic, I decided to let my travels inform my actions and bring a European perspective to the drug policy reform movement in the USA. In 2012, I co-sponsored Washington State Initiative 502 (or "I-502" for short), a ballot measure to legalize, regulate, and tax the

In this scene under the Washington Capitol dome (from *Evergreen: The Road to Legalization*, a documentary about the effort to pass I-502; www.evergreendocumentary. com), my attempt to explain the wisdom of legalizing marijuana met with vocal resistance not from the anti-pot lobby...but from the pro-pot crowd, who felt our initiative didn't go far enough.

responsible and recreational use of marijuana among adults. I-502 would allow adults to buy up to one ounce of marijuana from state-licensed stores (much like the liquor store model).

Legislating legal marijuana in the United States is a prickly proposition. The framers of I-502 learned from mistakes made by previous failed attempts at legalization, and designed the initiative to thread the needle: legalizing marijuana in a public safety way rather than a pro-pot way. It would need to come with regulations rigid enough to allay the fears of more conservative voters. Key safeguards of I-502 included ensuring that marijuana remained illegal for those under 21; enforcing strict DUI provisions; assuring employers they could maintain any standards they wanted in their workplace; and levying taxes on the legal sale of marijuana.

In my state, before I-502, marijuana was the second biggest cash crop—rivaling apples. And it was all a black market, empowering organized crime. We wanted to redirect those proceeds to legitimate business…with a cut for the state. Of the $100 million in annual tax revenue we estimated would flow into our state's coffers, a certain percentage was earmarked for healthcare and drug abuse prevention work, including public education, counseling for marijuana abusers, and an ongoing evaluation of the new law.

Surprisingly, I-502 seemed to rankle some marijuana advocates more than it did conservatives. The pro-pot crowd bristled about its DUI provisions (fearing that enforcement against "driving while stoned" would increase—and that this could be used against legitimate medical marijuana users, who may have a high level of THC in their blood even if not impaired). They fretted that the law did not include a home-grow provision; marijuana could be cultivated legally only by licensed producers. And because consumption in public would remain illegal, it would kill the chance of convivial, Amsterdam coffeehouse-type hangouts.

This opposition didn't surprise us. Rather than "pro-pot," my partners and I were anti-prohibition. We knew that over time, the legislature can easily fine-tune parts of the law that were either too strict or too loose. For us, the big goal was simply to be the first political entity to actually legalize marijuana, recognizing its adult recreational use as a civil liberty. In other words, we wanted to solve the puzzle of how to break the black market and regulate the legal production and wholesale of marijuana.

In October of 2012, I went on a fascinating road trip through Washington State, speaking at 10 stops in 7 days in support of I-502. I shared an inspirational message at a Unitarian church in Spokane, hiked across a field with a farmer to see his huge "Hemp for Washington" sign overlooking the freeway outside of Yakima, sipped wine in a trendy Walla Walla winery with a pragmatic Republican legislator open to finding an alternative to our country's tired war on pot, and shared the stage with a Baptist minister whose African American community was taking the brunt of a war on drugs he considered racist.

Working diligently on our laptops and cellphones as we drove up the Columbia River Gorge, across the Palouse, through Spokane, and over Blewett Pass—and determinedly lobbying legislators, mayors, and city council members each lunch and evening—it occurred to us as kind of funny how different we were from many of the people whose civil liberties we were defending.

I got pretty good at framing legal pot in conservative terms, and it seemed to resonate with lots of people. (You can watch my stump speech by searching for "Rick Steves Spokane" on YouTube.) It wasn't just liberal newspapers that endorsed I-502. Thoughtful and open-minded people of all political stripes saw the wisdom of taking crime out of the equation. The only vigorous opposition we encountered was at the Washington State Capitol—from a noisy pro-marijuana gang who felt our law didn't go far enough. I suspect these were what I like to call "Pot Prohibition Profiteers"—people who profited from the fact that marijuana was illegal, and who saw legalization as a threat to their bottom line.

When the results came in on election night, the people of both Washington and Colorado voted to legalize, tax, and regulate marijuana. And it was a decisive win. In fact, more people in both states voted for marijuana than voted to re-elect President Obama.

It soon became clear that the stakes of Washington's and Colorado's legalization were global. While the US typically lags behind most of Europe on progressive issues, Washington's I-502 and Colorado's Amendment 44 thrust these two states ahead of even the most progressive European countries. Soon after the historic vote, a famously liberal European country (Denmark) imported Seattle know-how (City Attorney Pete Holmes) for help in restructuring its drug laws. And shortly thereafter, Uruguay became the first country on earth to risk the wrath of the US trade policy and legalize marijuana.

Domestically, civic and political leaders nationwide could now openly discuss this issue. Two states legalized…and the sky didn't fall. Others realized, "We can do it, too!"

But, as with other legalization efforts, we found ourselves in a legal "gray area." Regardless of the will of two states' voters, federal law still said

marijuana was illegal. Drug policy reformers waited tensely to hear whether the Department of Justice would clamp down. We breathed a sigh of relief when President Obama decided not to stand in the way of implementation, reasoning, "We've got bigger fish to fry." The president seemed to recognize that our country was designed for states to be the incubators of change.

After Washington and Colorado legalized in 2012, Oregon and Alaska followed in 2014. Then, in 2016, California, Nevada, Massachusetts, and Maine all voted to legalize, tax, and regulate the responsible adult use of marijuana for recreational purposes. With each election, I hit the road to help out. Barnstorming through Oregon in 2014, we didn't yet have an established track record regarding the legal sale of pot to point to. But by 2016—spending eight days in Massachusetts and Maine—I enjoyed explaining that the numbers were officially in: In states with legal marijuana, teen use doesn't go up, crime doesn't go up, and DUIs don't go up. The only thing that goes up is tax revenue. In 2016 alone, in Washington State, we didn't have to arrest an estimated 8,000 people, and we generated $160 million.

The next chapter of drug policy reform—in the United States, and abroad—is yet to be written. But I find it heartening that so many states have finally stood up to Washington, DC, and voted to take the crime out of marijuana: treating its abuse as a health and education challenge; ending a massive black market that has enriched and emboldened gangs and organized crime; and finally accepting its use by mature and responsible adults as a civil liberty. For me, my ability to bring a European perspective to drug policy reform in the US has been a good example of making travel a political act—and it's been fun, too.

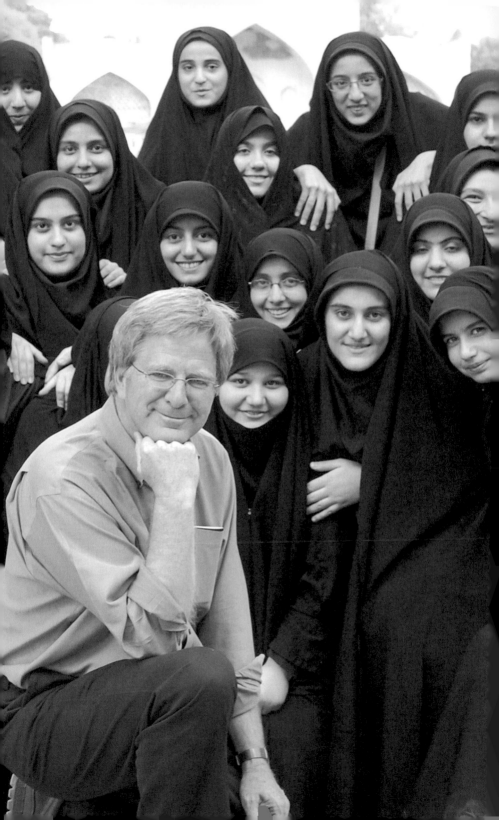

Chapter 8
Mission: Understand Iran

In early 2008, a friend from the Washington State chapter of the United Nations Association called me and asked what I could do to help them build understanding between Iran and the US, and to help defuse the tension that could lead to war. I answered, "The only thing of any consequence I could do would be to produce a TV show on Iran." Over the next few months, I wrote a proposal for a public television show—no politics, just travel. The title was *Iran: Yesterday and Today.*

When this project began, like most Americans, I knew next to nothing about Iran. It was a journey of discovery…all caught on film. My hope was to enjoy a rich and fascinating culture, to get to know a nation that's a leader in its corner of the world (and has been for 2,500 years), and to better understand the 70 million people who call Iran home.

I'm convinced that people-to-people travel experiences can be a powerful force for peace. Americans traveling to the Soviet Union helped us get through the Cold War without things turning hot. Travel to Vietnam has helped heal wounds left in the aftermath of that war. And, as the USA and Iran continue their dangerous flirtation with an avoidable war, travel there can help build understanding between our nations.

Knowing that many Americans won't likely actually travel to Iran, my TV crew and I wanted to bring the travel experience home to America. Rather than focus on Iran's well-documented offenses—their alleged funding of terrorists, threats to Israel, and nuclear ambitions—I simply wanted to better understand Iran's people and culture in the hopes that we can sort out our differences peacefully and more smartly. Contrary to the common practice of a nation dehumanizing the enemy as a prelude to war, I believe if you're going to bomb a place, you should know its people first. Even if military force is justified, it should hurt when you kill someone.

My Iran mission turned out to be not only an enjoyable travel experience, but one of the most gratifying projects I've ever taken on. In addition to addressing some of the deep rifts between our two societies, this chapter also offers a behind-the-scenes peek at traveling and filming in this mysterious country.

The Pilot Said, "We're Taking this Plane to Tehran"... and Nobody Was Alarmed

Flying from Istanbul's Atatürk Airport to Tehran's Khomeini Airport, I thought about other airports my fellow passengers likely used—Reagan and De Gaulle. The airports are named after four very different 20th-century leaders, but each one left an indelible mark on his nation.

Suddenly it occurs to our producer, Simon, that the plane is filled with Iranians...and everyone has been given a metal knife.

The plane was filled with well-off Iranian people. Their features were different from mine, but they dressed and acted just like me. As so often happens when I travel, I was struck by how people—regardless of the shapes of their noses—are so similar the world over. As we all settled into the wide-body jet, I wished the big decision-makers of our world weren't shielded from an opportunity to share an economy cabin with regular people like those who surrounded me.

I had made a similar Istanbul-to-Tehran trip 30 years before. Last time it took three days on a bus, and the Shah was on his last legs. Wandering through Iranian towns in 1978, I remember riot squads in the streets and the Shah's portrait seeming to hang tenuously in market stalls. Seeing dispirited peasants leaning against high-rise banks, I also recall being struck by the harsh gap between rich and poor in Tehran. I was 23 years old and confronted with realities that my friends who stayed home were oblivious to. I believe that was the first time in my life I was angered by economic injustice.

My Istanbul-Tehran trip was quicker this time—three hours rather than three days. And every main square and street that had been named "Shah" back then was now named "Khomeini." On my 1978 visit, all denominations of paper money had the same face on them. In 2008, they still did...but the face was different.

As the pilot began our descent, rich and elegant Persian women put on their scarves as routinely as buckling their seatbelts. With all that hair suddenly covered, I noticed how striking long hair can be—how it really does grab a man's attention. Looking out the window into the night, the lights of Tehran's millions of inhabitants seemed to stretch forever. Greater Tehran has more people than the entire country of Greece (where I had woken up that morning).

I thought of the chaotic path that had led me to this point. The permissions had been so slow in coming that the project only became a certainty about a week before the shoot. Because the US does not maintain a diplomatic relationship with Iran, the only way we could communicate was indirectly, via the Iranian Interest Section at the Pakistani Embassy. It was exhilarating to go into a relaxed, almost no-security Iranian Embassy in Athens…and walk out with visas.

Why was Iran letting us in? They actually want to boost Western tourism. I would think this might frighten the Iranian government, since tourists could bring in unwanted ideas (like those that prompted the USSR to restrict tourism back in the 1980s). But Iran wants more visitors nonetheless. They also believe that the Western media have made their culture look menacing, and never show its warm, human, and gracious side. They did lots of background research on me and my work, and apparently concluded that my motives were acceptable. They said that, while they'd had problems with other American network crews, they'd had good experiences with PBS film crews.

Not that we were planning to glorify Iran. While I was excited to learn about the rich

Our "welcome" included building-sized anti-US murals showing American flags with stars of skulls and dropping bombs painting the stripes.

tapestry of Iranian culture and history, I also recognized that I couldn't ignore some of the fundamental cultural differences. I felt a responsibility to show the reality that women face in Iran, and to try to understand why Iranians always seem to be chanting "Death to America." We wanted to be free-spirited and probing, but not abuse the trust of the Iranian government.

As the plane touched down, I felt a wince of anxiety. This was a strange land for me—and therefore frightening. We had considered leaving our big camera in Greece and just taking the small one. Nervous even about the availability of electricity, I had made sure all my electrical stuff was charged up before leaving Greece. And there were questions: How free would we actually be? Would the hotel rooms be bugged? Was there really absolutely no alcohol—even in fancy hotels? Would crowds gather around us, and then suddenly turn angry?

I was about to set foot in what just might be the most surprising land I've ever visited.

Tehran: Iran's Mile-High Metropolis

By my first night in Tehran, it was already clear that Iran was an intriguing and complex paradox: playful Revolutionary Guards, four-lane highways intersecting with no traffic lights, "Death to America" murals, and big, warm, welcoming smiles.

Tehran, a youthful and noisy capital city, is the modern heart of this country. It's a smoggy, mile-high metropolis. With a teeming population of 14 million in the metropolitan area, its apartment blocks stretch far into the surrounding mountains.

I stepped out onto the 15th-floor balcony of my fancy hotel room to hear the hum of the city. I enjoyed the view of a vast, twinkling city at twilight. Fresh snow capped the mountains above the ritzy high-rise condos of North Tehran.

As I looked straight down, I noticed the hotel's entryway buzzing with activity, as it was hosting a conference on Islamic unity. The circular driveway was lined by the flags of 30 nations. Huge collections of flags seemed to be common in Iran—perhaps because it provided a handy opportunity to exclude the Stars and Stripes. (The only American flags I saw during the trip were the ones featured in hateful political murals.)

A van with an X-ray security checkpoint was permanently parked outside the entrance, carefully examining the bags of each visitor. It was interesting to see that Iran, a country we feel we need to protect ourselves from, had its own security headaches.

Back in my room, I nursed a tall glass of pomegranate juice. My lips were puckered from munching lemony pistachios from an elegantly woven tray—the best I've ever tasted (and I am a pistachio connoisseur). I cruised the channels on my TV: CNN, BBC, and—rather than shopping channels— lots of programming designed to set the mood for prayer. One channel

showed a mesmerizing river with water washing lovingly over shiny rocks. Another featured the sun setting on Mecca, with live coverage of the pilgrim action at the Kaaba. I was a long way from home…and ready to explore.

Freedom to Film?

The nuts and bolts of filming in Iran were challenging. Our 12-day Iran shoot included Tehran, Esfahan, Shiraz, and Persepolis. I traveled with my typical skeleton crew of three: Simon Griffith (director), Karel Bauer (cameraman), and me. We also had the help of two Iranian guides: One was Abdi Sami, an Iranian-American friend who lived in Seattle. The other was Seyed, appointed by the Iranian government to be with us at all times. This combination was interesting…and tricky.

Traveling through Iran as a film crew presented us with some unique hurdles. On the first day, we dropped by the foreign press office to get our press badges. A properly covered woman took mug shots for our badges and carefully confirmed the pronunciation of our names in order to transliterate them into squiggly Farsi characters.

The travel agency—overseen by the "Ministry of Islamic Guidance"—assigned us what they called a "guide," but what I'd call a "government minder." Our guide/minder, Seyed, was required to follow our big camera wherever it went—even if that meant climbing on the back of a motorcycle taxi to follow our cameraman as he filmed a "point-of-view" shot through wild traffic. When

Our guide Seyed (far left) was expected to follow our camera at all times. Hang on tight and follow that taxi!

he wasn't holding on for dear life, Seyed slipped a tiny camera out of his pocket and documented our shoot—filming us as we filmed Iran.

While this sounds constraining, Seyed proved to be a big help to our production. Whenever we filmed a place of commercial or religious importance, a plainclothes security guard would appear. Then we'd

I like to sit cross-legged on the floor while writing. Routinely I'd look up from my note-taking and see Iranians gathered, curious, and wanting to talk.

wait around while Seyed explained who we were and what we were doing. In Iran, it seemed that no single authority was in charge—many arms of government overlapped and made rules that conflicted with each other. Seyed made our filming possible…or told us when it wasn't.

Permission to film somewhere was limited to a specific time window. Even if we were allowed to film a certain building on a given day, it didn't mean we could shoot it on a different day, or from the balcony of an adjacent tea house (where we didn't have permission), or from an angle, for instance, that showed a bank (since banks cannot be filmed).

My critics back home skeptically predicted that our access would be very limited—to only the prettiest sights. (Meanwhile, Iranians I met were convinced that I'd doctor our footage to make Iran look ugly and dangerous.) In reality, it was far less restrictive than we'd expected. Some subjects were forbidden for reasons of security (banks, government, military) or modesty ("un-veiled" women). But because we weren't filming an "exposé," we were allowed to shoot all that we needed to—including some provocative subjects, such as anti-American or anti-Israeli murals (more on these later).

We were also free to talk with and film people on the street, but this was a bit difficult. When our camera was rolling, it reminded me of my early trips to the USSR, when only those with nothing to lose would risk talking openly.

Welcoming travelers is a traditional Muslim value...and being an American makes you the most popular kid in the village.

At other times, such as when the crew was busy setting up a shot, I was free to roam about on my own and have fun meeting the locals. I have never traveled to a place where I had such an easy and enjoyable time connecting with people. Iranians were as confused and fascinated by me as I was by them.

Bombast and the "Axis of Evil"

Even from the first moments of this trip, it was clear that the people of Iran would be the biggest joy of our visit. Iranians consider visitors to be a gift from God…and treat them that way.

People greeted me with a smile. Invariably, they asked where I was from. I often said, "You tell me." They guessed and guessed, running through five or six countries before giving up. When I finally told them, "America," they'd be momentarily shocked. They seemed to be thinking, "I thought Americans hate us. Why would one be here like this?" The smile left their face. Then a bigger smile came back as they said, "Welcome!" or "I love America!"

In a hundred such interactions in our 12 days in Iran, never once did my saying "I am an American" result in anything less than a smile or a kind of "Ohhh, you are rich and strong," or "People and people together no problem, but I don't like your Mr. Bush." (It seemed that Iranians liked our president as much as Americans liked Iran's.) I found it ironic that during the Bush years, Americans found they were better off keeping a low profile in most foreign countries. But in a country I was told hated me, my nationality was a real plus absolutely everywhere I went.

The disparity between the warm welcome I received and the "Axis of Evil" and "Death to America" bickering of our two governments got me thinking about bombast and history.

The word "axis" conjures up images of the alliance of Hitler, Mussolini, and Hirohito that our fathers and grandfathers fought in World War II.

People in these countries now believe that each of these leaders helped maintain his power with his ability to stir the simplistic side of his electorate with fear-mongering bombast. Today, such exaggerated rhetoric still hogs the headlines, pitting good people from different countries against each other.

During my visit, Iran's president was Mahmoud Ahmadinejad, who had achieved a kind of Hugo Chavez notoriety around the West for his wild and provocative statements and actions: calling for Israel to be "wiped off the map," denying the existence of the Holocaust, insisting on Iran's right to nuclear arms, and persecuting gay people in Iran. Ahmadinejad was an ideologue, and Americans who found him outrageous were fully justified.

But, much as we might viscerally disagree with Ahmadinejad—or other Iranian rulers—it's dangerous to simply dismiss them as madmen. To these people, and to their followers, their logic does make sense: If Germany killed the Jews, why are Palestinians (rather than Germans) being displaced to house the survivors? Everyone in Iran seemed to understand—better, perhaps, than we foreigners—that Ahmadinejad was more extreme than the Supreme Leader, Ayatollah Ali Khamenei. And, crucially, the Supreme Leader is more powerful than the president. Many locals I talked with discounted Ahmadinejad's most outrageous claims as overstatements intended to shore up his political base. While that doesn't justify the hateful images and slogans I couldn't avoid as I explored his country, it might help explain them.

Meanwhile, Iranians get just as fired up about the rhetoric of American politicians. On the campaign trail in recent years, everyone from John McCain ("Bomb-bomb-bomb, bomb-bomb Iran") to Hillary Clinton (the US would "obliterate" Iran if it attacked Israel) to Donald Trump ("officially putting Iran on notice") has talked tough on Iran—making it clear that an anti-Iran stance is always in style. For Iranians, hearing high-profile representatives of the world's lone superpower talk this way was terrifying. Unfortunately, that fear enables people like Ahmadinejad to

Iranian government propaganda depicts the US and Israel as sinister partners in a quest for global domination.

Most Iranians genuinely like Americans.

demonize America in order to stay in power.

Like American children start school days pledging "allegiance to one nation, under God," Iranian kids are taught their nation's values. Rather than marketing products to consume, billboards sell an ideology. Some are uplifting, such as Shia scripture reminding people that there is wisdom in compassion. Many others glorify heroes who died as martyrs, taunt the US, cheer for Hezbollah, trumpet "Death to America" and "Death to Israel," and so on. These murals mix fear, religion, patriotism, and a heritage of dealing with intrusions from the West.

Many things I experienced in Iran fit the negative image that I'd seen back home. But the more I traveled there, the more apparent it became that the standard, media-created image of Iran in the USA was not the whole story. I simply couldn't reconcile the fear-mongering and hate-filled billboards with the huge smiles and genuine hospitality we received on the ground.

Ask anyone who has lived in a country where they disagree with the leaders: Attention-grabbing bombast does not necessarily reflect the feelings of the man or woman on the street. Throughout my visit, I kept thinking: Politicians come and go. The people are here to stay.

Death to...Whatever!

Traffic is notorious in Tehran. Drivers may seem crazy, but I was impressed by their expertise at keeping things moving. At some major intersections, there were no lights—eight lanes would come together at right angles, and everyone just shuffled through. The people are great drivers, and, somehow, it works. (It inspired me to drive more aggressively when I got home.)

While the traffic is hair-raising, it's not noisy. Because of a history of motorcycle bandits and assassinations, only smaller, less powerful (and therefore quieter) motorcycles are allowed. To get somewhere in a hurry, motorcycle taxis are a blessing. While most Iranians ignore helmet laws, I was more cautious. Being handed a helmet with paint scuffed onto it, I was warned, "It's better to leave a little paint on passing buses than a piece of scalp."

Adding to the chaotic traffic mix are pedestrians, doing their best to navigate the wild streets. Locals joke that when you set out to cross a big street, you "go to Chechnya" (the treacherous region of Russia infamously torn by civil strife). I was told that Iran loses more than 30,000 people on the roads each year (in cars and on foot).

While in Tehran, we were zipped smoothly around by Majid, our driver. Majid navigated our eight-seat bus like a motor scooter, weaving in and out of traffic that stayed in its lanes like rocks in a landslide. To illustrate how clueless I was in Iran, for three days I called him "Najaf." And whenever a bit of filming went well and we triumphantly returned to the car, I gave him an enthusiastic thumbs-up. But finally Majid patiently explained that I'd been confusing his name with a city in Iraq…and that giving someone a thumbs-up in Iran is very rude—like giving them the finger.

While the traffic is enough to make you scream, people are incredibly good-humored on the road. I never heard angry horns honking. One time, while stalled in a Tehran jam, people in a neighboring car saw me sitting patiently in the back of our van. They rolled down their window and handed Majid a bouquet of flowers, saying, "Give this to your visitor and apologize for our traffic."

Later, as we struggled to drive along a horribly congested street, Majid suddenly declared, "Death to traffic." This outburst caught my attention. I said, "I thought it was 'Death to America' or 'Death to Israel.'" He explained,

Cars merge through major intersections without traffic lights as if that's the norm. Surprisingly...it works.

"No, right now, it's 'Death to traffic.'" I asked him to explain. He said, "Here in Iran, when something frustrates us and we have no control over it, this is what we say. 'Death to traffic. Death to…whatever.'"

The casual tone of Majid's telling aside made me think differently about one of the biggest concerns many Americans have about Iranians: Their penchant for declaring "Death to" this and that. Did Majid literally want to kill all those drivers that were in our way? Of course not. His English was pretty basic, and he was merely attempting to translate the word "damn": "Damn this traffic jam!" If we say, "Damn those teenagers," do we really want them to die and burn in hell for eternity? Not yet…just turn down the music.

Don't get me wrong: The "Death to America" and "Death to Israel" murals are impossible to justify. But they seemed so incongruous with the gregarious people I met. Do the Iranians literally wish "death" to the US and Israel? Or is it a mix of language barrier, international road rage, fear, frustration—and the seductive clarity of a catchy slogan?

No Credit Cards, No Alcohol...No Urinals

While pondering weighty issues can be thought-provoking, the little everyday differences you encounter while traveling are vividly memorable. As I journeyed through Iran, my notebook filled with quirky observations. One moment, I'd be stirred by propaganda murals encouraging young men to walk into the blazing sunset of martyrdom. The next, a woman in a bookstore served me cookies while I browsed. Then, as I was about to leave without buying anything, she gave me—free of charge—a book I'd admired.

While English is the second language on many signs, and young, well-educated people routinely speak English, communication was often challenging.

Most Iranians are ethnically Persian. Persians are not Arabs, and they don't speak Arabic—they speak Persian (also called Farsi). This Persian/Arab

In this mural (filling the entire wall of a building), martyrs walk heroically into the sunset of death for God and country.

In a bookstore, a clerk patiently showed me fine poetry books. As we left, she gave me a book for free.

difference is a very important distinction to the people of Iran. I heard over and over again, "We are not Arabs!"

The squiggly local script looked like Arabic to me, but I learned that, like the language, it's Farsi. The numbers, however, are the same as those used in the Arab world. Thankfully, when I needed it, I found that they also use the same numbers we do.

Iran is a cash society. Because of the three-decade-old American embargo here, Western credit cards didn't work. No ATMs for foreigners meant that I had to bring in big wads of cash... and learn to count carefully. The money came with lots of zeros. One dollar was equal to 10,000 *rial*. A *toman* is ten *rial*, and some prices are listed in *rial*, others in *toman*...a tourist rip-off just waiting to happen. I had a shirt laundered at the hotel for "20,000." Was that in *rial* ($2)—or in *toman* ($20)?

People in Iran need to keep track of three different calendars: Persian (for local affairs), Islamic (for religious affairs), and Western (for dealing with the outside world). What's the year? It depends: After the great Persian empire—some 2,500 years ago; after Muhammad—about 1,400 years ago; or after Christ—just over 2,000 years ago.

Of course, the Islamic government legislates women's dress and public behavior (we'll get to that later). Men are also affected, to a lesser degree. Neckties are rarely seen, as they're considered the mark of a Shah supporter. And there seem to be no urinals anywhere. (I did an extensive search—at the airport, swanky hotels, the university, the fanciest coffee shops—and never saw one.) I was told that Muslims believe you don't get rid of all

While Washington made it on our one-dollar bill, Khomeini made it on every denomination in Iran.

your urine when you urinate standing up. For religious reasons, they squat. I found this a bit time-consuming. In a men's room with 10 urinals, a guy knows at a glance what's available; in a men's room with 10 doors, you have to go knocking. (And now I can empathize with women who do this all the time.)

Seyed made sure we ate in comfortable (i.e., high-end) restaurants, generally in hotels. Restaurants used Kleenex rather than napkins; there was a box of tissues on every dining table. Because Iran is a tea culture, the coffee at breakfast was Nescafé-style instant. Locals assured me that tap water was safe to drink, but I stuck with the bottled kind. Iran is strictly "dry"—absolutely no booze or beer in public.

From a productivity point of view, it seemed as if the country were on Valium. Perhaps Iranians are just not driven as we are by capitalist values to "work hard" in order to enjoy material prosperity. I heard that well-employed Iranians made $5,000 to $15,000 a year, and paid essentially no tax. (Taxes are less important to a government funded by oil.) While the Islamic Revo-

Because Iran is "dry," would-be beer-drinkers seem to fanta-size. They drink a "malt beverage" that tastes like beer and comes in a beer can, but is non-alcoholic.

lution is not anti-capitalistic, the business metabolism felt like a communist society: There seemed to be a lack of incentive to really be efficient. Measuring productivity at a glance, I assessed that things were pretty low-energy.

I couldn't help but think how tourism could boom here if they just opened up. There were a few Western tourists (mostly Germans, French, Brits, and Dutch). All seemed to be on a tour, with a private guide, or visiting relatives. Control gets tighter or looser depending on the political climate, but basically American tourists could visit only with a guided tour. I met no one just exploring on their own. The Lonely Planet guidebook, which is excellent, dominated the scene—it seemed every Westerner in Iran had one. Tourists are so rare, and major tourist sights are so few and obvious, that I bumped into the same travelers day after day. Browsing through picture books and calendars showing the same 15 or 20 images of the top sights in Iran, I was impressed by how our short trip would manage to include most of them.

With my travel sensibilities tingling from all these discoveries, I was excited to visit the University of Tehran. There I hoped to find another side of Iran: highly educated, liberated women and an environment of freedom.

I assumed that in Iran, as in most societies, the university would be where people run free…barefoot through the grass of life, leaping over silly limits just because they can.

But instead, the University of Tehran—the country's oldest, largest, and most prestigious university—made BYU look like Berkeley. Subsidized by the government, the U. of T. followed the theocracy's guidelines to a T: a strictly enforced dress code, no nonconformist posters, top-down direction for ways to play, segregated cafeterias…and students toeing the line (in public, at least).

Hoping to interact with some students, I asked for a student union center (the lively place where students come together, as on Western campuses). But there was none. Each faculty had a canteen where kids could hang out, with a sales counter separating two sections—one for boys and one for girls.

In the US, I see university professors as a bastion of free thinking, threatening (in a constructive way) to people who care about the status quo more than freedom. In Tehran, I found a situation where the theocracy was clearly shaping the curriculum, faculty, and tenor of the campus. Conformity on any university campus saddens me. But seeing it in Iran—a society that desperately needs some nonconformity—was the most disheartening experience of my entire trip.

Imagine Every Woman's a Nun

My visit to the university jolted me back into the reality of traveling in a society where morality is legislated—where a crime is a sin, and a sin is a crime. In their day-to-day lives, the women of Iran are keenly aware of the impact of living in a theocracy. The days when the Shah's men boasted that miniskirts were shorter in Tehran than they were in Paris are long gone. In the post-Islamic Revolution Iran, modesty rules, and the dress and behavior of women are carefully controlled.

While things are casual at home, Iranian women are expected not to show their

Given the strict dress code, the face is an Iranian woman's powerful tool. If the nose isn't quite right, it can be fixed. We saw many nose jobs healing. And those eyes…truly a contact sport.

hair or show off the shape of their body in public. This means that, when out and about, a proper woman covers everything except her face and hands. There are two key components to traditional dress: Hijab ("hih-JOB") means to be dressed modestly, with the head covered under a scarf. The chador ("shah-DORE") is a head-to-toe black cloak wrapped around the front and over the head. In public, all women must follow hijab rules, and many older, rural, and traditional women choose to wear a chador.

In addition to the dress code, Iranian women face other limitations. They're relegated to separate classrooms. While they are welcome at more genteel sports, they're not allowed to attend soccer games (for fear that they might overhear some foul language from the impassioned fans).

From a Western viewpoint, it's disrespectful to impose various modesty regulations on women. But from a strict Muslim perspective, it's the opposite: Mandated modesty is a sign of great respect. In the Islamic Republic of Iran, women's bodies are not vehicles for advertising. Having scantily clad babes selling cars at a trade show makes perfect sense to most Americans. But that would be considered disrespectful, and therefore unacceptable, in Iran. You don't see sexy magazines. There is almost no public display of affection. In theory, the dress code provides a public "uniform," allowing men and women to work together without the distractions of sex and flirtation.

Still not buying it? You're not the only one. Local surveys indicate that about 70 percent of these women would dress more freely in public, if allowed. Many push the established bounds of decency— with belts defining the shape of their bodies and scarves pulled back to show voluptuous cascades of hair—when out on the streets. When

On the subway, there are women-only cars. When I questioned an Iranian woman about this—mentioning that, for many Americans, a "women-only car" struck them as an affront to women's rights—she said, "Women are welcome to ride with the men in the regular cars, but many times they are more comfortable in the women's cars. Perhaps the women of New York wish they had a car only for them, to avoid the men on their subway trains."

filming, I found the women's awareness of our camera fascinating—they
seemed to sense when it was near,
and would adjust their scarves to be
sure their hair was properly covered.

In spite of attempts to enforce
modesty, vanity is not out of bounds.
Women still utilize their feminine
charms. In a land where showing
any cleavage in public is essentially
against the law, a tuft of hair above the
forehead becomes the exciting place a
man's eye tends to seek out. Cosmetic

Women are covered, yet beautiful...
a wisp of hair can be ravishing.

surgery—especially nose jobs—is big business here among the middle class.
Faces are beautifully made up, and—when so much else is covered—can be
particularly expressive and mysterious. Throughout Iran, I was enthralled
by the eye contact.

Trying to grasp Iran's mandated modesty in Christian terms, I imagined
living in a society where every woman is forced to dress like a nun. Seeing
spunky young Muslim women chafing at their modesty requirements, I kept
humming, "How do you solve a problem like Maria?"

Iran's "Revolution of Values": Living in a Theocracy

The status of women in Iranian society is just one of many ways in which
Iran's theocracy affects everyday life. For example, as I settled into a plane
that flew our crew between two Iranian towns, the pilot announced, "In
the name of God the compassionate and merciful, we welcome you to
this flight. Now fasten your seatbelts." Even though Iran is technically a
"Shia democracy" with an elected president, the top cleric—a man called
the "Supreme Leader"—has the ultimate authority. His picture (not the
president's) is everywhere.

The seeds of the Islamic Republic of Iran were sown during the Islamic
Revolution in 1979. The rebellion, with its spiritual leader Ayatollah Khomeini,
led to the overthrow of the US-backed Shah and the taking of 52 Americans
hostage for 444 days. As a gang of students captured the world's attention
by humiliating the US, this was a great event for the revolutionaries...and
a wrenching one for Americans.

The former US Embassy, where the crisis took place, was a stop on our filming route. Our minder/guide, Seyed, seemed almost proud to let us walk the long wall of anti-American murals. He encouraged us to film it, making sure we knew when the light was best for the camera.

As I walked along the wall, it occurred to me that the crisis had happened three decades ago. While it remains a sore spot for many Americans, Iranians—most of whom weren't even born at the time—appeared content to let the murals fade in the sun. The murals seemed to drone on like an unwanted call to battle…a call that people I encountered had simply stopped hearing. In fact, looking back, many Iranians believe that the hostage crisis hijacked their Revolution. By radicalizing their country, it succeeded in putting things in the hands of the more hardline clerics.

Today the Islamic Revolution has become deeply ingrained. After chatting with one young man, who didn't look particularly compliant with the Revolution, we said goodbye. Later—after he'd thought about our conversation—he returned to tell me, "One present from you to me, please. You must read Quran. Is good. No politics." Looking at the evangelical zeal in his eyes, I realized that he had just as earnest a concern for my soul as a pair of well-dressed Mormons who might stop me on the street back home. Why should a Muslim evangelist be any more surprising (or annoying, or menacing) than a Christian one? He simply cared about me.

Thirty years later, the former US Embassy wall is still lined with hateful political posters.

Seeing the Ayatollah Khomeini from the Iranian perspective was jarring: Rather than the impression I'd long held—of a threatening, unsmiling ideologue—many Iranians consider Khomeini a lovable sage...unpretentious, approachable, and a defender of traditional values. After the Shah's excesses and corruption,

For many Iranians, what they would call "family values" trumps democracy and freedom. That's why they follow a supreme leader: Khomeini (right) and his successor Ali Khamenei (left).

locals seemed to overlook Khomeini's sanctioning of brutal tactics. Khomeini's simplicity and holiness had a strong appeal to the Iranian masses. Locals told me that Khomeini had charisma, and if he walked into a room, even I, a non-Muslim, would feel it. To the poor and the simple country folk, Khomeini was like a messiah. As the personification of the Islamic Revolution, he symbolized deliverance from the economic and cultural oppression of the Shah. Khomeini gave millions of Iranians hope. (Khomeini's less charismatic successor, Ayatollah Ali Khamenei, has had much less of an impact on the people.)

Iranians who support the Revolution call it a "Revolution of Values." Many conservative Iranians I met told me they want to raise their children without exposure to cheap sex, disrespectful clothing, drug abuse, and materialism—all things they associate with America, and all things that, they believe, erode character and threaten their traditional values. It worries them as parents. It seemed to me that many of them willingly trade democracy and political freedom for a society free of Western values (or, they'd say, "lack of values"). It's more important to them to have a place to raise their children that fits their faith and their cherished notion of "family values."

One day, while filming on the street, a woman walked up to me and asked if I was an American journalist. I said yes. She tapped her finger repeatedly on my chest and said, "You go home and tell your friends the truth: We're strong...we're united...and we just don't want our little girls raised to be like Britney Spears." She had heard the rhetoric of "regime change," and she worried that if we installed "another shah" on the throne, her daughter's values would be hijacked—Westernized—and she'd become a boy toy, a drug addict, and a crass materialist.

Of course, there's plenty of drug addiction, materialism, and casual sex in Iran. But these vices are pretty well hidden from the determination of the theocracy to root them out. In general, the Revolution seems to be well-established. For example, in terms of commercialism, Iran and the US stand at opposite extremes. Back home, just about everywhere we look, we are inundated by advertising encouraging us to consume. Airports are paid to drone commercials on loud TVs. Magazines are beefy with slick ads. Sports stars wear corporate logos. Our media are shaped and driven by corporate marketing. But in Iran, Islam reigns. Billboards, Muzak, TV programming, and young people's education all trumpet the teachings of great Shia holy men…at the expense of the economy. Consequently, many in Iranian society tune into Western media via satellites, the Internet, and social media, and barely watch Iranian media.

Despite all of this, when it comes to religion, I was surprised by the general mellowness of the atmosphere in Iran compared to other Muslim countries I've visited. Except for the strict women's dress codes and the lack of American products and businesses (because of the US embargo), life on the streets in Iran was much the same as in secular cities elsewhere. In fact, ironically, despite the aggressively theocratic society, the country felt no more spiritual than neighboring, secular Muslim nations. During my visit, I didn't see spiny minarets and didn't hear calls to prayer—a strong contrast to my visit to Istanbul during Ramadan (described in Chapter 6).

Iranians are constantly reminded that charity is Muhammad-like. With a religious offering box on literally every street corner, extra money is raised for orphanages, schools, and hospitals.

While the focus of my trip was on the people rather than the politics, Iran's theocracy makes civil rights concerns unavoidable. Civil liberties for women, religious minorities, and critics of the government are the mark of any modern, free, and sustainable democracy. I believe that, given

Esfahan's great Imam Mosque is both a tourist attraction and a vibrant place of worship.

time and a chance to evolve on their cultural terms, the will of any people ultimately prevails. But in Iran, that time is not yet here. For now, this country is not free. (And no one here claims it is—locals told me, "Iranian democracy: We are given lots of options…and then the government makes the choice for us.") A creepiness that comes with a "big brother" government pervaded the place. Every day during my visit, I wondered how free-minded Iranians cope.

While the Islamic Republic of Iran's constitution does not separate mosque and state, it does allow for other religions…with provisions. I asked Seyed if people must be religious here. He said, "In Iran, you can be whatever religion you like, as long as it is not offensive to Islam." Christian? "Sure." Jewish? "Sure." Bahá'i? "No. We believe Muhammad—who came in the seventh century—was the last prophet. The Bahá'i prophet, Bahá'u'lláh, came in the 19th century. Worshipping someone who came after Muhammad is offensive to Muslims. That is why the Bahá'i faith is not allowed in Iran."

I asked, "So Christians and Jews are allowed. But what if you want to get somewhere in the military or government?" Seyed answered, "Then you'd better be a Muslim." I added, "A practicing Shia Muslim?" He said, "Yes."

Friday: Let Us Pray

Esfahan, Iran's "second city" with over three million people, is a showcase of ancient Persian splendor. One of the finest cities in Islam, and famous for its dazzling blue-tiled domes and romantic bridges, Esfahan is also just plain enjoyable. I'm not surprised that in Iran, this is the number-one honeymoon destination.

Everything in Esfahan seems to radiate from the grand Imam Square, dominated by the Imam Mosque—one of the holiest in Iran. Dating from the early 1600s, its towering facade is as striking as the grandest cathedrals of Europe.

We were in Iran for just one Friday, the Muslim "Sabbath." Fortunately, we were in Esfahan, so we could attend (and film) a prayer service at this colossal house of worship.

Filming in a mosque filled with thousands of worshippers required permission. Explaining our needs to administrators there, it hit me that the Islamic Revolution employs strategies similar to a communist takeover: Both maintain power by installing partisans in key positions. But the ideology Iran is enforcing is not economic (as it was in the USSR), but religious.

President Ahmadinejad had inspired a fashion trend in Iran: simple dark suit, white shirt, no tie, light black beard. Reminiscent of apparatchiks in Soviet times, it seemed to me that all the mosque administrators dressed the part. They actually looked like their president.

To film the service—which was already well underway—we were escorted in front of 2,000 people praying. When we had visited this huge mosque the day before, it was nearly empty—a lifeless shell with fine tiles for tourists to photograph. An old man had stood in the center of the floor and demonstrated the haunting echoes created by the perfect construction. Old carpets had been rolled up and were strewn about like dusty cars in a haphazard parking lot. Today the carpets were rolled out, cozy, orderly, and covered with worshippers.

I felt self-conscious—a tall, pale American tiptoeing gingerly

As everyone bowed down in prayer, they revealed soldiers providing security and a "Death to Israel" banner.

over the little tablets Shia Muslim men place their heads on when they bend down to pray. Planting our tripod in the corner, we observed.

As my brain wandered (just like it sometimes does at home when listening to a sermon), I felt many of those worshippers were looking at me rather than listening to their cleric speaking. Soldiers were posted throughout the mosque, standing like statues in their desert-colored fatigues. When the congregation stood, I didn't notice them, but when all bowed, the soldiers remained

standing—a reminder of the tension within the Islamic world. I asked Seyed to translate a brightly painted banner above the worshippers. He answered, "Death to Israel."

Despite this disturbing detail, I closed my eyes and let the smell of socks remind me of mosques I'd visited in other Muslim countries. I pulled out my little Mecca compass, the only souvenir I'd purchased so far. Sure enough, everyone was facing exactly the right way.

Watching all the worshippers

After the service, the cleric was eager to talk with us.

bow and stand, and pray in unison, at first seemed threatening to me. Then I caught the eye of a worshipper having a tough time focusing. He winked. Another man's cell phone rang. He struggled with it as if thinking, "Dang, I should have turned that thing off." The mosaics above—Turkish blue and darker Persian blue—added a harmony and calmness to the atmosphere.

I made a point to view the service as if it were my own church, back in Seattle. I was struck by the similarities: the too-long sermon, responsive readings, lots of getting up and getting down, the "passing of the peace" (when everyone greets the people around them), the convivial atmosphere as people line up to shake the hand of the cleric after the service, and the fellowship afterward as everyone hangs out in the courtyard.

On our way out, I shook the hand of the young cleric. He had a short, slight build, a tight white turban, a trim Ahmadinejad-style beard, big teeth, and a playful smile. He reminded me of Rafsanjani, Iran's moderate former president. In the courtyard, a man hit the branches of a mulberry tree with a pole as giddy kids scrambled for the treasured little berries.

Esfahan TV, which had televised the prayer service, saw us and wanted an interview. It was exciting to be on local TV. They asked why we were here, how I saw Iranian people, and why I thought there was a problem between the US and Iran. (I pointed out the "Death to Israel" banner, for starters.) Suspicious of our agenda, they fixated on whether our show would actually air…and if we'd spin our report to make Iran look evil.

Leaving the mosque, our crew pondered how easily the footage we'd just shot could be cut and edited to appear either menacing or heartwarm-

ing, depending on our agenda. Our mosque shots could be juxtaposed with guerillas leaping over barbed wire and accompanied by jihadist music to be frightening. Instead, we planned to edit it to match our actual experience: showing the guards and "Death to Israel" banner, but focusing on the men with warm faces praying with their sons at their sides, and the children outside scrambling for mulberries.

After prayer service at the mosque, a proud dad grabs a photo of his children.

It occurred to me that the segregation of the sexes—men in the center and women behind a giant hanging carpet at the side—contributes to the negative image many Western Christians have of Islam. Then, playing the old anthropologist's game of changing my perspective, I considered how the predominantly male-led Christian services that I'm so comfortable with could also be edited to look ominous to those unfamiliar with the rituals. At important Roman Catholic Masses, you'll see a dozen priests—all male—in robes before a bowing audience. The leader of a billion Catholics is chosen by a secretive, ritual-filled gathering of old men in strange hats and robes with chanting, incense, and the ceremonial drinking of human blood. It could be filled with majesty, or with menace…depending on what you show and how you show it.

After the prayer service, we set up to film across the vast square from the mosque. My lines were memorized and I was ready to go. Then, suddenly, the young cleric with the beaming smile came hurrying toward us with a platter of desserts—the local ice cream specialty, like frozen shredded wheat sprinkled with coconut. I felt like Rafsanjani himself was serving us ice cream. We had a lively conversation, joking about how it might help if his president went to my town for a prayer service, and my president came here.

Persepolis: The Palace of Persia's King of Kings

The sightseeing highlight of our time in Iran was Persepolis. Back when the Persian Empire reached from Greece to India, Persepolis was its dazzling ceremonial capital. Built by Darius and his son Xerxes the Great around 500 B.C., this sprawling complex of royal palaces was—for nearly two hundred years—the awe-inspiring home of the "King of Kings." At the time, Persia was so mighty, no fortifications were needed. Still, 10,000 guards served at the pleasure of the emperor. Persepolis, which evokes the majesty of Giza or Luxor in Egypt, is (in my opinion) the greatest ancient site between the Holy Land and India.

My main regret from traveling through Iran on my first visit, back in 1978, was not trekking south to Persepolis. And, I wanted to include Persepolis in our TV show because it's a powerful reminder that the soul of Iran is Persia, which predates the introduction of Islam by well over a thousand years. Arriving at Persepolis, in the middle of a vast and arid plain, was thrilling. This is one of those rare places that comes with high expectations…and actually exceeds them.

Persepolis is pharaoh-like in its scale. Emperors' tombs are cut into the neighboring mountains.

About 2,500 years ago, subjects of the empire (from 28 nations) would pass in "we're not worthy"-style through the Nations' Gate, bearing gifts for the "King of Kings."

We got to Persepolis after a long day of driving—just in time for that magic hour before the sun set. The light was glorious, the stones glowed rosy, and all the visitors seemed to be enjoying a special "sightseeing high." I saw more Western tourists visiting Persepolis than any other single sight in the country. But I was struck most by the Iranian people who travel here to savor this reminder that their nation was a mighty empire 2,500 years ago.

Wandering the site, you feel the omnipotence of the Persian Empire and gain a strong appreciation for the enduring strength of this culture and its people. Immense royal tombs, reminiscent of those built for Egyptian pharaohs, are cut into the adjacent mountainside. The tombs of Darius and Xerxes come with huge carved reliefs of ferocious lions. Even today—2,500 years after their deaths—they're reminding us of their great power. But, as history has taught us, no empire lasts forever. In 333 B.C., Persepolis was sacked and burned by Alexander the Great, replacing Persian dominance with Greek culture...and Persepolis has been a ruin ever since.

The approach to this awe-inspiring sight is marred by a vast and ugly tarmac with 1970s-era parking lot light poles. This paved hodgepodge is

Iranians—quick to smile for the camera of a new American friend—visit Persepolis to connect with and celebrate their impressive cultural roots.

Tarmac is all that remains of the Shah's big party in 1971.

a reminder of another megalomaniac ruler. In 1971, the Shah threw a bash with unprecedented extravagance to celebrate the 2,500-year anniversary of the Persian Empire—and to remind the world that he was the latest in a long string of great kings who ruled Persia with the omnipotence of a modern-day Xerxes or Darius. The Shah flew in dignitaries from all over the world, along with dinner from Maxim's in Paris, one of the finest restaurants in Europe. Iranian historians consider this arrogant display of imperial wealth and Western decadence—which so offended his poverty-stricken subjects—the beginning of the end for the Shah. Within a decade, he was gone and Khomeini was in. It's my hunch that the ugly asphalt remains of the Shah's party are left here so visiting locals can remember who their Revolution overthrew…and why.

Martyrs' Cemetery: Countless Deaths for Allah and Country

I make a point to visit war cemeteries in my travels. They always seem to come with a healthy dose of God—as if dying for God and country makes a soldier's death more meaningful than just dying for country. That is certainly true at Iran's many martyrs' cemeteries.

There were several hundred thousand casualties in the Iran-Iraq War. While the United States lives with the scars of Vietnam, the same generation of Iranians lives with the scars of its war with Iraq—in which they, with one-quarter our population, suffered an estimated three times the deaths. Iran considers anyone who dies defending the country to be a hero and a martyr. This bloody conflict left each Iranian city with a vast "martyrs' cemetery." Tombs seem to go on forever, and each one has a portrait of the martyr and flies a green, white, and red Iranian flag. All the death dates are from 1980 to 1988.

Could be anywhere: A mother remembers her son—lost for God and country.

Two decades after the war's end, the cemetery was still very much alive with mourning loved ones. A steady wind blew through seas of flags on the day of our visit, which added a stirring quality to the scene. And the place was bustling with people—all mourning their lost loved ones as if the loss happened a year ago rather than twenty. The cemetery had a quiet dignity, and while I felt a bit awkward at first (being part of an American crew with a big TV camera), people either ignored us or made us feel welcome.

We met two families sharing a dinner on one tomb (a local tradition). They insisted we join them for a little food and told us their story: They met each other twenty years ago while visiting their martyred sons, who were buried side by side. They became friends, their surviving children married each other, and ever since then they gather regularly to share a meal on the tombs of their sons.

A few yards away, a long row of white tombs stretched into the distance. A lone figure interrupted the visual rhythm created by the receding tombs: a mother cloaked in black sitting on her son's tomb, praying—a pyramid of maternal sorrow that silhouetted in the sun.

Nearby was a different area: marble slabs without upright stones, flags, or photos. This zone had the greatest concentration of mothers. My friend explained that these slabs marked bodies of unidentified heroes. Mothers whose sons were never found came here to mourn.

I left the cemetery sorting through a jumble of thoughts:

How oceans of blood were shed by both sides in the Iran-Iraq War—a war of aggression waged by Saddam Hussein and Iraq (with American support) against Iran.

How invasion is nothing new for this mighty and historic nation. (When I visited the surprisingly humble National Museum of Archeology in Tehran, the curator apologized, explaining that the art treasures of his country were scattered in museums throughout Europe and the West.)

How an elderly, aristocratic Iranian woman had crossed the street to look me in the eye and tell me, "We are proud, we are united, and we are strong. When you go home, please tell your people the truth."

How, with careless diplomacy or a reckless military action, this society could be set ablaze and radicalized. The uniquely Persian mix of delightful shops, university students with lofty career aspirations, gorgeous young adults with groomed eyebrows and perfect nose jobs, hope, progress, hard work, and the gentle people I encountered here in Iran could so easily and quickly be turned into a fiery hell of dysfunctional cities, torn-apart families, wailing mothers, newly empowered clerics, and radicalized people.

My visit to the cemetery drove home a feeling that had been percolating throughout my trip. There are many things that Americans justifiably find outrageous about the Iranian government—from supporting Hezbollah and making threats against Israel; to oppressing women and gay people; to asserting their right to join the world's nuclear club. And yet, no matter how strongly we want to see our demands met by Iran, we must pursue that aim carefully. What if our saber-rattling doesn't coerce this country into compliance? In the past, other powerful nations have underestimated Iran's willingness to be pulverized in a war to defend its ideals…and both Iran and

How has this boy's loss shaped his worldview?

their enemies have paid the price. Leaving this cemetery, I was haunted by the thought that America could do to a stable Iran what it did to a once-stable Iraq.

I have to believe that smart and determined diplomacy can keep the Iranians—and us—from having to build giant new cemeteries for the next generation's war dead. That doesn't mean "giving in" to Iran…it means acknowledging that war is a failure, and we'd be wise to find an alternative.

Back to Europe: Tight Pants, Necklines, Booze…and Freedom

My flight out of Iran was scheduled for 3 a.m. For whatever reason, planes leaving for the West depart in the wee hours. The TV crew had caught an earlier flight. Seyed had gone home. I was groggy and alone in the terminal. Standing face-to-face with uniformed customs officials who spoke no English, there was a delay. I started getting nervous. It seemed like forever until they said, "You may go."

Finally walking down the jetway toward my Air France plane, I saw busty French flight attendants—hair flowing freely—greeting passengers at the door. It was as if the plane was a lifeboat, and they were pulling us back to the delicious safety of the West. People entered with a sigh of relief, women pulled off their scarves…and suddenly we were free to be what we considered "normal." The jet lifted off, flying the exact opposite route the Ayatollah had traveled to succeed the Shah.

For 12 days, I'd been out of my comfort zone, in a land where people live under a theocracy. I tasted not a drop of alcohol, and I never encountered a urinal. Women didn't show the shape of their body or their hair (and were beautiful nevertheless). It was a land where people took photos of me, as if I were the cultural spectacle.

Landing in Paris was reverse culture shock. I sipped wine like it was heaven-sent. I noticed hair, necklines, and the curves revealed by tight pants like never before. University students sat at outdoor cafés—men and women mingling together as they discussed whatever hot-button issue interested them. After the Valium-paced lifestyle of Iran, I felt an energy and efficiency cranked up on high. People were free to be "evil" and able to express their joy any way they wanted. And, immersed in that vivid whirlpool of life, I was thankful to be a Westerner. I was grateful for the learning experience that gave simple things—from visiting the men's room to dealing with traffic jams, from valuing nonconformity to respecting women—a broader cultural context.

Reflecting on My Motives—
and the Real Souvenir I Carried Home

Returning home to the US, I faced a barrage of questions—mainly, "Why did you go to Iran?" Some were skeptical of my motives, accusing me of just trying to make a buck. (As a businessman, I can assure you there was no risk of a profit in this venture.) Reading the comments readers shared on my blog—some of whom railed against me for "naively" acting as a Jane Fonda-type mouthpiece for an enemy that has allegedly bankrolled terrorists—was also thought-provoking. The whole experience made me want to hug people and scream at the same time. It was intensely human.

I didn't go to Iran as a businessman or as a politician. I went as what I am—a travel writer. I went for the same reasons I travel anywhere: to get out of my own culture and learn, to go to a scary place and find it's not so scary, to bring distant places to people who've yet to go there, and to talk to people who have a dramatically different world view than I do…and to gain empathy. To me, understanding people and their lives is what travel is about, no matter where you go.

I have long held that travel can be a powerful force for peace. Travel promotes understanding at the expense of fear. And understanding bridges

Young couples—regardless of their presidents—share the same basic dreams and aspirations the world over.

As a traveler, I've often found that the more a culture differs from my own, the more I am struck by its essential humanity. Since our TV show on Iran, I've met countless Americans who have been inspired by our work and traveled in Iran. The unanimous consensus: Iran is a friendly and fascinating place to explore. For travel details, see www.ricksteves.com/iran.

conflicts between nations. As Americans, we endured the economic and human cost of war engulfing Iran's neighbor, Iraq. Seeing Iraq's cultural sites destroyed and its kind people being dragged through the ugliness of that war, I wished I'd been able to take my film crew to Baghdad before that war to preserve images of a peacetime Iraq. As our leaders' rhetoric ramped up the possibility of another war—with Iran—I didn't want to miss that chance again. It's human nature to not want to know the people on the receiving end of your "shock and awe"—but to dehumanize these people is wrong. I wanted to put a human face on "collateral damage."

It's not easy finding a middle ground between the "Great Satan" and the "Axis of Evil." Some of Iran's policies and statements (such as their leader denying the Holocaust) are just plain wrong. But I don't entirely agree with many policies in my own government, either. Yes, there are evil people in Iran. Yes, the rhetoric and policies of Iran's leaders can be objectionable. But there is so much more to Iran than the negative image drummed into us by our media and our government.

I left Iran impressed more by what we have in common than by our differences. Most Iranians, like most Americans, simply want a good life and a safe homeland for their loved ones. Just like my country, Iran has one dominant ethnic group and religion that's struggling with issues of diversity and change—liberal versus conservative, modern versus traditional, secular versus religious. As in my own hometown, people of great faith are suspicious of people of no faith or a different faith. Both societies seek a defense against the onslaught of modern materialism that threatens their traditional "family values." Both societies are suspicious of each other, and both are especially suspicious of each other's government.

My Iranian travels gave me insight to how a great nation can vote for a bombastic blowhard for a leader. Meeting that woman who didn't want her daughter to be like Britney Spears, I realized who the 51 percent of Iranians who elected Ahmadinejad were: Not the big-city elites. Not the educated liberals. But the salt-of-the-

Who voted for Ahmadinejad? Good people motivated by fear and love.

earth people in what we might call "flyover country"...small-town, less-educated fundamentalists...good people who are riddled by fear and motivated by love.

When we travel—whether to the "Axis of Evil" or just to a place where people yodel when they're happy, or fight bulls to impress the girls, or can't serve breakfast until today's croissants arrive—we enrich our lives and better understand our place on this planet. We undercut groups that sow fear, hatred, and mistrust. People-to-people connections help us learn that we can disagree and still coexist peacefully.

Thoughtful travel teaches us that countries like Iran are on evolutionary tracks that come with strong headwinds of fear. Impatience can make a bad situation worse—as we've seen in places like Iraq or Egypt. With patience and an understanding that progress is more successful when it comes organically from within rather than forced from outside, it's my hope that societies like Iran can become free on their terms.

Recent changes in Iran's post-Ahmadinejad government are reason to be hopeful and exercise continued patience. Granted, there's no easy solution, but surely getting to know Iranian culture is a step in the right direction. Hopefully, even the most skeptical will appreciate the humanity of 70 million Iranian people. Our political leaders sometimes make us forget that all of us on this small planet are equally precious children of God. Having been to Iran and meeting its people face-to-face, I feel this more strongly than ever.

Chapter 9
The Holy Land:
Israelis and Palestinians Today

The land that Israelis and Palestinians occupy is, for a third of humanity, literally Holy Land. For Christians, this is where Jesus was crucified and rose from the dead. For Muslims, this is from where Muhammad journeyed to heaven. And for Jews, it's where the Temple of Solomon stood. The epic stories of the three great monotheistic religions on this planet have played out on this tiny piece of real estate, which has been coveted and fought over for centuries. The struggles here are difficult, and the stakes are high. While one man's terrorist may be another man's freedom fighter, the fact is that in recent decades, people on both sides have suffered terribly.

Conflict in the Middle East is a huge issue for the US. Like it or not, we are deeply involved in this problem. And considering our unwavering commitment to Israel's security, we have a responsibility to be engaged in finding a durable solution. When you travel to a faraway place where your country is a major stakeholder, it's hard not to travel as a political act.

"Travel is a force for peace" is a nice slogan. To help make that slogan a reality, I traveled to Israel and Palestine in 2013 with the goal of producing a television documentary to help my American viewers better understand this troubled land. Several of my friends asked me whether I really wanted to wade into the quagmire of Israel and Palestine, where it seems like anyone who probes for the truth will anger people on one side or the other. But I believe that the vast majority of Americans are not partisan on the issues here. My agenda was simply to be balanced and honest. I espoused a "dual narrative" approach: Giving voice to reasonable and rational people from both sides of the thorny issues. It seems to me that open-minded people want to hear a variety of perspectives, and be given the opportunity to form their own opinions.

For me, exploring the Holy Land wasn't just educational—it was actually fun, because I flew there knowing so little. I find that being steep on the learning curve is a joy. Old dogs can learn new tricks when traveling to complicated places with an appetite to learn. And the best way I can do that is to get out of my comfort zone and simply talk to people. In this chapter, I'll share the lessons I brought home. Equipped with open minds, we'll visit each side, in alphabetical order: first Israel, then Palestine. Let's go.

How Did We Get Here?

Troubled regions like the Middle East often struggle with a "Who was here first?" debate. And in the Holy Land, that question has no easy answer. The Arabs and Jews who call this region home share a family tree that goes back nearly 4,000 years. That's when, according to tradition, the prophet Abraham—called the patriarch—had two sons: From Isaac came the Israelites, while Ismael spawned the Arabs. That means that today's Jews and Arabs are cousins: They share similar DNA, speak closely related languages, and each have a genuine historical claim to this land.

This ancient ethnic mix is complicated by religions. Israelites were Jewish. Christians worship Jesus, a Jew who brought his own message. And today, most Arabs here are Muslim—a religion that arrived much later, in the seventh century, with their prophet, Muhammad. Here in the Holy Land—where Muslims, Jews, and Christians celebrate their Sabbath on different days—Friday, Saturday, and Sunday are each holy days for some part of the population.

Throughout the centuries, this region endured waves of conquerors—from pagan Roman legions to Christian Crusaders to Muslim Ottomans. In A.D. 70, the Romans destroyed the main Jewish temple in Jerusalem, laid siege to a valiant last stand of Jewish rebels at the mountaintop fortress of Masada (which ended in mass suicide), and exported Jews as slaves. This catastrophic event began what's known as the Diaspora. The Jews dispersed throughout the world, mostly settling in Europe, where they suffered centuries of oppression culminating in the Holocaust.

During those centuries, the Arabs (and a small minority of Jews) continued living in this land as it was batted between various outside powers. Until the 20th century, the entire area was called "Palestine," as it had been in Roman times.

Meanwhile, beginning in the late 19th century, "Zionism"—a movement inspired by visionaries such as Theodor Herzl in the Austro-Hungarian Empire—spurred Jews worldwide to dream of creating a modern state in their ancestral homeland. During World War I, when Palestine was ruled by British mandate, the Balfour Declaration set the stage to make this a reality, and Jews began to return to Palestine to claim the land. After the Holocaust, in 1948, the modern state of Israel was officially formed. That trickle of immigration became a flood, as Jews from Europe, Arab lands of the Middle East, and beyond came here to create Israel.

As Jews returned to build their nation, hundreds of thousands of Palestinians were displaced. And to this day, both peoples struggle to find an equitable and peaceful way to share what they each consider their rightful homeland.

The dividing of the Holy Land hasn't been easy. At first, the United Nations established a border known as the Green Line. Then, in 1967's Six-Day War, Israel launched a surprise offensive to take over land held by Jordan, Syria, and Egypt, substantially increasing its territory. Palestinians managed to hold two enclaves within Israel: the Gaza Strip (a tiny yet densely populated coastal area adjoining Egypt) and the West Bank (between Jerusalem and the Jordan River).

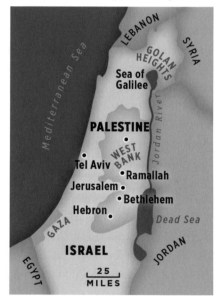

Palestinians—chafing at the loss of their land and freedom—lashed out with terrorist attacks, and Israelis retaliated by turning Palestinian territories into a virtual police state. Palestinians launched their First Intifada, an armed rebellion that employed violent riots and suicide bombings (1987-1991). In 1993, the Oslo Accords (negotiated by Yitzhak Rabin and Yasser Arafat) attempted to create peace by recognizing the Palestinian Territories. The treaty was designed as a transitional agreement, until it could be phased out (in five years, they hoped) to make way for a more permanent solution.

But extremists both in Israel and in Palestine worked hard to undermine the peace. From 2000 to 2005, the Second Intifada brought a rash of bloody terrorist attacks in Israel, killing more than a thousand Israelis—more than three-quarters of them civilians. Israel retaliated, and Palestinians suffered three times the casualties as Israel. During the Second Intifada, Israel began to build a controversial barrier around the West Bank in the name of security from terrorism. From about 2005 through my visit in 2013, terrorist attacks from the West Bank declined dramatically, and my impression was that most West Bank Palestinians had decided to pursue a nonviolent approach to resolving the conflict.

The Jewish population of Israel is just over six million. Four out of every five Israelis are Jewish, but most are non-practicing. About 20 percent of Israel's population are Palestinians—many internally displaced persons who were not pushed over the borders of Israel in 1948, but are not allowed to return to their homes. The government calls them "Arab Israelis," but they generally call themselves "Palestinian citizens of Israel." Most are Muslim, while Christians make up a tiny minority. Palestinians living in Israel are, by law, full citizens with nearly the same rights as Jewish Israelis. But many feel that they're treated as second-class citizens; they compare their situation to the plight of pre-Civil Rights-era African Americans in the USA.

On this trip (and for my TV show), I focused on the West Bank, which is governed by the Palestinian Authority. I did not travel to the Hamas-ruled Gaza Strip—the more densely populated, poverty-stricken, and war-torn of the "Palestinian Territories." While Hamas is more extreme, the Palestinian Authority does not endorse violence and is willing to recognize the state of Israel.

In the Holy Land, terminology is charged with symbolic meaning and controversy. As a travel writer, I struggle with simply what to call the land of the Palestinians. Many conservative Jews and Evangelical Christians, believing this is the land God promised to the Jews, use the biblical name "Judea and Samaria." The non-loaded "West Bank" or "Occupied Territories" would be the cautious choices. But this area was historically called "Palestine," and in 2012, the UN General Assembly voted to grant Palestine (with that name) "non-member observer state" status. I've decided to follow the example of the international community. For the title of my TV show, I went with "Palestine: Yesterday and Today." I realize—and accept—the fact that even using the name "Palestine" alienates many people. These are the people who, I believe, would benefit the most from actually traveling to both sides of the wall that divides the Holy Land.

Fabled Jerusalem: Steeped in History, Politics, and Religion

Before Columbus and the illustrious class of 1500, many maps showed Jerusalem as the center of the world. Jerusalem—holy, treasured, and long fought over among the three great monotheistic religions—has been destroyed and rebuilt 14 times. Its fabled ramparts were so strong that its defeats often came by starve-'em-out sieges.

Modern Jerusalem is a sprawling city with about 800,000 people. Exploring its American-style shopping boulevards and malls, you'll feel right at home. But its historic core, the Old City—home to around 35,000—feels lost in time. Its venerable two-mile-long Ottoman wall corrals a tangle of vibrant sights. It's a bustling maze of winding cobblestone paths and streets, each stone carrying within it the shadows and stories of prophets, leaders, and infamous invaders of the past. Each alley, each doorway, each church, each mosque, each store, and each vendor—everyone and everything in Jerusalem has a story, waiting to be discovered and unleashed by your own curiosity.

The golden Dome of the Rock is one of Jerusalem's enduring landmarks.

Under that glittering dome is a sacrificial stone with gutters to drain the blood spilled upon it by pagans long before there was a Jewish faith. It's the stone upon which— according to Jewish, Christian, and Muslim tradition—Abraham prepared to prove his faith by sacrificing his son, Isaac.

The mighty walls and gates of Old Jerusalem define the Old City, which is divided into four quarters: Jewish, Armenian, Christian, and Muslim.

(When it became clear that Abraham would be obedient to God's will, God intervened, saving Isaac.) Many consider this spot to be both the starting point or foundation stone of creation, and the closest place on earth to God in heaven. Jews believe this place to be the center of the earth, and have worshipped here for 3,000 years. Muslims believe Muhammad journeyed to heaven from here 1,300 years ago. Pondering the tumult and persistent tragedy caused by the fact that three religions share a single holy rock, I wondered if God doesn't just have a wicked sense of humor.

Jews call the hill capped by the Dome of the Rock "Temple Mount"—the holiest site in Judaism. A thousand years before Christ, King David united the 12 tribes of Israel and captured Jerusalem. His son, Solomon, built the First Temple right here. It was later burned by invaders, and the Second Temple was built. Then came that catastrophic year for the Jews: A.D. 70, when the

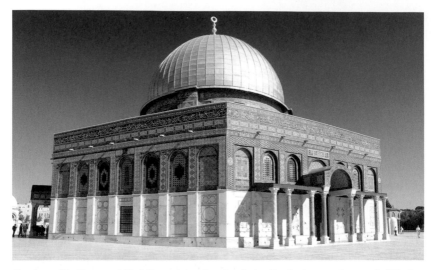

For Jews, Muslims, and Christians, Jerusalem is a holy city. And ground zero of all that holiness is a much-venerated rock marked by this golden dome.

Romans destroyed their temple, ushering in the Diaspora. Only a bit of the western foundation of the wall surrounding this ancient temple complex survived. Over the centuries, throughout the Diaspora, Jews returning to Jerusalem came here to the Western Wall—the closest they could get to that holy rock—to pray and to mourn their temple's destruction. That's why it's often called "the Wailing Wall."

Today, Jews still gather at the Western Wall, not only to recall a horrible past but also to pray for a better future. The square operates as an open-air synagogue, divided into a men's section and a women's section. The faithful believe prayers left in cracks between the stones of the Western Wall will be answered. It's a lively scene, with intense yet private worship mixing with the joyous commotion of

For nearly 2,000 years, Jews have prayed at the Western Wall, all that survives of their destroyed temple complex on Temple Mount.

Jewish families from around the world celebrating bar mitzvahs—a ritual coming of age.

Christians know Jerusalem as the place where Jesus was crucified, buried, and resurrected 2,000 years ago. Just a few minutes' walk from Temple Mount is the Via Dolorosa—the "Way of Grief" where, it's believed, Jesus walked as he carried his cross to be crucified. Pilgrims come from around Christendom to worshipfully retrace his steps. Today most of the Via Dolorosa feels like a touristy shopping mall, but the presence of devout pilgrims, retracing Jesus' steps, gives it a sacred feeling.

Their journey culminates at the site of Jesus' crucifixion, marked by the Church of the Holy Sepulcher on the summit of Calvary Hill, or Golgotha. This dark, sprawling church is the most sacred site in Christendom. Built around the tomb, or sepulcher, of Jesus, it's shared by seven different denominations. Because it's holy for all kinds of Christians (who see things differently and don't always cooperate), it's a cluttered religious hodgepodge of various zones, each controlled by

Within the Church of the Holy Sepulcher, this stone—generally surrounded by pilgrims touching it and praying—marks the spot where Jesus' dead body was placed when taken down from the cross.

a separate sect. There are chapels for Greek Orthodox, Coptic Christians, Armenians, Ethiopians, Roman Catholics, and so on. A Greek Orthodox chapel marks the site believed to be where Jesus was crucified. A few steps away, under a grand dome, pilgrims line up to enter the Holy Sepulcher itself and place a candle near the tomb of Jesus.

Local Christians like to believe that even if God is everywhere, all prayers go through Jerusalem (as if it's a sacred cell-phone tower), and the Holy Spirit comes down to us via Jerusalem. One local joked that the Vatican has a golden phone with a direct connection to God, but the toll is $1,000. Meanwhile, the golden phone offering the same service in Jerusalem only costs 25 cents. Why? "It's a local call."

Ultra-Orthodox: Every Religion's Got 'Em

Roughly eight percent of Israeli Jews are ultra-Orthodox—very religious and living lives that require them to be apart in many ways. Entire districts of Jerusalem are known as ultra-Orthodox, including the fascinating quarter called Mea She'arim. I stopped by for a visit on a Friday, and found the place bustling. Since its population takes the Shabbat (holy day of rest on Saturday) very seriously, Friday is the day when everyone is preparing.

The diversity of Israel—a nation made up mostly of Jewish immigrants from around the globe—shows itself in the way people dress and wear their hair. This is especially evident in the ultra-Orthodox neighborhoods. Most people in Mea She'arim dress very conservatively. Women's stores have a huge selection of wigs, hats, and scarves, because after marriage, Orthodox Jewish women must cover their hair in public. And yet, there's a surprising degree of variety within these narrow constraints.

Simply people-watching comes with fun cultural insights. As I sat with my local friend at a café and surveyed the scene, he offered a running commentary: "The yarmulke is a constant reminder that God is always above us. The ear locks are because some embrace the scripture that says not to cut the hair on the side of your face. Men wear black as a symbol of mourning of the destruction of the Second Temple nearly 2,000 years ago. The black top hats come in many varieties, and from them, you can guess which specific brand of Orthodoxy they profess—and, in some cases, which country they emigrated from."

Among ultra-Orthodox Jews, there are many groups who follow different teachers or rabbis. Rabbis are typically charismatic and have huge followings. (One died the day I arrived in Jerusalem, and the streets of the city were at a standstill as thousands came out to mourn.) In Mea She'arim, storefronts are lined

Israel's ultra-Orthodox community dresses in black and sticks together.

Leading rabbis have enthusiastic followings. They're like pop stars...without the pop.

with posters and paintings of the top rabbis. A quick survey tells you which are the most popular.

Israelis are split on the role that Orthodox Jews play in their society: Some see them as leaders of their faith, while others have a more negative view. One secular Israeli told me, "To these Hassidic Jews, I—with my modern ways—am the enemy. And to me, they are parasites. They don't work. Our taxes pay them to just sit around and learn the Torah. Their 'job' is to be religious."

All of this got me thinking about other charismatic religious leaders, and how Evangelical Christians back home can also get caught up in the teachings of one particular dynamic minister. Meanwhile, in both Christianity and Judaism, mainstream worshippers have a spiritual keel provided not by an individual, but by a steady liturgy or theology that doesn't flex with the comings and goings of various leaders.

Religions around the world seem to always be stoking turmoil—even though the teachings of those religions say "love your neighbor," and all of them have the "do unto others..." Golden Rule. I've decided that fundamentalism is the crux of the problem. I think the rainbow of religions on this planet is a delight—except for the fundamentalists in each. Perhaps there are "different strokes for different folks" fundamentalists, but it seems to me that, in a nutshell, a fundamentalist (Christian, Jew, or Muslim) believes, "I am correct in my understanding of God, and you are wrong"...and then proceeds to intrude into the lives of people who see their relation with God differently. And that's reason enough to be thankful we live in a nation that is vigilant about protecting the separation of church and state.

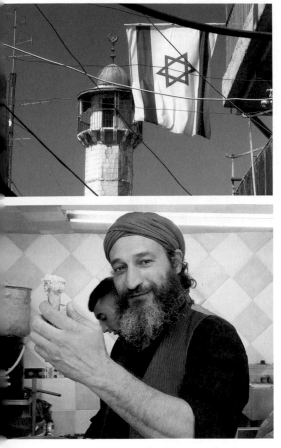

Radiating out from Temple Mount is Jerusalem's Old City, divided into four quarters. The Jewish Quarter springs from the Western Wall. The Muslim Quarter faces the Dome of the Rock. And north of the Armenian Quarter, the Christian Quarter surrounds the Church of the Holy Sepulcher. The Old City is fraught with endless little games of interfaith one-upmanship. For example, in the Muslim Quarter, the volume of call to prayer is turned up high…just to annoy the Jews.

The Jewish Quarter is more orderly and modern than the others. Much of this area was destroyed in the 1948 fighting, or during the ensuing period of Jordanian occupation. After the Israelis took control of Jerusalem in 1967, they rebuilt this quarter. Today, when you see new stones, you're probably in the Jewish Quarter. While it's not conve-

Top: Deep in the Muslim Quarter, a few houses boldly fly Israeli flags. Bottom: In Jerusalem's Old City, the little things in life are celebrated.

nient or economical to live in this medieval tangle, devout Jews find great joy in raising their families so close to Temple Mount.

The Muslim Quarter, with over half of the Old City's population, is mostly Arab. But wandering the Muslim Quarter, I noticed several houses fortified and festooned with Israeli flags. These are homes of ultra-Zionist families determined to stake out this bit of the Old City for their Jewish community. Considering the rich historic heritage of each of these communities, it's understandable that both vie for this sacred real estate.

This struggle over control of Jerusalem is a huge political challenge. While complete Muslim control of Jerusalem is unrealistic, many Arabs envision an independent Palestinian state with this part of Jerusalem—East Jerusalem—as their capital. It's a contentious issue, and Israel seems determined to keep Jerusalem whole and under its control.

And yet, exploring Jerusalem's Old City—with its tight quarters and religious passions—I was impressed by the diversity, the feeling of community, and how things all seem to work together. Life is a celebration here, from the man who's evangelical about the quality of his falafel and the woman who serves the sweetest pomegranate juice to the song of the merchants in the market and the kids who still need their training wheels to bike down tiny lanes amid the chanting pilgrims.

Jerusalem's Unforgettable Yad Vashem Holocaust Memorial

In 2013, for the first time, Israel's Jewish population passed six million. This is considered highly significant because it's symbolic of the number of Jews killed in the Holocaust.

Understandably, Israel works to keep the memory of the millions of Jews killed by Hitler alive and strong. I imagine that with the passing of the generation that actually lived through that horror, this will become a bigger and bigger challenge. To help accomplish this, Israel has constructed a memorial and museum, called Yad Vashem, to honor those victims.

A visit to Yad Vashem is part of every Israeli's upbringing. All visiting heads of state are also brought here. The modern state of Israel rose from the

Yad Vashem tells a compelling story and stirs powerful emotions.

Yad Vashem's Hall of Names is an archive with a mission: to give each victim of the Holocaust the dignity of being remembered by name.

ashes of the Holocaust—and to understand the history of modern Israel, you must comprehend the cause and the enormity of that massacre. Yad Vashem imprints on visitors a searing impression of the suffering of the Jewish people under Nazi Germany, turning tourists into pilgrims.

The museum brings the hate-filled horror of Nazism to life. It primes you for the garden-like grounds, which are a place to think. A train car—one of countless German wagons once jammed with people en route to death camps—sits on rails that stop in midair, high above.

In the Hall of Names, a vast archive surrounds a powerful collection of faces of Jews killed during the Holocaust. Of the roughly six million Jews murdered, about half have been identified by surviving family and friends. Pages of their testimony are archived here. The purpose: to give victims—whose deaths were as ignominious as their killers could manage—the simple dignity of being remembered.

The Children's Memorial starts with a gallery of photos showing the faces of adorable kids from many countries lost to the Holocaust. You learn that a quarter of Hitler's victims were children. Then, stepping into a dark chamber, you'll see one small light reflected by mirrors 1.5 million times to make a galaxy of flickering souls while a somber voice reads their names in a steady roll call. Emerging back into the daylight, I found myself trying to imagine how such a heritage would impact my outlook if I were Jewish.

Along the "Avenue of Righteous Gentiles," trees are planted to honor non-Jews who risked their lives to help the persecuted. The memorial honors 24,000 Europeans who aided the Jews...while reminding us that another 160 million turned a blind eye. A recurring theme at Yad Vashem is how humanity ignored the plight of the Jews in the 1930s and 1940s. The memorial reminds us that when Hitler was warned that his plan to exterminate the Jewish race would damage his image, he responded, "Who remembers the Armenian genocide?"

For a powerful finale, the Yad Vashem memorial finishes with a platform overlooking the land Israelis have worked so hard to establish as the one nation on earth that is Jewish.

An Appreciation for Israel's Determined Pioneers

One of the great joys of travel—particularly in the Holy Land—is the rich insight you gain by talking with the people you meet.

To many, Israel represents a beacon of democracy, stability, and prosperity in the middle of a bunch of very troubled states. (Having traveled recently in Egypt and Iran, I can certainly appreciate that.) To others, its very existence is an offense against groups who were displaced after living here for centuries. As with everything here, it all depends on which people you talk to. And first, I talked to the Israelis. (Palestinian partisans, your turn is coming up.)

There are Jews who don't concern themselves about Israel at all. There are Jews (particularly devout Jews) who think the state of Israel is a terrible, even un-Jewish idea. And there are Jews who believe that their people should live together in the single homeland God chose for them. These Jews are the Zionists who built Israel.

During my visit, Israel was celebrating 65 years as a

This iconic photograph of determined Zionists—still wearing their concentration camp stripes as they labor to create their country in the late 1940s—stirs the Israeli soul.

nation. Star of David flags flew everywhere. Perhaps caught up in the excitement, I welcomed the opportunity to gain an appreciation for the Zionist pioneers who built the country—slowly in the early 20th century, then very quickly after its modern founding in 1948—and to see how far the nation has come.

After World War II, a generation of Holocaust orphans helped end the Jewish Diaspora. Back then, there was an inspiring slogan: "A land without a people for a people without a land." The problem was that this land wasn't empty—it was inhabited, albeit sparsely, by thousands of Palestinians. Still, when you look at a photo of the early Zionists who came here and mixed sand, sweat, brainpower, and a determined vision into a powerful nation, you can understand the passion Israelis have for their homeland. In the countryside, lush valleys farmed by co-operative communities called kibbutzes recall generations of patriotic Israelis who turned the desert into orchards.

I find the poignancy of nation-building most inspiring in the big coastal city of Tel Aviv. In 1908, Tel Aviv was just a big sand dune. Today the city feels like San Diego. The skyscrapers of Tel Aviv are exclamation points that seem to declare, "We've come a long way."

Tel Aviv's waterfront promenade is the place to rock to the rhythm of contemporary Israel—foamy cafés, sugar-sand beaches, and the beckoning Mediterranean. With a "use it or lose it" approach to the good life, young Israelis embrace the present. I see Tel Aviv as a fun-loving resort, just the opposite of Jerusalem. People in Tel Aviv told me that many don't like the

Tel Aviv, born in 1909, must be the youngest major city on the Mediterranean.

Each year on Israel's Independence Day, the happy soundtrack of families enjoying BBQs fills the parks. It's like the Fourth of July, only with Stars of David rather than Stars and Stripes.

A few blocks away, just over the wall, Palestinians in the West Bank mark that same day, which they call "The Day of Catastrophe," with sadness and demonstrations.

religiosity of Jerusalem. "The cities have two different mindsets. The sea makes you open. There's no sea in Jerusalem, and no beach. In Jerusalem, everybody is political, religious, or a tourist."

The relative prosperity between Israel and its neighbors is striking. Waking up on my first morning here, I looked out my hotel window at the wonderful sandy beach (which is made of sediment blown and washed over from the Nile River). Pondering the joggers and kayakers getting in their morning exercise, I kept thinking it's as if someone put Southern California in the middle of Central America.

The historic port town of Jaffa—now consumed by the sprawl of Tel Aviv—was the Ellis Island of the new state. This was where new arrivals first set foot in Israel. Much of historic Jaffa was destroyed in 1948, in what Israelis call their "War of Independence." As in any war, there were winners and there were losers. When Israel celebrates its Independence Day each spring, the same day is mourned as "The Day of Catastrophe" on the other side of the wall. While Israelis set off fireworks, Palestinians remember the destruction of entire Arab communities that once thrived here and elsewhere, and how hundreds of thousands of those who survived ended up in refugee camps over a newly drawn border.

How do you build a new nation? For one thing, it's national policy to welcome all Jews into Israel. The "Law of Return" entices Jewish immigrants from around the world with grants and loans, subsidized housing, and classes

Half of Israel's population consists of first-generation immigrants. Those who are 18 years old go into the military—providing them with a crash course on how to be an Israeli.

to facilitate their assimilation. No matter how poor, foreign, and rough the returning Jew may be, the program expects to create well-educated, Hebrew-speaking Israelis out of his family within two generations. Israel claims to have successfully absorbed at least a million penniless refugees this way.

When you're surrounded on all sides by enemies, military readiness is serious business. All Jewish Israelis go into the military at age 18: men for three years, women for two years. While the primary purpose is to protect the country, a strong secondary purpose for the universal draft is to build social cohesion. Military service functions as a kind of cultural boot camp for first-generation Israelis—new arrivals from places like Russia, Iraq, and Ethiopia. After three years in the army, they're no longer F.O.B. ("fresh off the boat").

While the "Law of Return" sounds wonderful, it's a policy that angers many Palestinians I met. They recall how their parents were evicted from their villages—now plowed under and providing foundations for forests and parks—and wonder why a Russian Jew who has no connection with Israel is welcomed as if royalty, while a person whose family had lived there for 2,000 years is not allowed to go home.

Israel's Dogged Determination to Keep the High Ground
High in the mountains at the far-north end of Israel, the Gadot Lookout in the Golan Heights overlooks the upper Jordan River Valley. After Israel

was created in 1948, its neighbors generally held the high ground around its borders. For a generation, Arabs could lob shells into the towns, kibbutzes, and farms of Israel below. Then, with their victory in the Six-Day War in 1967, Israel surprised all of its enemies (essentially destroying Egypt's air force on the ground in minutes) and substantially increased its size. To the north, they could have waltzed right into Damascus. But Israel just wanted buffer territory. Today, Israel—determined never again to live under its enemies—controls this and all of the high ground around its borders.

A similar spot is the fortification atop Mount Bental. From this Golan Heights viewpoint, you can look into Syria toward its capital, Damascus—just 35 miles to the north. As long as things are peaceful, the fort is treated as a scenic tourist depot. The trenches and barbed wire here provide a kind of commando playground for visiting Israelis. There's even an open-air modern art gallery with installations made of rusty military hardware and barbed wire. The café on Mount Bental is named "Coffee Annan," a clever reminder that former United Nations Secretary-General Kofi Annan once led the UN troops stationed below.

Towering above the Dead Sea is yet another fortified mountaintop—but this one's 2,000 years old and in ruins. The powerful and historic Masada fortress was built back when the Jews were the rebellious subjects of Roman occupation. In A.D. 70, Roman Emperor Titus, in an effort to put down the Jews once and for all, destroyed much of Jerusalem, including the main Jewish

Hearing an Israeli explain the importance of keeping the high ground while overlooking the Sea of Galilee from a former Syrian pillbox atop the Golan Heights, it was easy to get the point.

Mount Bental's fortifications are a fun tourist attraction in good times...and a strategic military stronghold in bad.

temple. Nearly 1,000 Jewish rebels—the original Zealots—fled to this fortress to defend their families and faith. An army of 15,000 Romans attacked the rebels at Masada. Preferring a direct attack to a drawn-out siege, the Roman army had a huge ramp built up this mountain. Knowing the Zealots wouldn't kill their own countrymen, the Romans forced Jewish slaves to do the back-breaking construction. Slowly, under the frustrated gaze of the rebels, the ramp was completed. The Zealots realized they were doomed to a life of slavery or worse. So, on the eve of the inevitable Roman breakthrough, Masada's rebels methodically took their own lives.

At Masada in A.D. 70, Jewish rebels—facing imminent defeat by Roman soldiers—committed mass suicide. The hilltop ruins remain an important symbol for defense-minded Israelis.

Today, Masada reminds us that Israel's staunch "they'll never take us alive" commitment to independence started 2,000 years ago. This patriotic site is popular for Israeli schoolchildren, for the ceremony swearing in Israeli soldiers, and for tourists.

Imagine a people maintaining their culture and traditions for nearly two millennia without a homeland. Imagine them remembering the holy temple destroyed and that epic last stand ending in mass suicide on a fortified hilltop. Imagine a generation of people whose parents were killed in the Holocaust and who, with a love of their heritage, found themselves in the position to retake what they believed to be their homeland. A rallying cry among these Zionists is "Masada shall never fall again."

More and more Israeli Jews, along with people around the world who care about peace in the Middle East and believe in the survival of a strong and secure Jewish state, think Israel would be wise to lighten up a bit on the Palestinian issues. But when you travel here and interact with the older generation, you appreciate why most of them take every threat to their nation extremely seriously—and make their own rules for security without waiting for anyone else's approval. These people remember 1967, when Hebrew-language propaganda radio from Egypt broadcast to a young generation of Israelis: "Dear fish of the Mediterranean, don't bother eating now—because in a few days, you'll be dining on two million Jews."

Christian Pilgrims Flock to the Sea of Galilee

As a Christian, I enjoy making travel a spiritual experience—whether hiking on a ridge high in the Swiss Alps with nothing but nature around me and the heavens above, or stepping into the great cathedrals of Europe to be bathed in sunlight filtered through exquisite stained glass created by poor and simple people with a powerful faith nearly a thousand years ago. I'm touched by the delicate yet mighty love of parents for their little children in hardscrabble corners, and I'm inspired by the faith of people who see God differently than I do. Being tuned into my spirituality as I travel enhances my experience.

Meditating on Bible lessons where they actually took place helps a Christian better connect with the word of God.

For a person of faith to travel without letting the experience stir what's inside them is a lost opportunity. Of course, many people actually go on religious trips—pilgrims on pilgrimages. While

The faithful believe John the Baptist baptized Jesus in the Jordan River. And today, Christians from all over the world come here in droves to affirm their baptism with a dip in that same storied river.

I've never done exactly that, every time I'm at a pilgrimage site, I endeavor to keep a positive attitude about the devotion that surrounds me. It's easy to be cynical about the reverence given to relics I don't understand, the determination many have to believe in what seem like silly miracles, or the needless pain someone suffers in the name of their faith—whether by climbing a mountain in bare feet or a long staircase on their knees. But it's far more constructive and meaningful to let your heart be warmed.

The biggest share of the tourist industry in the Holy Land is religious tourism. While Jesus was born in Bethlehem (in the south, near Jerusalem), he grew up and spent much of his three-year ministry farther north, in Nazareth, near the Sea of Galilee—where the Bible says Jesus walked on water, calmed the storm, and talked fishermen into changing careers. For Christians, making a pilgrimage to the places they've imagined since their childhood Sunday school classes can be a transforming experience. Experiencing "the fifth gospel," as pilgrims call the Holy Land, helps them better understand the other four gospels. While I rarely saw a tour group elsewhere, I was stuck in traffic jams of tour buses at the great Bible sights.

The Sea of Galilee—700 feet below sea level, 13 miles long by 8 miles wide, and fed and drained by the Jordan River—is Israel's major source of fresh water. The Jordan River dumps into the north end of the lake, oxygenating the water and attracting a high concentration of fish—and fishermen. In the Bible, Matthew writes, "As Jesus walked by the Sea of Galilee, he saw two brothers, Simon, who is called Peter, and Andrew his brother, casting a net into the lake—for they were fishermen. And he said to them, 'Follow me, and I will make you fishers of men.'"

Churches are built on sites where, for 2,000 years, stories of miracles have inspired worship. Christians gather to worship on Mount Beatitude, high above Galilee, where Jesus gave the Sermon on the Mount. "Beatitude" is Latin for "blessing." And here, Jesus said, "Blessed are the meek, for they will inherit the earth. Blessed are the merciful, for they will receive mercy. Blessed are the peacemakers, for they will be called children of God." Peacenik priests and pastors enjoy making the point that Christ said "peacemakers" rather than "peacekeepers." Traveling here in the Holy Land, this Beatitude has a particular poignancy and relevance.

The Church of the Primacy of St. Peter, delightfully set on the Sea of Galilee, is especially important for Roman Catholic pilgrims. The church is built upon the rock where, tradition holds, the resurrected Jesus ate with his disciples and told Peter to "feed my sheep." For Catholics, this is a very important site, as it established the importance of Peter—the first pope—among the disciples.

At each pilgrimage site, my Jewish guide read with passion passages from the Bible. I found the scriptures about the Sermon on the Mount, feeding the masses with a few loaves and fish, Jesus calming the stormy sea, and the Beatitudes particularly moving in the places where those events occurred.

Gazing out over the fabled Sea of Galilee and imagining Jesus walking on the water, I became more emotional than I had imagined I would be. Closing my eyes, I let the song of pilgrim groups singing in the distance, the sound of the little waves cresting at my feet, and the breeze off the lake come together in a touching, personal moment. If you'd like to share the experience enjoyed by pilgrims over the centuries, travel can be a spiritual act as well as a political one.

Bethlehem: Gateway to Palestine

For me, no Holy Land visit is complete or balanced without learning from both narratives—Israeli and Palestinian. Crossing from Jerusalem to Bethlehem (in

Crosses and crescents share Bethlehem's skyline.

While pilgrims line up at the Church of the Nativity, the people of Bethlehem go about their daily chores under this memorial to locals locked up in Israeli prisons.

Palestine), suddenly there's not a yarmulke in sight. Wandering Palestinian streets and markets, I kept thinking how easy it is to get here, how little I knew of it, and how rarely visited this land is.

No longer just the little town of Christmas-carol fame, Bethlehem is a leading Palestinian city. The classic Bethlehem panorama shows a delightful town capping a hill with spires and minarets. But this view is impossible to find today, as the city sprawls and is almost indiscernible from greater Jerusalem. If it weren't for the border crossing—and the traffic—you could ride a bike from the place Jesus was born (Manger Square in Bethlehem) to the place he died (Calvary Hill in Jerusalem) in about 20 minutes.

While beloved among Christians as Jesus' birthplace, Bethlehem's skyline is a commotion of both crosses and crescents—a reminder that historically, the town has held a mix of Christians and Muslims. The main square bustles with commerce. And the traffic circle comes with a memorial to locals doing time in Israeli prisons. Here, immersed in a sea of Palestinian people going about their daily lives, preconceptions are challenged.

In Palestine, a clean plate just gets you more food.

I checked into my guesthouse, and within minutes met my Palestinian tour guide. He took me to a tourist-friendly restaurant that posted a "families only" sign so they could turn away rowdy young men. I guess we looked harmless enough, as they let us right in. We sat down, and an impressive array of Palestinian dishes appeared.

For over a thousand years, a mosque has also stood on Nativity Square. Muslims consider Jesus a major prophet and have a special reverence for Mary, who has a big role in the Quran.

There's a rhythm to eating here. You're presented with a delicious and irresistible array of little appetizer plates: hummus, salads, cheeses, meats, eggplant, and various dips to eat with pita bread. Then, just when you're about full, the real meal arrives—generally a plate full of various meats and grilled vegetables. And save room for dessert! If food is love, there's an abundance of that in this land.

In fact, a frustration when traveling in Palestine is being overfed. I don't like to overeat or to waste food. And it seemed I had to do both twice a day. But then my local friend taught me that, according to Palestinian culture, whenever a guest finishes the food on his plate, it's only hospitable to refill it. So I found the solution: not to finish my food.

As in Israel, nearly all tourism in Palestine is religious tourism. And, of course, Bethlehem is a hugely important pilgrimage site to Christians as the birthplace of Jesus. While our image of "no room at the inn" is brick and wood, the "inn" of Bible fame was very likely a series of caves. And "no room" meant that a woman about to give birth would not be welcome in the main quarters, as childbirth was considered unclean. Mary was sent to the manger cave, where the animals were stabled, to give birth to Jesus.

Today, the place where the Baby Jesus first entered the material world is marked by the Church of the Nativity, established by St. Helena—mother

of the Roman Emperor Constantine—in 326. Inside, you feel the history. A
steady stream of tourists and pilgrims come here from all across Christendom
to remember that first Christmas and to pray.

For too many, unfortunately, the word "Palestinian" raises an automatic
association with terrorism. Because of this fear, the typical Christian pilgrimage tour visits Bethlehem as a side-trip from Israel. They zip through the
wall into the West Bank, head directly to Manger Square, visit the Church
of the Nativity, and make a beeline back to safety in Israel. These unfortu-
nate travelers miss a lot and come home with only one narrative. This means
that pilgrims who visit the Holy Land to "walk where Jesus walked" seldom
walk with the people Jesus walked with. They rarely interact with Palestinian Christians.

The fact that not all Palestinians are Muslims surprises some.
When meeting an Arab Christian,
many tourists ask when their family was converted. The answer is
usually, "About 2,000 years ago,
back when Jesus' disciples were
doing missionary work around
here." A century ago, about 20 percent of Palestinians were Christian.
But many Arab Christians fled the
draft during World War I (since
the ruling Ottomans were neither
Arab nor Christian, these Arab

According to scripture, angels were heard on
high at Beit Sahour—the Shepherds' Fields just
outside Bethlehem.

Christians saw no reason to fight in their army). And many more have fled
with the rising sectarian tensions of recent decades. Today, Christians make
up a tiny sliver of the Palestinian population...and most of them live here in
Bethlehem. With the rise of Islamists across the region making parishioners
nervous, the Church needs people to stay. Christian leaders meet monthly
with Muslim imams to discuss growing extremism in the Muslim community
and a growing uneasiness among Christians.

The village of Beit Sahour, just a 30-minute walk east of Bethlehem, is
the site of the famous Shepherds' Fields. In these fertile fields, the Bible tells
of an angel who said to ancient shepherds, "Do not be afraid; for see—I am
bringing you good news of great joy for all the people: to you is born this

day in the city of David a Savior, who is the Messiah, the Lord. This will be a sign for you: you will find a child wrapped in bands of cloth and lying in a manger." Today, pilgrims still come to these fields to hear the good news, and then spread it throughout the world. (Locals say that God knew what he was doing, because this town is still notorious in Palestine for its gossiping. Even news less important than the coming of the Messiah spreads fast from Beit Sahour.)

That evening, back at my Bethlehem hotel, I bumped into a dozen Lutheran pastors in the lobby. They were heading into the 2,000-year-old cave upon which the hotel was built for a devotional service. They invited me along. Although I was really tired, I followed my travel ethic: If an opportunity presents itself, say "Yes." I climbed down into the cave with them and enjoyed a wonderful hour of singing, reading, and sharing. It was, simply, beautiful. You meet far fewer tourists in the West Bank than elsewhere, but those you do meet are really interesting.

Walls and Settlements: It's About Land...
Like Holy Land Monopoly

As long as I've been politically active (since my first trip to Central America back in the Contra/Sandinista days), I've been impressed by how land issues are so fundamental to peace with justice. And land—it seems to me—is what the struggles in the Holy Land are all about.

Whether you call it a "Security Fence" or a "Separation Wall," this 300-mile-long structure has become an icon of the Israeli-Palestinian conflict.

Two hot-button land issues dominate much of the debate: Israel's erection of a barrier around the West Bank, and the Israeli construction of settlements within West Bank territory. In an effort to get a balanced-as-possible take, I made a point to talk with people on both sides (physically and philosophically) of this divide.

Begun in 2003, a 300-mile-long fortified barrier now separates Israel from the West Bank. What Israelis call the "Security Fence" or "Anti-Terrorism Barrier," Palestinians—who consider it an affront to their dignity—call the "Separation Wall," the "Apartheid Wall," or simply "The Wall."

Israelis explain that the barrier is essential to their national security, and needed to be built after losing hundreds of its citizens to suicide bombers in the previous decade. And they claim it's been effective—noting that since its construction, there has been far less violence.

Palestinians would counter by saying that the wall was built only with the pretense of security. (Several locals assured me that if anyone really wants to get through the wall—which is far from finished—it's very easy to do.) They don't credit the wall for the decline in violence, but say it's because the West Bank, its leaders, its security forces, and most of its people have all realized that violence is a losing strategy.

Palestinians also view the wall as a land grab designed to hobble a Palestinian state. The wall generally runs well within Palestinian territory: It's nearly twice as long as the border it claims to defend—gerrymandered in order to secure Israel settlements, aquifers, good farmland, and religious and

Over 500,000 Israelis live in planned and fortified communities built mostly in the last generation on ridges and hilltops within the West Bank.

archeological sites within the West Bank. While it can look landscaped and attractive from the Israeli side, the wall is gloomy and oppressive from the Palestinian side.

Walking through the border checkpoint is enlightening and, for some people, uncomfortable. For a Western tourist, it's easy: Leaving Jerusalem, I took a cab to the checkpoint, flashed my passport, walked through the turnstile, and hopped into one of the many taxis waiting on the Palestinian side for the quick ride into downtown Bethlehem. Most of the traffic passing through the border checkpoint is not tourists, but Palestinians heading to and from work in Jerusalem. Like border towns between rich and poor lands all over the world, workers with spe-

For Israeli parents, settlements in the West Bank are a great place to raise children. I could have played all day with the kids I met.

cial passes cross every day on their commute for higher-paying jobs in the more affluent country.

I can understand Israel's need for security, but my hunch is that the wall is designed at least partly to separate people from people. At least, it functions that way—and, to me, that's part of the problem. I sensed that the younger generation on both sides wanted to get beyond the baggage of their parents and connect. But with this barrier, there's literally no common ground where people from opposite sides can come together. Walls are ugly. They may be necessary at times, but they represent a diplomatic failure.

In addition to the wall, Israel has steadily encroached upon Palestinian territory by building hilltop settlements in the West Bank. Today more than half a million Israeli Jews live in settlements in Palestinian land (about a third of them in East Jerusalem, claimed both by Israel and Palestine). These are planned communities—beautifully landscaped and designed— offering the same modern conveniences and efficiency you'd expect in an American gated community. And thanks to Israeli governmental subsidies for housing and transportation, young Jewish families can afford to live here and comfortably commute to jobs back in Israel. For many, it's simple economics—a deal too good to refuse.

When Palestinians complain about Israelis building homes here, they hear many justifications. Supporters of these settlements make the case that developing this land is reasonable because it was unused, and because the language of the treaty designating it Palestinian was open-ended ("until a final status agreement is reached"). Israel also explains that settlement construction creates a needed buffer zone (an action they can defend by simply pointing to their recent history). They say that according to international law, if land is used to attack a nation, that nation has the legal right to both occupy and settle that land for its

This Israeli couple—enjoying their community's sleek shopping mall—explains why they choose to live in a West Bank settlement. To watch my interview with them and many others featured in this chapter, see www.ricksteves.com/holy-land.

own defense. And many Jews (and Evangelical Christians who are inclined to support them) believe it is God's will that they occupy this land. (A certain breed of Christian believes that, according to the Bible, Judgment Day will only happen when Jews control the entire Holy Land. And they support Israel simply because they'd like to move things along.)

To better understand the settlers' perspective, I spent some time in a few Israeli settlements that were built during the last decade or so in the West Bank. Strolling along *Leave It to Beaver* streets under the red-tiled roofs of cookie-cutter homes, I felt as if I were in suburban America. Gangs of happy-go-lucky children on their bikes were eager to befriend me, and there was a relaxed vibe.

I spoke to one couple who's raising 10 children in one of Israel's biggest and most modern settlements. Chatting in a café at their mall, they acknowledged that the rest of the world may not like it (referring to the "rest of the world" as just another opinion). Describing their community as a "city" rather than a "settlement," they were thankful to have a place to raise their children according to their values in a secure and affordable environment.

I also enjoyed a beer and a chat with a resident of a simple and rustic settlement in the Jordan River Valley. He said he was here not as a Zionist, but because it was quiet and offered his young family a back-to-nature home with wonderful neighbors. "You never see the stars in Tel Aviv like we do here," he told me.

In another settlement, I met a 24-year-old man who had just bought his house and was thrilled to invite me in. He and his buddy talked with me on their balcony, overlooking a vast and unpopulated view. They said that the land was going unused anyway, so why shouldn't industrious Israeli Jews develop it? They can pump in water from desalination plants and build a slick freeway to provide a fine place for people to live within a short drive to jobs back in Israel proper. When I asked these young men if there's a good and peaceful future in this region, I was struck by how matter-of-factly they said, "Only if the Palestinians move east across the Jordan River and into the country of Jordan."

Walking through an Israeli settlement, I can see the appeal of these neighborhoods. But history has taught us that when a government plants its citizens in disputed territory, the descendants of those original settlers are likely to pay the price. Ultimately, rather than cheap, that land is very costly. (For more thoughts on this, see "Nations without States," Chapter 3, page 70.)

I've also learned that these Israeli enclaves embitter the Palestinians as much as violent resistance embitters Israelis. And the more settlements are built, the more the West Bank becomes fragmented, and the more difficult a mutually agreeable two-state solution—or any solution—may become. While I hope it's not true, I worry that the aggressive establishment of these settlements today could haunt Israel's prospects for a peaceful resolution of the tensions in the Middle East tomorrow.

This map, posted in many places around Palestine, illustrates how with each passing decade, Israeli control of the Holy Land is becoming greater, while Palestinian control (the green area) is shrinking.

I see three possible outcomes to the Israeli-Palestinian conflict: The first scenario is two independent and secure states (a Jewish Israel and Palestine). The second scenario is one modern, pluralistic, and democratic secular state with a dominant

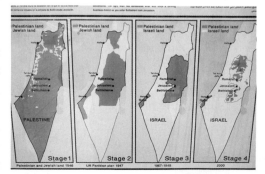

Palestinian Borders: Complex as ABC

As a visitor, zipping from Palestinian city to city on fine modern freeways, it's easy to underestimate the complexity of the region and the extent of Israeli control. Palestinians living in the West Bank, while nominally autonomous, feel they're under Israeli occupation. Palestinian cities are generally Palestinian-run with their own security forces. But these islands of relative independence are surrounded by land and roads controlled by Israeli military.

Since the 1993 Oslo Peace Accords, the West Bank has been subdivided into pockets of land classified into three zones: Areas A, B, and C.

Area A (18 percent of the land in the West Bank, with about 55 percent of the people) is made up of urban islands within the West Bank. It contains most of the Palestinian cities and towns, and is entirely controlled by the Palestinian Authority.

Area B is filled mostly with infrastructure connecting the islands of autonomy that combine to make Area A.

The West Bank is not as contiguous as simple maps imply. Locals say it's more like Swiss cheese, with the holes being densely populated islands of Palestinian autonomy surrounded by roads and open land controlled by Israel.

As you approach any Palestinian city, a bold red sign makes it clear in Hebrew, Arabic, and English: You are leaving the realm of the Israeli military and entering the zone controlled by Palestinian security.

At checkpoints, stalled and frustrated drivers have plenty of time to ponder political art decorating the walls. People living difficult lives are expert at coping—whether through hero-worship, venting with a spray can, or dark humor.

While Area B is technically under Palestine civil authority, it's effectively controlled by the Israeli military. Palestinian license plates are green and Israeli plates are yellow. When times are good, all cars are allowed. In troubled times, traffic is yellow plates only. If there's unrest or a problem, Israel can shut down Area B border crossings all over the country and stop all traffic in the West Bank. In minutes, they can isolate and lock down every Palestinian city.

Area C, holding most of the West Bank's uninhabited land, is under complete Israeli authority. While Area C is nominally a part of Palestine, there can be no Palestinian building in Area C without Israeli permission (which is rarely granted). Area C also includes modern Israeli highways that cut through the West Bank, connecting Jewish settlements in Palestine with Israel proper.

Checkpoints stand sternly at the boundary between Israeli-controlled land and Palestinian territory. Some are manned; others are empty and a simple drive-through; and "flying checkpoints" can pop up unexpectedly in the middle of nowhere. But all checkpoints come with a watchtower reminding everyone that Israel is keeping an eye on things. For Palestinians, the needless wasted time spent sitting at these checkpoints is aggravating and humiliating. Driving by one, I saw two soldiers checking papers one car at a time (holding up traffic in the opposite direction and creating a huge traffic jam in the baking sun).

Although Palestinians still feel that they live at least partly under Israeli occupation, they try to remember what an historic accomplishment it is that the land in Area A is free and self-ruled, and has been since 1993—for the first time after centuries of foreign control.

Jewish population and an equal and protected Palestinian minority. Unfortunately, this is untenable for anyone who believes in a Jewish state, as over time—according to demographic trends—the Muslim minority would grow to outnumber the current Jewish majority, tipping the balance of power. The third option is one Jewish state with its Palestinian minority kept on the equivalent of Indian reservations—what some would call an "Apartheid state."

I don't believe an Apartheid state is what Israel wants, and I don't believe it's the best option for Israel. But as Israel continues to build settlements that carve up the West Bank, I fear the country may be forcing itself into an ugly and undesirable corner. With a two-state scenario becoming less and less likely, Israel will have to be one state. And if that state is to be Jewish, Israel may ultimately have no option but to become what most Israelis don't want it to be in order to simply be.

The Beauty of Palestine: Olives, Bedouins, and Salty Seas

After just a couple of days in Palestine, I was really impressed by how much fun it was to simply be there. I sensed a resilience, a welcoming spirit, and a warmth that was striking. While I rarely saw fellow Americans, everywhere I went, I heard over and over, "Welcome to Palestine!" It's as if people were just thrilled that they have a name for their country…and someone from the outside world was there to see their flags flapping in the West Bank breeze.

Driving through the Palestinian countryside, the vistas feel timeless—I couldn't help but imagine Abraham, Jesus, or Muhammad traversing these same valleys. One place that stole my heart was a natural preserve for hiking near the village of Battir, west of Bethlehem. A fine trail snaked along the same terraces that defined this terrain in ancient times. These

3,000-year-old "Biblical Terraces" were lined with stately and graceful olive trees.

Here in the Holy Land, the land itself is holy to its inhabitants. For Palestinians, the olive tree—a symbol of steadfastness and faith in the future—is a kind of lifeblood for the culture. The tree of poor people, it gives without taking. As they say, "It was planted by our grandfathers for us to eat, and we plant it for our grandchildren to eat."

Each autumn, across the

Top: In Palestine, olive trees have been tended by locals for millennia. Bottom: Families still come together to harvest olives, just as they have since biblical times.

land—as they have since ancient times—families gather in the olive groves for the harvest. Children are let out of school for the week so they can work the trees with their parents. Then families take their olives to the communal village press to make oil. Stumbling upon one of these village presses in action is a treat. The traditional technique survives—though boosted by hardworking machinery—as a busy crew in oil-soaked shirts meets the demand of the harvest season. Rounds of olive paste are pressed into a weeping mass of fresh oil, which after filtering becomes a golden liquid poured into jugs to be taken home.

Scattered through the Palestinian countryside, like timeless limpets, are the settlements of nomadic Bedouin tribes—filling dusty gullies with their scrappy shacks and goat corrals. Children and sheepdogs follow their flocks of goats and sheep as they search for something to munch on.

While hardscrabble communities still eke out an off-the-grid existence, their way of life is dying. Like nomads everywhere, Bedouins are being driven into a world where people have addresses and send their children to school to learn the prevailing val-

Bedouin people, while settling down, are retaining as much of their heritage as the modern world allows.

ues of that society. With the political tensions between Israel and Palestine (the walls, settlements, freeway construction, and aggressive water politics), I was told that Bedouin camps are now less mobile and stick to land near roads where they can tap into water mains. After so many centuries, more and more Bedouin families are finally settling down in towns and villages. As their ability to roam free is disappearing and their access to water is becoming more limited, they are, by necessity, adapting.

And yet, these Bedouins are trying to maintain their traditions as much as a nomad with a roof over his head can. Visiting a Bedouin settlement and watching the man of the house roast coffee with a reverence for tradition is

Bedouin settlements pepper the Palestinian countryside.

mesmerizing. Observing him at work, it was clear to me that the dignity of these people and their closeness to the land is emblematic of Palestinians in general. And tasting his fresh-brewed coffee was like sealing a new friendship.

Also hiding in folds of the desert are fabled monasteries, which, since ancient times, have given hermits the isolation of their dreams. The dramatically set Monastery of St. George, built on cliffs above a natural spring, welcomes pilgrims and tourists alike.

Top: The Monastery of St. George is tucked away deep in the Judean Desert. Bottom: The Orthodox icons at the Monastery of St. George are a reminder of how the meditation, isolation, and hermetic way of life can all help the monks—and pilgrims—to better understand the message and will of Jesus.

For 15 centuries, the faithful have ventured to this remote spot, hiked into the ravine, quenched their thirst, and nourished their souls. Orthodox Christians—whether from Palestine, Greece, Russia, or Ethiopia—enliven these monasteries today, as they have since the sixth century.

I ascended the dramatic Wadi Qilt viewpoint for a thrilling panorama over the Judean Desert. Then my ears popped as I dropped below sea level and passed through the ancient city of Jericho. Dating back some 10,000 years, it's one of the oldest continuously inhabited cities on earth. Locals claim that the thick air that comes with this low altitude—nearly a thousand feet below sea level—makes their bananas, oranges, and dates particularly tasty.

The road ends where the Jordan River does, at the lowest place on earth (about 1,400 feet below sea level): the fabled Dead Sea. The Jordan continually empties into this inland sea. Because there's no outlet for the water, and the scalding sun—almost unbearable in the summer—causes constant evaporation, the minerals concentrate. That's why the water is more than one-third minerals (bromine, magnesium, and iodine).

Tourists are more than welcome here, and they enjoy bobbing like corks in water that's about six times as salty as the ocean. A dip rubs salt on cuts you didn't know you had. Keep the water out of your eyes and float near a shower.

Dead Sea spas have an impressive brag list. The soothing air is thick—there's 10 percent more oxygen here than at sea level—and hazy with bromine, a natural tranquilizer. Visitors rub the Dead Sea's magically curative black mud on their bodies. Many believe the mud's minerals make their skin younger and more beautiful.

Palestinians living in the West Bank have no access to waterfront. Israel even adjusted the border to control the entire Dead Sea shoreline. But when tensions are low, Palestinian families who can afford the admission are allowed to enjoy some Israeli Dead Sea resorts.

Traveling through the West Bank, you become attuned to telltale symbols of a divided society. For example, the skylines of Palestinian cities and towns are dotted with black water tanks. (Tanks are black to better absorb the solar heat and warm the water.) While Israeli settlers have running water

The Dead Sea, the lowest place on earth, has a special mystique at twilight.

whenever they like, Israel controls and limits water service in Palestinian-held areas. These rooftop water tanks give Palestinians a private reservoir when the water is shut off—and help you identify Arab houses.

Each community has its concerns: They say the first thing an Israeli considers when building a house is a bomb-hardened safe room, and the first thing a Palestinian considers is building a cistern. Along with water tanks and

Top: Palestinian rooftops are punctuated with countless black water tanks. Bottom: This Israeli water pump, in the West Bank, is caged in and surrounded by barbed wire—a reminder of what is the most important natural resource around here.

solar panels, Palestinian rooftops also sport satellite dishes to connect to Arab and international satellites, which serve as their window on the world. Palestinians told me that many here keep the TV on at all times. To them, "breaking news" stories aren't just entertainment, but critical updates about a constantly shifting political reality.

Driving through the West Bank at night was also instructive. In the countryside, there were no streetlights unless I was under an Israeli settlement or military base—in which case, the highway was well-lit, including powerful spotlights facing away from the road, illuminating the land nearby.

In the distance, the faint flicker of open fires, lanterns, and makeshift dangle lighting marked off-the-grid Bedouin camps. And I could identify Palestinian towns on the horizon by the proud green lights festooning their minarets.

A Synagogue, a Mosque, and Bulletproof Glass: Jews and Muslims Sharing Abraham in Hebron

Hebron is the West Bank's biggest city (with 700,000 people), and is also home to one of the holiest sites in the Holy Land: The Tomb of Abraham, revered by Jews, Muslims, and Christians. According to scripture, Abraham had one son

by his wife, Sarah (Isaac, the ancestor of the Israelis), and another son by their Egyptian servant, Hagar (Ismael, from whom the Arabs are descended). That's why both Jews and Muslims come to the Tomb of Abraham to be close to their great patriarch. While this confluence could have been an opportunity for unity and cooperation, instead it has turned the tomb into a divisive place with an uneasy aura.

The Tomb of Abraham stands right in the center of town, where Israeli troops are posted in the name of security. In the surrounding streets, Jews live literally atop Muslims as the two communities struggle to be near the shrine of their common patriarch. While the city is mostly Palestinian, a determined and well-protected community of several hundred Israeli settlers has staked out the high ground. The tension between the communities is illustrated by a wire net that protects the Arab food and

Top: Hebron, the biggest city in the West Bank, is a jostle of activity.
Bottom: In Hebron, the bustling market comes with a net to protect it from falling Israeli garbage.

clothing market from the garbage tossed down by the Jewish residents above. Observing this, I wondered what Abraham would think about the inability of his feuding descendants to live together.

And it's all about one complicated and tragic sight: The Tomb of the Patriarchs, an ancient structure capped by a medieval church, which now

In Hebron, turnstiles and checkpoints are a way of life.

functions both as a mosque and a synagogue holding the tombs of Abraham and his family. Abraham purchased this burial plot almost 4,000 years ago, as explained in Genesis 23.

For centuries, Jews were generally not allowed to worship here. Then, after the Israeli victory in 1967's Six-Day War, this holy site was shared by Muslims and Jews. But during a Muslim service in 1994, a Jewish settler entered with his gun and killed 29 Palestinian worshippers. Since then, this holy space has been smothered with security and divided—half mosque and half synagogue—with Abraham's tomb in the middle, granting both communities partial access.

Sadly, this shrine comes with bulletproof glass and barred windows so that his two sons' feuding descendants can respect his grave. On one side of the glass, Jews worship in the synagogue, enlivened with singing, studying, and praying among the tombs of their great patriarchs. And the other half is a mosque, where Muslims worship with equal fervor.

The tomb of the great patriarch Abraham, venerated by both Jews and Muslims, is shared by a synagogue and a mosque—and split by a pane of bulletproof glass.

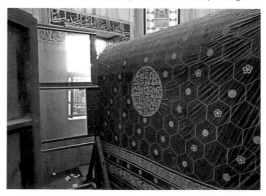

Hebron is the place where I feel the most tension in the West Bank. Jews expect access, as do Muslims—and, with a history of

Top: A virtual no-man's-land with closed buildings divides Hebron's two communities. Bottom: A giant key is a powerful symbol among Palestinians.

massacres on both sides, any trust is fragile. Palestinians can do little but annoy the huge number of Israeli soldiers stationed here—and vice versa. During my visit, I noticed that they were putting down protective mats over the venerable carpets in the mosque. When I asked why, I was told that they expected an inspection by Israeli soldiers, and they never knew if the soldiers would remove their boots before entering.

I sensed a sad and unsettling sentiment of occupiers' vengeance among these young Israeli soldiers, who seemed to have little empathy for the people they were controlling. I remembered learning how, in World War I, the French and Germans were so willing to slaughter each other on the Western Front because the vast majority of them had never broken bread with someone from the other side. The society here seems purposefully structured to prevent people from knowing each other. These seemingly likeable young soldiers were fun to chat with. Then, when it was time to go, one of them said, "Time to go bust down a door." His friends in uniform laughed, and they were off.

A Stroll Through Balata Refugee Camp

Refugees are a big issue in the Holy Land. When Jews returned to their ancestral homeland after World War II to create the modern state of Israel, they displaced hundreds of thousands of Palestinians. Many of these families still live in refugee camps in the West Bank. The biggest, with over 20,000 people, is Balata, just outside the city of Nablus.

The original ten-foot-by-ten-foot platting—marking where tents were pitched in 1948—survives. Only now the tents are gone, replaced by multi-story cinderblock tenements. Exploring these narrow lanes, I tried to imagine living in such tight quarters: being a parent with children and little money...

the feeling of desperation and no way out. The density is horrible, and there's little privacy. It's a land of silent orgasms.

Walking through the Balata camp, I made a point to remember that throughout the world, there are refugee camps filled with people living this way. When we travel, we draw a tiny line of experience across our globe. But what we experience hints at a much broader reality; although we see very little, we can learn a lot. From one country to the next, a gated community is a gated community. A happy person with clean running water is a happy person. And a refugee camp—regardless of who lives there and why—is filled with destitution, frustration, and faint but persistent hope.

Wandering the streets of Balata offered a vivid glimpse of life here. Mothers send their sons out for chicken, and they bring home a very fresh bird ready to cook. The boy selects a bird from the cage. The butcher slits its throat, drains it, and tosses the bird into a spinner to remove all its feathers. Then he guts it, washes it, puts it in a plastic bag, and collects a few coins. Palestinians call the spinner a *ma a'ta*— the same word they use for the turnstile they have to go through at security checkpoints.

Balata's political art—typical of the graffiti decorating the wall separating Israel and Palestine—comes with powerful symbolism. And for Palestinian refugees, one of the most poignant symbols is a key. In 1948, when the families now living in Balata left their homes, they were told it would be for a short time. They locked up and took their

Top: The claustrophobic Balata Refugee Camp is home to more than 20,000 Palestinians. Bottom: Political art in Palestine comes with unmistakable symbolism: Here, along with the Dome of the Rock (sacred to Muslims), a shattered wall, and an olive branch, is a key.

At an Internet café in the refugee camp, kids spend a few pennies playing violent shoot-'em-up games. One cute little boy turned to me, saying, "Shalom." Another boy, just as cute, said, "F__k you, rich man." Part of me was impressed.

keys. Now, more than 60 years later, many of these people treasure those old keys and are eager to share their story.

For over 60 years, the United Nations has kept a calming presence in Balata Refugee Camp. When the UN-run-and-funded school lets out, the streets are flooded with children eager to practice their English with a rare tourist venturing into their world.

In Balata—and throughout the West Bank—I saw Palestinian kids with toy guns shooting imaginary Jews. It was disturbing to me. But then, in the Israeli settlements, I also saw Jewish kids with plastic guns gunning down imaginary terrorists. And it occurred to me that, if we're being honest, what American man today didn't grow up with a toy gun happily shooting Indians or Soviets in their imagination? Whether it's cowboys and Indians, Commies and Capitalists, or Jews and Arabs, little boys throughout the world are raised with a toy gun in their hands to shoot their parents' bad guys.

But many parents take the opposite tack. I asked a Palestinian whether

children here are taught in schools to hate Jews (as some Israelis allege). He said, "As a parent raising my family under this Jewish occupation, it's my challenge to teach our children *not* to hate Jews."

The conditions in Balata are dismaying, particularly when you think that people have been living

Top: Like many other Palestinian cities and towns, Nablus is encrusted with posters honoring young men killed or imprisoned in the struggle against Israel. While considered "terrorists" by many, these Palestinians are viewed as freedom fighters and martyrs in their hometowns. Bottom: Just being a tourist in Palestine for a week, I can understand the toll it must take on any "love thy neighbor" person to live in a land where they say, "To exist is to resist."

this way here for decades. But Israelis point out that Israel has taken in many Jewish refugees and assimilated them into their prosperous society. Meanwhile, they claim that Palestine—and the Arab world—has intentionally kept the West Bank refugee camps in squalor in order to stir public opinion against Israel.

Observing the Holy Land from a distance through a media lens, we can't really get an honest picture of the reality here. I might see a news clip of Palestinians destroying a synagogue. It looks so hateful. And then I learn that during a land swap, Israel agreed to give back land upon which they had built a luxurious modern settlement. And, before retreating, they destroyed every building in the settlement except the synagogue. When hardscrabble Palestinians, so poor and needy, walked into their land, they saw only rubble except for one building—and they got mad and destroyed it. It's ugly both ways, but television coverage without context leaves the viewer with the wrong impression.

Many Palestinians I met resent the "terrorism" tag that is typically applied to their community. One Palestinian said to me, "Maybe terrorists are 'terrorists' only because they lack uniforms, tanks, and warplanes."

Ramallah, Palestine's De Facto Capital

Ramallah is the boomtown of the West Bank. As, bit by bit (under the settle-ment policy of Israel), the likelihood of East Jerusalem being the capital of Palestine is fading, Ramallah is emerging as a natural stand-in, hosting the Palestinian government and international agencies. The PLO headquarters is here. Yasser Arafat is buried here. And it's busy with NGOs and interna-tional agencies working on Palestine's problems.

As many Palestinian Americans have moved back home and live here, there are lots of American accents. The city of 340,000 people sits at about 3,000 feet above sea level. Its name means "God's Mountain." As it lacks the trouble-causing religious sites—and is more liberal and cosmopolitan than other Palestinian cities—I found it the most relaxed city in the country.

With its international professionals and university students, Ramal-lah has an almost cosmopolitan energy. Whether coming together at the Square of the Lions or browsing down a stylish shopping street, the people of Ramallah inspire me to envision a peaceful and prosperous Pales-tine of the future.

Top: Ramallah proudly flies the flag of Palestine.
Bottom: The tomb of Yasser Arafat.

The number one sight in Ramallah is the tomb of Yasser Arafat. While he cer-tainly has plenty of detractors, this Pal-estinian statesman, who led the PLO from 1969 to 2004, is without a doubt the father of modern Palestine. Call him what you like—people here celebrate Arafat as the man who did

The Hijab: The Meaning of a Scarf

At Ramallah's Birzeit University, I enjoyed a fascinating conversation with three smart, young, female Palestinian university students about the role of women in a Muslim society. Along with many other things, I was curious about the hijab, or traditional head covering. Throughout the country, I noticed that some women wear it, while others don't.

Like many Westerners, I'm intrigued and perplexed by the tradition of women in religious families or communities needing to be covered in public for modesty. Modesty requirements are not unique to Muslims. Some conservative Christian women are expected to cover their heads in church. Some ultra-Orthodox Jewish women are expected to shave their heads and to wear a wig in public. And many Muslim women cover their heads. In Palestine, far more women wear scarves in Hebron and Nablus than in the more cosmopolitan cities of Bethlehem and Ramallah. For a Muslim man, it's a sin to look lustfully at a woman who's not his wife. Around here, hair is sexy, and in the strictest of Muslim societies, women carefully cover up every strand in public. (Of course, in the privacy of their own domestic world, they are welcome to be as sexy as they like for their husbands.)

But the scarf—while meant to downplay a woman's beauty—has morphed into something stylish and sexy in itself. Women can be technically proper with their faith while still looking good. These days, scarves

are worn like peacock tails. For many women, much care is put into coordinating their scarves, nail polish, handbags, and lipstick. One woman I met told me that she has over a hundred scarves, and each morning, she enjoys choosing one that fits her mood. It's an ensemble. You never wear pattern-on-pattern or solid-on-solid. If the dress is solid, the hijab will be patterned. I picked up another fashion tip: Propping up the back end with an empty yogurt cup as you tie it gives your scarf a fetching lift.

The women I talked with agreed that women are free to be individuals in Palestine, and that choosing to wear the hijab was entirely up to them. The woman who covers up is just as socially active, and in on all of the jokes and fun. But when she walks in public, she feels she gets more respect.

As for the broader role of women in Palestinian society, they pointed out that there were more women than men in higher education, and feel that they can do anything they want, if they work hard. Still, the consensus was that a woman's role is generally to raise children and run the family, while the man's role is to be out making the money.

My favorite Palestinian dessert is *kunafeh*, made of fine shreds of pastry with honey-sweetened goat cheese in the center. It's drenched in sweet syrup and then sprinkled with crushed pistachios.

more than anyone else to raise awareness of the Palestinian struggle for independence. I found that, while many Palestinians believe Arafat squandered some opportunities for peace that they would love to have now, nearly all respect him as an important leader who committed his life to forging a free Palestinian state.

Growing up, the only Palestinian I was aware of was Yasser Arafat. Today, Arafat's tomb stands next to the Palestinian president's headquarters. A thoughtful museum at the tomb of the Palestinian poet Mahmoud Darwish introduced me to the author and poet who wrote the Palestinian Declaration of Independence. Darwish, who died in 2008, worked with Arafat, but used a pen rather than a gun as his weapon—a reminder of the wide range of approaches the Palestinians have used to make their message heard.

To get a more well-rounded feeling for modern Palestine both in its people and its institutions, I popped into Birzeit University. Its campus, at the edge of Ramallah, has an enrollment of about 10,000. With beautiful landscaping connecting modern buildings and a student body that represented the future leaders of this young country, the campus was a sharp contrast with the intense and chaotic cities. A stroll through the campus gave me a chance to connect with young students and learn a bit about both their culture and their aspirations (see facing page). It was inspiring.

Israelis and Palestinians: Who's Right, Who's Wrong... Who Knows?

My Holy Land trip had the best possible outcome: It challenged my preconceptions. I learned that people whose language always sounded to me like terrorists conspiring are actually gentle souls with big challenges. And it taught me that there are two sure things: Violence doesn't work, and neither the Israelis nor the Palestinians are going to move. The only workable road is one of peaceful coexistence. It's clear to me that if you care about the future of Israel, you must find a viable solution for Palestine. Creating security, dignity, and independence for Palestine is actually in Israel's best interest—part of the long-term, sustainable solution to this region's troubles. I know—the hurdles are high. But hearing both narratives, I can envision a peaceful and prosperous Holy Land—with a secure Israel and a free Palestine.

Another thing is clear: Good travel is all about connecting with people and better understanding their perspective. I learned what Muslims think of Jesus while sitting on a carpet with an imam; talked about raising kids while sipping coffee with Israelis who live in a settlement overlooking the West Bank; and visited with a Palestinian refugee as he clutched the key his parents took with them when they fled their village in 1948. I talked with soldiers in guard towers, roasted coffee with a Bedouin, and gained insight into why a proud and independent young woman would choose to wear a hijab. And I chatted

Good travel is all about meeting people, talking with them, and learning.

with a Hebron butcher—next to the swing-
ing head of a camel he just slaughtered—for
insight into his world.

   I remember when I first went on a political trip. It was back in the 1980s, to Nicaragua and El Salvador. Seeing me off, my Dad
(suspicious of communism) said, "Don't be
duped." Now, after a few weeks in the Holy
Land—the latest chapter in more than 30
years of satisfying my curiosity about our world and its challenges by traveling and talking to people—I believe that the people most in danger of being
duped are actually those who stay home.

   Traveling through the Holy Land, my heart was a shuttlecock, flipping
back and forth between sympathy for Israel and solidarity with Palestine. I'm
saddened by the many people—in Israel, Palestine, or the USA—who are so
hardened on one side or the other that they cannot allow themselves to find
empathy with the society they consider the enemy. Even if one side is the
enemy, it's not the entire society—just its leaders or its extremists. Just like
American children of Catholic parents tend to be Catholic, and children of
Lutheran parents tend to be Lutheran, children of the Holy Land have their
parents' baggage from the start. And very few are packing light around here.

   I'm concerned that—as a result of the societal and physical barriers
that separate them—people on both sides will not get to know each other.
It's next to impossible for Israelis and Palestinians to connect in any way.
Consider this: Israelis and Palestinians who are soccer fans, curiously, root
for the same Madrid and Barcelona teams—but many don't realize that

No trip to the Holy Land is complete,
nor is the learning experience balanced,
without spending time in Palestine
as well as in Israel. I found travel in
Palestine comfortable and safe in part
because I hired a local guide to be
with me each day I was there (pictured
here are Kamal, one of my Palestinian guides, and Abie, one of my Israeli
guides). For contact information for my
Palestinian and Israeli guides and for a
list of companies doing "dual narrative" tours of the Holy Land, see www.
ricksteves.com/holy-land.

they have this fandom in common. There's no way mutual fans of Real Madrid could be mutual enemies. They are completely reliant upon hometown media, parents, and schooling to shape their opinion of the younger generation of the people on the other side of the wall—a generation they are destined to share their historic homeland with.

In this land, so treasured by Jews, Muslims, and Christians, I'm reminded that the prophets of each of these religions taught us to love our neighbors.

There's a little turnout on the Palestine side of the wall where passengers can conveniently change from a Palestinian car to an Israeli one. When I left Palestine, my Israeli driver was there, waiting for my Palestinian driver to drop me off. While I barely knew either of these men, I'll never forget their handshake—in the shadow of an ominous Israeli watchtower blackened by the flames of burning tires and tagged with angry Palestinian graffiti. These men were each beautiful, caring people, trapped in a problem much bigger than either of them. In the exchange, I was little more than a suitcase shuttling from one back seat to the other. I watched as they quietly shook hands, looked into each other's eyes, and said a solemn and heartfelt "Shalom." And I thought, "With all these good people on both sides, there has got to be a solution—and a big part of it will be regular people making not walls...but bridges."

Chapter 10
Homecoming

After our whirlwind tour, it's time to wrap up our journey. No matter where you go, the final stop is always the same...and home is the best destination of all. Thankfully, our travels can inspire and empower us to make it even better.

Reverse Culture Shock

Having traveled makes being home feel homier than ever. Part of my re-entry ritual is a good, old-fashioned, American-style breakfast at the local diner. I know just how I like it: eggs—over medium, hash browns—burn 'em on both sides, and toast—sourdough done crispy with marionberry jam. As the waitress tops up my coffee and I snap my sugar packet before ripping it open, I think of how, across this planet, there are thousands of entirely different breakfasts eaten by people just as exacting as I am. And, of all those breakfasts, it's clear that this one is the right one for me. I am home.

Considering all the fun I have traveling, feeling thankful to be home affirms my sense that I'm rooted in the right place. I enjoy the same Olympic Mountains view from my kitchen window that I did as a kid. I look out my office window and still see my junior high school.

While I relish the culture shock of being in an exotic, faraway place, I also enjoy the reverse culture shock of returning to the perfect normalcy of home. As if easing from my traveling lifestyle into my home lifestyle, I still function out of my toiletries kit for a few days before completely unpacking. The simplicity of living out of a single bag slowly succumbs to the complexity of living out of a walk-in closet in a big house with light switches and an entertainment system I've yet to master.

Over time, I willingly fall back into the snappy tempo and daily routine of a busy home life. I do this because I am not fundamentally a vagabond. I love my children, have fun running a business, enjoy the fellowship of the social hour after church each Sunday, and savor my daily stroll across town for coffee. If I had a top hat, I'd tip it to the ladies I pass along the way.

And yet, after every trip, things remain a bit out of whack...but only to me. There's a loneliness in having a mind spinning with images, lessons, and memories that can never adequately be shared—experiences such as finding out why the Salvadoran priest ignores his excommunication, why the Dutch celebrate tolerance, and why the dervish whirls.

Travel Changes You

Travel doesn't end when you step off the plane into your familiar home airport. The preceding chapters—while ranging far and wide across the globe—all illustrate how travel is rich with learning opportunities, and how the ultimate souvenir is a broader outlook. I enjoy splicing what I've learned into who I am and what I do. By incorporating those lessons into my being, I am changed. Any traveler can relate to this: On returning from a major trip, you sense that your friends and co-workers have stayed the same, but you're...different. It's enlightening and unsettling at the same time.

A wonderful byproduct of leaving America is gaining a renewed appreciation for our country. When frustrated by overwrought bureaucracies overseas, I'm thankful that it's not a daily part of my life back home. When exasperated by population density, I return home grateful to live in a sparsely populated corner of the world. Traveling, I sample different tempos, schedules, seasonings,

Even when this Afghan girl and her mother can no longer see me, I live my life at home knowing the world is watching.

For a High-Contrast Look at Your Own Country...Leave It

When we travel, we can enjoy a fresh and often clearer perspective on challenges facing our nation. We can see how other nations are dealing with the same issues. We can see the consequences of ignoring a budding problem that has ballooned into a big one. And, we can see the beauty that results when a challenge is dealt with thoughtfully and successfully.

From a distant land, you can look back at your own country and see its beauties and its shortcomings in higher contrast. The problems and the triumphs pop. Consider the gap between rich and poor. Consider the blessing of good governance and of a peaceful transition of power. Consider the benefits of a meritocracy, as opposed to a more corrupt society. Appreciate a relatively small and efficient bureaucracy. Consider the impact of violent weather resulting from climate change. Consider the absence of anxiety about medical bills in a country with universal healthcare. Consider the results of legislating morality. Consider the beauty of involving seniors in everyday life rather than siloed away.

When you travel thoughtfully, you understand your own country better. It becomes clearer what's working well...and what's not. And you can see where you can best contribute.

business environments, and political systems. Some I like better—others I'm glad don't follow me home.

When I return home from any trip, I realize that I am a part of the *terroir* of my home turf, just as the people who so charm me in distant corners of the world are part of theirs. Those people might visit me here, find it interesting, incorporate a few slices of my lifestyle into theirs, and be just as thankful to fly back home. While seeing travel as a political act enables us to challenge our society to do better, it also shows us how much we have to be grateful for, to take responsibility for, and to protect.

Settling back into my hometown life, I embrace the idea that life is good, the world is not a scary place, and—considering everything—these are good times. While I may seem to many like "an activist," I've also learned that activism can be good stewardship of the status quo. I find that, after a good trip, I'm quicker to celebrate and support what undergirds the stability and goodness in my community.

Travel helps us better see both sides of our privileged reality: In addition to gaining a keen appreciation of how blessed we are, travelers also understand that with these blessings come responsibilities. Protecting the poor, civil rights, and our environment are basic to good global citizenship. Travelers experience lands that have a wide gap between rich and poor, places without basic freedoms an American might take for granted, and regions where neglect has led to ruined environments. Packing that experience home, we can become more compassionate, even (or especially) during difficult times. Because we've seen the extremes in faraway lands, we can better understand the consequences of continued neglect in our own community.

After a thought-provoking trip, I consume news differently. Since I've wandered through war debris with Alen in Mostar, news footage of any city being devastated by bombs suddenly aches with humanity. My memories of friends stiff with shrapnel, and former parks filled with tombstones, push me toward pacifism.

During times of saber-rattling, I fly a peace flag from my office building. A neighbor once asked if I knew how much business I've lost by flying that flag. Because of what I've learned about the human costs of war in places such as Bosnia-Herzegovina, El Salvador, and Iran, it hadn't occurred to me to measure the economic costs to my business of speaking out for peace. In fact, it's hard for me to understand how someone could support a war they didn't believe in because it was good for their business.

Mark Twain wrote, "Travel is fatal to prejudice, bigotry, and narrow-mindedness." These wise words can be a rallying cry for all travelers once comfortably back home. When courageous leaders in our community combat small-mindedness and ignorance—whether it's pastors contending with homophobia in their congregations, employers striving to make a workplace color-blind, or teachers standing up for intellectual and creative freedoms—travelers can stand with them in solidarity.

I strive, not always successfully, to be tolerant. As a comfortable, white, Protestant, suburban American, a warm welcome always awaits me over at the tyranny of the majority. I recognize that intolerance can be a natural state of rest. I'm inspired by lands that have morals but don't moralize…lands that make tolerance a guiding virtue and consider peaceful coexistence a victory. I want to celebrate the diversity in American life by making room for people representing the entire range of human experience. And I want to help shape an America that embraces that openness on a global scale as it works to be a constructive member of the family of nations.

Putting Your Global Perspective into Action at Home

Traveling to learn, you find new passions. Had I not seen shantytowns break out like rashes in Cairo, I might not have gotten tuned into affordable housing

Once you've met these girls living on a garbage dump in El Salvador, it's hard not to take them along when you enter the voting booth.

issues in my own community. After observing the pragmatic Dutch and Swiss approach to drug abuse, I chose to speak out on drug law reform and co-sponsor Washington State's initiative to legalize the recreational adult use of marijuana. Having traveled in the Islamic Republic of Iran, where religion and government are thoroughly interwoven, I've seen the troubling consequences of mixing mosque or church and state. In my church, some want the American flag right up there in front, while others in my community would like to hang the Ten Commandments in our City Hall. And because I care both for my church and my state, I work to keep my church free of flags and my City Hall free of religious commandments.

Travel becomes a political act only if you act—if you do something positive with your broadened perspective once you return home. The challenges on the horizon can be so overwhelming that they freeze caring people into inaction. While trying to save the planet singlehandedly can be disheartening, taking a few concrete and realistic baby steps in that direction can be empowering and bring fine rewards. Because of my work, I've had some exciting opportunities in this regard. Below are a few personal examples of how I've incorporated passions sparked by my travels into real action back home. While we may have different wattage in our light bulbs, we all bring light to our communities. Teachers teach, preachers preach, shoppers shop, parents parent, leaders

My daughter Jackie's high school trip—a month in a Moroccan village—was her most eye-opening experience yet in life. A trip like that doesn't happen without parents and teachers who appreciate the value of sending students abroad.

lead, those with money fund, and voters vote. I'm sharing these examples of making a difference in the hopes of demonstrating a few creative ways that you may do the same—on a larger or smaller scale:

Be an advocate for those outside of the US who have no voice here, but are affected by our policies. See our government policy through a lens of how will this impact the poor. Travel forces voters to consider a new twist on "representative" democracy. Whom should your vote represent? Because I've made friends throughout the developing world, my vote is based on more than simply, "Am I better off today than I was four years ago?" Travelers recognize that the results of an election here in the US can have a greater impact on poor people half a world away than it does on middle-class American voters. My travels have taught me that, even if motived only by greed, you don't want to be really rich in a desperately poor world. With this in mind, I think of it not as noble or heroic, but simply pragmatic to bring a compassion for the needy along with me into the voting booth.

Share lessons, expect more from your friends, and don't be afraid to ruin dinners by bringing up uncomfortable realities. In a land where the afflicted and the comfortable are kept in different corners, people who connect those two worlds are doing everyone a service. To paraphrase Finley Peter Dunne, strive to afflict the comfortable in order to comfort the afflicted. By saying things that upset people so they can declare they'd fight and die for my right to be so stupid, I feel I'm contributing to the fabric of our democracy.

Taking a principled stand—on any issue—can be inspirational (both personally and socially). What do you care about? Civil liberties, tasty food eaten in season, the downside of prisons for profit, states' rights, the danger to society of a single chain bookstore driving independent bookstores out of business, public funding of the arts, pedestrian zones in city centers, the corrosive effect on democracy of money in politics, the beauty of professors being free to say what they like, the way Airbnb threatens the character of a community, public access to waterfront...there are countless causes that your thoughtful travels can cause you to realize you care about.

THINK MULTILATERALLY

Promote multilateralism. Join your local chapter of the UN. In the lead-up to the Iraq War, I designed bumper stickers with the blue-and-white UN flag that said simply "Think Multilaterally" so my neighbors and I could fly our flag without implying we supported a unilateral foreign policy.

Get involved. After observing alarming trends in other countries, it's easier to extrapolate and appreciate where small developments in our own society may ultimately lead—whether it's the impact of a widening gap between rich and poor, a violation of the separation of church and state, the acceptance of a tyranny of the majority, or the loss of personal freedoms in the interest of national security. Then, for the good of your community, you understand the importance of becoming active and speaking out against those trends.

Encourage others to travel. For example, support student exchange programs. Many people have the resources to travel, but live within a social circle where "travel" means Las Vegas and Walt Disney World. High schools and universities are putting more priority than ever on foreign study programs. For many, the funding is a challenge. One trip can help forever broaden the perspective of a young person with a big future. Hosting a foreign student—while much easier to afford—can help create the same amount of international understanding as funding an American student's trip abroad.

Every community has nonprofit organizations whose mission is to foster understanding between cultures—bringing the same benefits of travel to people at home who may not be able to travel. They do this by facilitating inbound travel and opportunities for people from distant lands to interact with American communities. For example, the World Affairs Council hosts students, businesses, and cultural exchanges—bringing the world into the USA (www.world-affairs.org). Your local chapter of the United Nations provides a great way to travel vicariously, and would love to have you on their team (www.un.org). The Rotary Club recognizes the value of future community leaders being open to the world (www.rotary.org). Know which of these organizations are active in your community, support them, and celebrate their work.

You have choices. Do a survey of causes that interest you, choose a couple that resonate, then tackle these as a hobby. Working on my favorites—debt relief for the developing world, drug policy reform, and affordable housing—brings me great joy. I have an excuse to focus my studies, I meet inspirational people, and I enjoy the gratification that comes with actually making a difference. Organizations like Jubilee USA Network need grassroots help in reaching their goal of relief for the world's most heavily indebted nations (www.jubileeusa.org). Bread for the World (www.bread.org) is a Christian citizens' organization that effectively lobbies our government in the interest of poor and hungry people both in our country and overseas. (I'm donating all the royalties I earn from this book to support Bread's exciting work.) If you want to advocate for smarter US drug laws, join NORML (www.norml.org) and talk about drug policy reform in polite company. There are a host of good organizations and a world of worthy causes to support.

When sorting through your options to make a difference, distinguish between charity, development, and advocacy. Let's say there's a struggling community of fishermen at a place called Desperation Delta. Giving fish to hungry people there is charity. Giving them nets and skills to fish, along with matching funds to build a safer harbor, is development. And, lobbying our government to create legislation that protects fish during spawning season, cleans up industrial pollution, and prohibits large corporations from detonating explosives that kill fish en masse—that's advocacy. While charity and development certainly have their place, advocacy is my personal choice for getting the most bang out of my philanthropic dollar.

Promote the wisdom and importance of talking to your political opponents, even in everyday life. Confront problems—at home, at work, in your community—with calm, rational, and respectful communication. Support politicians who do the same with foreign policy. France and Germany still mix like wine and sauerkraut, but they've learned the hard way that an eternity of agreeing to disagree beats an eternity of violent conflict.

Reach and preach beyond the choir. Don't hold back in places where progressive thinking may seem unwelcome. I was tempted to move to a church downtown that welcomed progressive thinkers, but chose instead to continue sharing a pew with a more conservative gang at my suburban church. Rather

Conquering fear and ethnocentrism through world exploration rewards the traveler with a grand and global perspective.

than switch churches, I've stayed and contributed: teaching poverty awareness workshops, sharing my political travels at special events, and—after realizing that many in our congregation were homophobic—inviting the Seattle Men's Chorus (America's largest gay chorus) to provide music one Sunday.

While conservatives and liberals may see things differently, they care equally. I've found that, deep down, any thinking person wants to be challenged respectfully and thoughtfully. (That's why, after a little discussion, rather than install a new air-conditioning system for our auxiliary chapel, we re-directed that money to build a well in a thirsty Nicaraguan village.)

Travel inside the United States to appreciate the full diversity of culture and thought within our vast, multifaceted society. Assume that subcultures—even scary ones—provide basic human necessities. At home and abroad, the vast majority of people who look scary aren't.

I remember the first time I walked through Seattle's Hempfest—a party of 100,000 far-out people filling a park to celebrate what they considered the civil liberty to smoke marijuana. A man named Vivian wearing a Utili-kilt and dreadlocks yelled, "Give it up!" for a band whose music sounded like noise to me...and people went wild. It was intimidating. Then I got to know Vivian, who explained to me that this is a subculture that gets to come together out of the shadows once a year on Seattle's waterfront. I walked through the crowd again, with a different attitude. I celebrated the freedom and tolerance that made that tribal gathering possible. At the same "protestival," a few years later, I noticed I got strangely emotional when talking with police who said they enjoy the Hempfest assignment as a two-way celebration of respect and tolerance.

Take your broader outlook to work. Until we have "cost accounting" that honestly considers all costs, there is no real financial incentive for corporations to consider the environment, the fabric of our communities, the poor at home or abroad, or our future in their decisions. Executives of publicly held corporations are legally required to maximize profits in the short term, but with leadership and encouragement coming from their stockholders and workforce, they are more likely to be good citizens as well as good business-men. I encourage my employees to guard my travel company's ethics and stand up to me if I stray. And they do. (For example, because of encourage-ment from my staff to be more green in our travels, my company is powered by renewable energy and is working on ways to help us travel with a zero carbon footprint.)

Remember that many would love to travel and gain a broader perspective, but cannot. Find creative ways to bring home the value of travel by giving pre-sentations to groups of curious people not likely to have passports. I did this back in my twenties by hosting a monthly "World Travelers' Slide Club," and do essentially the same thing on a bigger scale today by producing a radio show that I offer free each week to 400 public radio stations around our country.

Consider an educational tour for your next trip. (I've assembled a list of recommended organizations that offer "reality travel"—see the sidebar). Even if you normally wouldn't take a tour, visiting trouble zones with a well-connected organization is safer, makes you an insider, and greatly increases your opportunities for learning. I've taken several such tours, and each has been powerfully informative and inspirational. Educational tourism is a small but important part of the tourism industry and offers options worldwide.

Seek out balanced journalism. Assume commercial news is entertain-ment—it thrives on making storms (whether political, military, terrorist-related, or actual bad weather) as exciting as they can get away with in order to increase their audience so they can charge more for advertising. (For more on this topic, see page 16.) Money propels virtually all media. Realize any information that comes to you has an agenda. If you're already consuming lots of TV news, read a progressive alternative source that's not so corporation-friendly (such as *The Nation* magazine, www.thenation.com). If you have a problem with entertainment masquerading as news (along with media that

Take an Educational Tour

I've taken several wonderful trips with organizations that offer "educational" or "reality" tours. My best experiences were with the Center for Global Education and Experience, which creates custom tours (www.augsburg.edu/global). It's clear to me that if you want to get the most out of visiting a complicated corner of our world, your best bet is to go with an organization that has a network of people on the ground who can provide an insider's understanding. Here are a few of the many fine organizations that offer educational travel experiences.

Friendship Force (www.friendshipforce.org): A nonprofit cultural organization, FF focuses on person-to-person exchange, with locals welcoming travelers into their homes. Each one- to three-week program includes cultural experiences, such as learning to make traditional *lavash* bread in Armenia, visiting historic Brazilian fishing villages, or tobogganing on sand hills in Australia's Hunter Valley.

Global Exchange Reality Tours (www.globalexchange.org/tours): An international human rights organization, their five- to sixteen-day Reality Tours focus on personal connections and give travelers a firsthand look at the effects of intractable global problems. Whether meeting with health organizations in Haiti, observing Cuban teachers and musicians at work, or visiting a farming co-op in North Korea, participants build real understanding.

New Community Project (www.newcommunityproject.org): This small organization designs their one- to

Educational tours build in time to share and reflect.

two-week Learning Tours to introduce tour members to people from all walks of life, from human trafficking survivors to indigenous shamans to farmers. Travelers learn about difficult challenges that people are facing with resilience and hope.

Xperitas Community Partnership Programs (www.xperitas.org): A nonprofit educational organization, Xperitas offers one- to two-week immersive programs with local, grassroots organizations in indigenous and marginalized communities around the world. Travelers eat what the locals eat, help with community-led local development projects, and get to know the community in ways a tourist cannot.

AFSNext (www.afsusa.org/afsnext): Part of AFS-USA (the study abroad organization), AFSNext offers international internship programs geared for close engagement with local communities through volunteer work, and professional development through internship opportunities on global issues such as wildlife conservation.

numbs us to violence, objectifies women, and generally dumbs us down), recognize public broadcasting (radio and TV) as a service worth supporting.

Read books that explain the economic and political basis of issues you've stumbled onto in your travels. A basic understanding of the economics of poverty, the politics of empire, and the power of corporations are life skills that give you a foundation to better understand what you experience in your travels. Information that mainstream media considers "subversive" won't come to you. You need to reach out for it. The following are a few of the books (listed in chronological order) that have shaped and inspired my thinking from my student days until now: *Bread for the World* (Arthur Simon), *Food First* (Frances Moore Lappé), *The Origins of Totalitarianism* (Hannah Arendt), *Future in Our Hands* (Erik Dammann), *Manufacturing Consent* (Noam Chomsky), *War Against the Poor: Low-Intensity Conflict and Christian Faith* (Jack Nelson-Pallmeyer), *Unexpected News: Reading the Bible with Third World Eyes* (Robert McAfee Brown), *The United States of Europe* (T. R. Reid), *The European Dream* (Jeremy Rifkin), *Escaping Plato's Cave* (Mort Rosenblum), and *The End of Poverty* (Jeffrey Sachs).

Find ways to translate your new global passions to local needs. As the saying goes, "Think globally...act locally." Travel has taught me the reality of homelessness. Talking with a proud and noble woman like Beatriz in El Salvador does more to humanize the reality of poverty than reading a library of great books on the subject, and inspired me to action back home. Thinking creatively, I used part of my retirement savings to purchase a small apartment complex that YWCA used to house local homeless mothers. For years, I could sleep easy, knowing that the value of my property was appreciating even as I was using my savings to house 25 needy moms and their kids. I promote this as a model of how people who care can put their personal savings to good use without diminishing their long-term financial security. (In 2017, realizing that my retirement will be comfortable enough without that equity, I outright donated the complex to the YWCA.)

When you can learn to vicariously enjoy the consumption of someone who's dealing with more basic needs than you are, and then help that person, you become richer for it. With this outlook, helping to provide housing to people in need is simply smarter, more practical, and more gratifying than owning a big yacht. (This can be done on a smaller scale with much less equity, too.)

Find creative ways to humanize our planet while comfortably nestled into your workaday home life. Sweat with the tropics, see developing-world debt as the slavery of the 21st century, and feel the wartime pain of "enemy losses" along with the pain of American losses. Do things—even if only symbolic—in solidarity with people on the front lines of struggles you care about.

Put your money where your ideals are. Know your options for local consumption and personal responsibility. Don't be bullied by non-sustainable cultural norms. You can pay more for your bread to buy it from the person who baked it. You can buy seasonal produce in a way that supports family farms. You can, as a matter of principle, shun things you don't want to support (bottled water, disposable goods, sweatshop imports, your least favorite fast food joint's burgers, and so on). You can use public transit or drive a greener car. Consume as if your patronage helps shape our future. It does.

Keep on Whirling

With the fall of the USSR, I remember thinking, "Wow, the USA will reign supreme on this planet through the rest of my lifetime." It seemed that American values of democracy and the free market would be unstoppable. And, American economic might, coupled with our hardball approach to maintaining our relative affluence, would be insurmountable. We would just keep getting richer and more powerful.

Of course, the outlook today is more sober. America has been humbled by many things: dysfunctional government, the limits of our military power, periodic financial woes, the advent of corporate money shaping our government as "free speech," the meteoric rise of India and China as economic giants, the costly specter of global climate change, and a general inability to shape events both overseas and at home.

In this Global Age, the world's problems are *our* problems. And we have a responsibility to address these challenges honestly and wisely. Our nation is grappling with a hard choice: Will we look out exclusively for American interests? Or will we try to be a good steward of the planet—dealing with challenges generously and compassionately? As I see it, ironically, taking a globalist view actually is in our self-interest—making us both more affluent and safer in the long run.

That's why I believe that lessons learned from our travels can better equip us to address and help resolve the challenges facing our world. We travelers are both America's ambassadors to the world...and the world's ambassadors to America.

Whether you're a parent, a schoolteacher, a celebrity, a realtor, or a travel writer, it's wrong to stop paying attention. It's wrong to let others (motivated by their own self-interest) make political decisions for us. Our founding fathers didn't envision career politicians and professional talking heads doing our political thinking for us. All are welcome in the political discourse that guides this nation. And those who've gained a broader perspective through traveling have lots to contribute.

Thoughtful travelers know that we're all citizens of the world and members of a global family. Spinning from Scotland to Sri Lanka, from Tacoma to Tehran, travelers experience the world like whirling dervishes: We keep one foot planted in our homeland, while acknowledging the diversity of our vast world. We celebrate the abundant and good life we've been given and work to help those blessings shower more equitably upon all—at home and abroad...in our lifetime and beyond.

Acknowledgments

I'm grateful to work with people at my company who share my vision and commitment. Special thanks to my lead editors, Cameron Hewitt and Risa Laib, for bringing clarity, depth, and focus to my writing. If this book has struck a chord with you, it's due largely to their tuning—and even downright overhauling—of my work. Cameron, who co-authors many of my books, artfully carries out my desire to convey complex realities simply and clearly, and refines my writing into material that's both readable and accurate. For over 20 years, Risa has overseen our growing family of Rick Steves travel books with a passion nurtured by her strong belief in the value of smart travel and a commitment to excellence. Thanks to Rhonda Pelikan for designing the original edition of this book so thoughtfully. I also appreciate the talented help of Gene Openshaw, Jennifer Madison Davis, Barb Geisler, and Lauren Mills.

I had experts in various fields and from various countries review the portions of my work that relate to their area of expertise. For their insightful guidance, my thanks to Marijan Krišković (tour guide, on the former Yugoslavia), Dr. Benjamin Curtis (tour guide and scholar, on the European Union), Fabian Rueger (German guide extraordinaire, on the EU), Francesca Caruso (licensed Italian guide, on the EU), Edit Herczog (member of the European Parliament, on the EU), Ann Butwell (Center for Global Education at Augsburg College, on El Salvador), Richard Karpen (a.k.a. "Hans Christian Andersen," on Denmark), Jane Klausen (insider's look at Denmark), David Hoerlein (tour guide, on Denmark), Jakob Nielsen (Danish journalist, on Denmark), Lale Surmen Aran (tour guide and author, on Turkey), Tankut Aran (tour guide and author, on Turkey), Aziz Begdouri (tour guide, on Morocco), Norm Stamper (former Seattle Police Chief, on drug policy), Dr. Craig Reinarman (Professor of Sociology, UC Santa Cruz, on drug policy), Abdi Sami (Associate Producer of *Rick Steves' Iran* public television show), Abie Bresler and Benny Dagan (tour guides, on Israel), and Kamal Mukarker and Husam Jubran (tour guides, on Palestine).

This book is dedicated to the memory of Mehlika Seval (1949-2017). Meli, the consummate Turkish tour guide, introduced me and countless American travelers to the complex wonders of Anatolia with passion and abandon.

Thanks to the people mentioned in the anecdotes in this book for giving such meaning and wonder to my travels. And finally, thanks to you, my thoughtful reader, for knowing that travel can—and should—be a positive force for change. Happy travels!

Index

This big-picture index is designed to point you to some of my favorite themes, topics, and destinations. The page numbers direct you only to the main discussion of the item (not each passing mention). The list, shaped by my own preferences, is not comprehensive and admittedly quirky…just like each traveler's own journey.

Public Television:
Rick Steves' Europe

Rick's award-winning travel series has become a public television institution, appearing for two decades on more than 300 stations nationwide. Every

Rick Steves' Europe episode gives viewers a chance to experience Europe's most interesting destinations, from the windswept coast of Scotland to the scalps of the Alps to the markets of Istanbul—watching Rick Steves' Europe is the next best thing to a plane ticket. All 100 Rick Steves' Europe shows are available to view free and on demand at ricksteves.com/tv, or for purchase as a DVD box set. For details on all of Rick's TV shows, visit ricksteves.com.

Public Radio:
Travel with Rick Steves

Every week Rick Steves, his guest experts, and callers share a lively, ear-opening hour of travel talk that connects public radio listeners with the sights, sounds, and cultures of the world. Going far beyond Rick's "home base" of Europe, Travel with Rick Steves explores global topics, such as encounters with Islam, bicycle adventures in Asia, ecotourism in Latin America, road trips in the USA, local cooking, cultural quirks, travel as a force for peace, and much more. The

show is broadcast by more than 400 radio stations nationwide, and also available as free podcasts. For a complete list of stations and archived shows, visit ricksteves.com/radio.

Free Travel Podcasts

It's easier than ever to enjoy Rick's expert travel information as a podcast. You can listen or watch any time, on demand, for free. Choose from our rich archive including the weekly one-hour Travel with Rick Steves radio show, weekly video snippets from the Rick Steves' Europe TV show, Rick's video travel talks, and more! Either subscribe or download from iTunes.

Rick's Free Audio Europe™ App

Rick Steves Audio Europe™ brings Europe's history and art to life. Enjoy dozens of self-guided audio tours of Europe's top museums, sights, and neighborhood walks—plus hundreds of tracks filled with cultural insights and sightseeing tips from Rick's radio interviews—all organized into geographic playlists that you can listen to offline before or during your trip.

Explore Europe

Browse thousands of articles, videos, photos, and radio interviews, and find a wealth of money-saving travel tips for planning your dream trip. You'll find up-to-date information on Europe's best destinations, packing smart, getting around, finding rooms, staying healthy, avoiding scams, and more. And with our mobile-friendly website, you can easily access all this great information anywhere you go.

Travel News & Blog

Subscribe to our free Travel News e-newsletter, and get monthly dispatches from Rick packed full of fresh information about Europe's top destinations, the latest travel tips, and special offers. You can also follow Rick's latest adventures on his travel blog and Facebook page.

Travel Forums

Learn, ask, share! Our online community of savvy travelers is a great resource for first-time travelers to Europe, as well as seasoned pros. You'll find forums by country, travel tips, and restaurant and hotel reviews. You can even ask one of Rick's well-traveled staff to chime in with an opinion.

Rick Steves Travel Gear

Pack light and right—on a budget—with Rick's affordable, custom-designed luggage including rolling carry-on bags, backpacks, day packs, and shoulder bags. Plus find travel accessories, guidebooks, phrase books, maps, and more at Rick's online travel store.

Rick's European Tours

Rick Steves tours take you to Europe's most interesting places with great guides and small groups of 24-28 travelers. We follow Rick's favorite itineraries, ride in comfy buses, stay in centrally located hotels, and bring you intimately close to the Europe you've traveled so far to see. Find out more at ricksteves.com, where you can also order a free tour catalog.

The travel-savvy staff at Rick Steves' Europe is eager to help you turn your travel dreams into affordable reality.

Other Books by Rick Steves

Europe Through the Back Door:
  The Travel Skills Handbook
Europe 101: History and Art for the
  Traveler
Mediterranean Cruise Ports
Northern European Cruise Ports
European Christmas
European Easter
European Festivals

Country Guides

Croatia & Slovenia
Eastern Europe
England
France
Germany
Great Britain
Ireland
Italy
Portugal
Scandinavia
Scotland
Spain
Switzerland

City and Regional Guides

Amsterdam & the Netherlands
Barcelona
Belgium: Bruges, Brussels, Antwerp & Ghent
Berlin
Budapest
Florence & Tuscany
Greece: Athens & the Peloponnese
Istanbul
London
Paris
Prague & the Czech Republic
Provence & the French Riviera
Rome
Venice
Vienna, Salzburg & Tirol

Best of Guides

Best of England
Best of Europe
Best of France
Best of Germany
Best of Ireland
Best of Italy
Best of Spain

Pocket Guides

Amsterdam
Athens
Barcelona
Cinque Terre
Florence
London
Munich & Salzburg
Paris
Prague
Rome
Venice
Vienna

Snapshot Guides

Basque Country
Berlin
Copenhagen & the Best of Denmark
Dublin
Dubrovnik
Edinburgh
Hill Towns of Central Italy
Lisbon
Loire Valley
Kraków, Warsaw & Gdansk
Madrid & Toledo
Milan & Italian Lakes
Naples & the Amalfi Coast
Normandy
Northern Ireland
Norway
Sevilla, Granada & Southern Spain
St. Petersburg, Helsinki & Tallinn
Stockholm

Phrase Books

French, Italian & German Phrase Book
French Phrase Book & Dictionary
German Phrase Book & Dictionary
Italian Phrase Book & Dictionary
Portuguese Phrase Book & Dictionary
Spanish Phrase Book & Dictionary

Learn More About Topics in this Book

You can learn much more about topics covered in this book at ricksteves.com. There you can watch free, full-length public television specials (including *Rick Steves' Iran: Yesterday and Today*; *Rick Steves' The Holy Land: Israelis and Palestinians Today*; and—coming in 2018—*Rick Steves' The Story of Fascism in Europe*); read Rick's original journals from his travels in Latin America; watch Rick's one-hour "Travel as a Political Act" slideshow lecture; listen to thought-provoking interviews from Rick's public radio show; find out more about how you can turn traveling as a political act into philanthropic action back home; connect with worthwhile causes that Rick is personally involved in and passionate about; and much more.

This book is also available as an audiobook, read by the author, through Hachette Audio (hachetteaudio.com).

About the Author

Rick Steves, born in 1955 and raised in Edmonds, Washington (just north of Seattle), still looks out his window each morning at Puget Sound. He has two adult children, Andy and Jackie. Rick ventured to Europe for the first time as a teenager in 1969, visiting relatives in Norway and touring German piano factories with his piano-importer father. Rick was hooked...and ever since, he's spent four months each year overseas. After a few trips and lots of learning from his mistakes, Rick was inspired to teach his fellow travelers how to enjoy smoother and more culturally broadening travels. What began as a series of lectures evolved into guidebooks, guided tours, a public television series (*Rick Steves' Europe*), a public radio show (*Travel with Rick Steves*), a blog (on Facebook), a website (ricksteves.com), and a syndicated newspaper column. Rick wrote his first book, *Europe Through the Back Door*, in 1980. Since then, he has researched and written dozens of different European travel guidebooks (all published by Avalon Travel). His Edmonds-based travel company, Rick Steves' Europe, employs a hardworking and well-traveled staff of over 100. An active Lutheran, Rick has hosted several educational videos for the Lutheran Church (ELCA), received the Wittenberg Award in 2007 for his social activism, and in 2017 produced the public television special, *Martin Luther and the Reformation*. In 2009, the National Council for International Visitors (funded by the US State Department) presented Rick with their Citizen Diplomat of the Year Award. The Society of American Travel Writers named the first edition of this book "Travel Book of the Year" in 2010, and named Rick "Travel Writer of the Year" in 2011. In 2013, the ambassador of the European Union to the United States awarded Rick the "Friend of Europe" award. Rick's public television specials include *The Holy Land: Israelis and Palestinians Today; Iran: Yesterday and Today; Luther and the Reformation*; and his latest, *The Story of Fascism in Europe* (2018). Every year, Rick travels to Europe to update his guidebooks, research new ones, and produce TV shows, as he has for three decades. And when he's home, Rick pursues a wide variety of philanthropic activities in his own community (for more, see www.ricksteves.com/politicalact).

Rick is donating all the royalties from the sale of this book to Bread for the World, which lobbies our government on behalf of hungry people in the USA and abroad (www.bread.org).